Hugh Robinson, Author of *Database Analysis and Design,* originally studied philosophy at the University of Keele, graduating in 1970. The attraction of applying the analytical approach and clear thinking of philosophy led him to a lasting involvement with computer science and a further degree from the University of London. Since 1973 he has worked in the area of analysis and design of large files and Databases. After some five years of working in industry, he joined Hatfield Polytechnic as a senior lecturer, although he has maintained his contact with industry through consultancy work. He is author of several papers on Data Analysis and Database design and is active in the work of Codasyl and Databases.

Hatfield Polytechnic Computer Science Series

Database Analysis and Design

Hugh Robinson

Chartwell-Bratt
Studentlitteratur

Chartwell-Bratt (Publishing and Training) Limited,
Old Orchard, Bickley Road, Bromley,
Kent, BR1 2NE, England
ISBN 0 86238 018 9

Studentlitteratur ab,
Box 141, S 22100 Lund, Sweden
ISBN 91 44 18781 5
Fourth Printing

Printed in Sweden
Studentlitteratur
Lund 1986

for
Robert O'Neill Montgomery and Rufus,
the "inheritors of promises"

FOREWORD

by Sir Norman Lindop MSc.,CChem.,F.R.S.C.,

It is a particular pleasure for me to introduce this series of books, which is designed to provide a coherent set of undergraduate texts in computer science. All the contributors to the series have been associated in one way or another with Information Sciences at The Hatfield Polytechnic, and the texts are based upon modules of the Honours degree course in Computer Science — a full-time course on the sandwich pattern which has evolved over the past 15 years.

One of the main features of the Hatfield computer science courses is that they provide a set of broadly-based studies, not unduly biased towards any particular aspects or applications though including many specialist topics and achieving a high final academic standard. It is intended that the modules upon which this series of books is based form a graduated set, from basic foundation studies up to advanced texts.

The development of computing and of computer science at Hatfield has been exciting and spectacularly successful and it is gratifying to present to a wider public some of the fruits of that experience.

Contents

ANALYSIS

DESIGN

PREFACE

Some years ago it became almost <u>mandatory</u> to introduce any new book on the topic of database with a statement that the book in question was aimed to fill a specific gap in teaching texts: the absence of any suitable book in a new and developing field. This situation is largely no longer the case. There are several excellent books on the market which treat, at varying depths, the issues of database systems, approaches to database models, database management system software, and so on.

The aim of this book is not to add to *that* particular collection of texts. Rather, it aims to fill another, quite different, gap. It addresses itself to *this* question:

"How do you *use* this new software in the traditional tasks of systems analysis and design? How do you *design* a database?"

And here a <u>gulf</u> does exist. On the one hand there is a body of database <u>expertise</u>, and on the other a body of traditional techniques well understood by analysts and designers. There seems no common ground, and many analysts and designers regard database with much the same mixture of horror and <u>awe</u> as did the <u>layman</u> when <u>confronted</u> by the <u>mystifying</u> computer that <u>intruded into</u> his life. This book attempts to <u>bridge</u> that gulf: to show that common ground not only <u>exsists</u>, but must exist, if we are to effectively use the new developments of database theory.

The book is divided into three Parts:

Fundamentals

Analysis

Design

Given the <u>intent</u> of the book, the latter two require no justification. **Fundamentals** has three main aims:

* to provide an introduction to database systems within some coherent framework; to remove some of the 'horror' and 'awe', but also to avoid providing a natural history of databases.

* to define *why* we are using the database approach.

* to define *what* the database approach provides as components with which we can construct systems using databases.

This text grew from a series of lectures to undergraduate & postgraduate students at Hatfield Polytechnic. During those lectures the need for a consistent example became apparent: to show for a given problem what you would do with a given approach. The problem was that any suitable example seemed to require almost as much time to describe as it did to use as an illustration. The example I finally settled on, and use in this book, concerns something students are intuitively familiar with: students, courses, lectures, degrees etc. — in short a Hypothetical University. However, it must be remembered that all that is said using this example applies equally well to operations such as stock control, invoicing, retail goods distribution, and so on.

No book is *just* the product of the immediate work and effort put into it. Its origins are embedded in the experience and perceptions of the author. I would like to acknowledge some of those seminal origins:

* to Birkbeck College, University of London for the opportunity of an absorbing introduction to Computer Science.
* to the various organisations where I have been employed and learnt my trade as systems analyst and designer.
* to Bernard Bennetto, Martin Joyce, David Long, Mike Newton, Gill Williams, and Christine Warner during my time with the Open University.
* to the members of the Data Base Administration Working Group.
* to the students of Hatfield Polytechnic, who have caused me to reflect on my ideas more times than I care to remember.

This book was substantially written in the first half of 1979. Circumstances allowed me subsequently to make minor changes to reflect some of the developments that have taken place more recently.

HMR
Tyttenhanger Green
1980

FUNDAMENTALS

The aim of this Part of the book is not to give an authoritative account of database systems. Rather it sets the necessary groundwork for the task of analysis and design of databases to support users' needs. It reminds us of *why* we are using the database approach, *what* a database system consists of and *how* various approaches have tackled the task of providing such systems.

Chapter 1

THE NEED FOR THE DATABASE APPROACH

"In these parts a man's life may depend on the existence of a mere scrap of information."

Don Miguel, A Fistful of Dollars

1.1 DATA AS AN ORGANISATIONAL RESOURCE

Any organisation will have certain *resources* which it uses to meet its objectives. As Fig. 1.1 illustrates, a reasonable large scale operation in a commercial, technical, administrative, or educational area might have resources such as:—

* people: the clerks, typists, assembly line workers, managers, lecturers, programmers, analysts.

* stock: the products, the raw materials the organisation uses.

* buildings: the warehouses, office blocks, shops, classrooms, factory units.

* machinery: the blast furnaces, steel mills, vehicles, computers, typewriters.

* money: the financial resource in terms of bank accounts, stocks, shares.

* **data:** what products are sold to whom, what lecturers teach what courses.

Fig.1.1
Resources of an Organisation

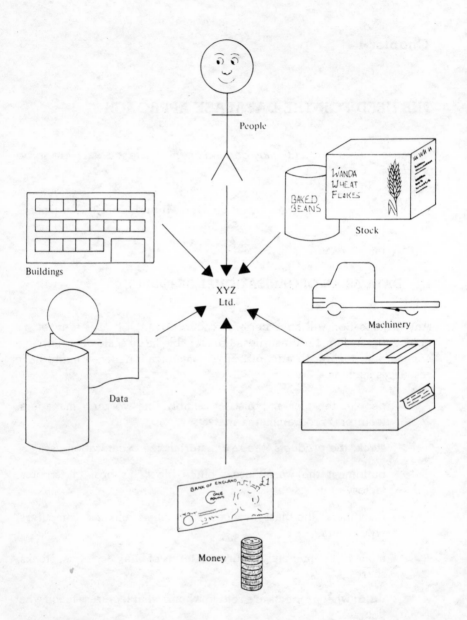

People

Stock

Buildings

XYZ
Ltd.

Machinery

Data

Money

4

requisites for others, some are recommended co-requisites, and so on. We can also note the two relationships between staff and faculty; one indicating the members of a faculty, the other indicating the head of a faculty.

3. No one department will be interested in the *whole* organisational data resource. However the areas of interest will often *overlap*. Student Administration, for example, will be interested primarily in *students*, and also in courses; the Faculties will be primarily interested in *courses* and *staff*, but also in students and degrees. Finance may be interested in *students* and *staff*, but will also be interested in courses and locations.

1.1.4 What organisations do with resources

Significant organisational resources are *managed* and *administered*. Questions such as:

How much have we got?

Where is it being used?

Is it being used effectively?

are asked and are answered.

The money resource, for example, is far too important to be just left lying around, unco-ordinated and unaccounted. Traditionally organisations have managed and administered the money resource by:

1. An administration function — a person, or group of persons, charged with the responsibility for managing and administering the money resource, e.g. the Chief Accountant.

   and

2. A set of techniques to aid them — accounting practice.

We *should* expect the same for the data resource. After all, any small business can produce a set of books which in the hands of a trained accountant could lead to a concise understanding of just what the business's assets were and how they were being used. *Surely*, a large scale organisation, such as a nation-wide distribution company, would have a similar approach for its data resource? Surely its documentation and data structure would be on a par with that of the money resource for a small business?

11

Unfortunately, our expectations will not always be matched by reality. The questions:

What are your data?

What are they used for?

Are they being used effectively?

have a certain strangeness to them. But this strangeness is not merely the result of grammar and syntax; it is a result of the way that data processing systems have treated the data resource, as we shall see in the following sections.

So far our example has centered on *data*, but we must now consider what this sample data is used for. We shall not be defining any sample processes, but rather will talk loosely about the data needs of *two* of UniHyp's departments: Student Administration and Course Administration.

Student Administration is primarily concerned with STUDENTs but does have a need to know what COURSEs a STUDENT is taking. On the other hand, the main interest of Course Administration is with COURSEs, with a secondary concern of the STUDENTs taking the COURSEs. UniHyp is very privacy conscious and decisions have been made as to who is allowed to access the data in this area. The issue is complex — reference (1.5) outlines the area — but for our purposes we can say that the following rules have been agreed by the staff/student body:

* data about a STUDENT and his academic progress can only be accessed by
  — lecturers directly involved in teaching the student,
  — staff directly involved in the administration of UniHyp's regulations to the student,
  — persons the student has authorised to have access.
* data about a COURSE, however, is in principle available to any interested party.

We now look at various approaches to these information processing requirements in order to see how the data resource *should* be administered and managed.

1.2 THE CONVENTIONAL FILE APPROACH AND ITS PROBLEMS

Recognising data as an organisational resource poses the general problem outlined in 1.1.4: how is it managed and administered? To answer this question we must look a little at the history of data processing and the conventional file approach to treating data as a resource. Although we shall be discussing points of *general* importance, it is helpful to illustrate them with a *specific* example. The example chosen is from a small aspect of UniHyp's data resource discussed earlier. Like all examples it is a *toy* and omits many of the complexities of a real life situation. However the problems it illustrates are very real ones that have been faced by many data processing departments over the years.

The area of UniHyp's data resource that will be examined is that of *students* and *courses*. This can be illustrated by some sample data which can naturally be displayed as tables as shown in Fig. 1.7. The immediate impact of Fig. 1.7 is the resolution of our outline relationship between students and courses from a single many-to-many relationship to two one-to-many relationships:

STUDENTS

REG. NO.	NAME	ADDRESS	DATE-OF-BIRTH	DATE-OF-REGISTRATION
9491	B. ROBERTS	9 INKERMAN ST.	8.6.58	1.10.77
3123	G. JUNG	26 SHAW ST.	19.11.59	2.10.78
7416	C. DAY	63 SPRING RD.	3.2.60	3.10.78
9372	D. THOMAS	14 CHURCH END	7.7.59	1.10.77
4739	D. WHITE	2 WARWICK AV.	21.1.61	1.10.79

COURSES

COURSE CODE	COURSE NAME	RATING	DATE-OF-INTRO	FACULTY
PHI 121	THE EARLY WITTGENSTEIN	1	1975	HUMANITIES
PHI 102	KANTIAN METAPHYSICS	2	1973	HUMANITIES
LIT 312	THE EXPATRIATES	2	1976	HUMANITIES
COMP 141	COMPUTER ARCHITECTURE	1	1975	MATHEMATICS
COMP 222	ADVANCED DATA STRUCTURES	2	1978	MATHEMATICS
CHEM 301	MOLECULAR GENETICS	1	1979	SCIENCE
ENG 111	BASIC SURVEYING	1	1974	ENGINEERING
COMP 272	CONCEPTUAL MODELS	2	1979	MATHEMATICS

STUDENTS AND COURSES

REG. NO.	COURSE CODE	RESULT
9491	PHI 121	PASS
9491	PHI 102	PASS
9491	LIT 312	PASS
9491	ENG 111	FAIL
3123	COMP 141	PASS
3123	LIT 312	PASS
3123	ENG 111	FAIL
3123	PHI 102	PASS
7416	ENG 111	PASS
7416	CHEM 301	–
7416	LIT 312	PASS
7416	COMP 141	PASS
9372	PHI 121	FAIL
9372	PHI 102	FAIL
9372	ENG 111	PASS
9372	CHEM 301	–

Fig 1.7
The Sample Data as Tables

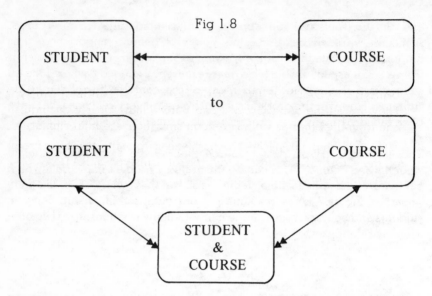

Fig 1.8

to

We have some data — a RESULT — about a STUDENT and a COURSE that belongs neither to the STUDENT nor to the COURSE; it is data about the relationship between the two; so-called *intersection data*. We can see this more clearly if we draw out an example of the many-to-many relationship as in Fig. 1.9.

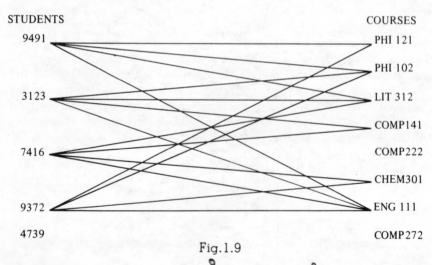

Fig.1.9

The natural place to write the RESULTs on this diagram would be on the relationship lines, and this is effectively what the table STUDENTS AND COURSES is doing.

14

The data in the tables is aimed to be self-explanatory. However, some points are worth noting.

1. We have several DATEs involved: the DATE-OF-BIRTH of a STUDENT, the DATE-OF-REGISTRATION of the STUDENT with UniHyp, the DATE-OF-INTRODUCTION of a COURSE at UniHyp. They are all the same *sort* of thing but we must clearly distinguish one from the other as well as recognising their essential similarity.

2. A COURSE has a RATING which is a measure of the academic credit of the COURSE towards a degree of UniHyp: a RATING of 2 involving about twice the work from a STUDENT that a COURSE with a RATING of 1 would require.

3. Several values in the RESULT column in the STUDENTS AND COURSES table have an entry of "—", indicating a null value as a consequence of the fact that the STUDENT is still studying the COURSE in question.

4. One STUDENT is not taking any COURSEs; the implication being that he has just registered at UniHyp and has not yet elected for any specific COURSEs as such.

5. Similarly, two COURSEs have no STUDENTs; the implication being that they have just been introduced and as yet have no takers in the STUDENT community.

As mentioned in the Preface this example has been chosen deliberately since the semantics of the application are reasonably self-explanatory to students. However, many applications would not have this intuitive appeal: some form of rudimentary documentation — or "accounting" technique — would be needed. References (1.3) and (1.4) detail the need and scope for such documentation, and we shall be returning to this issue later, in Chapter 12. It is a sad reflection that many data processing installations would not possess documentation of their data resource to anything like the level that these references suggest.

1.2.1. Conventional file approach I

When such information processing requirements were initially computerised in the 1950s and 1960s each individual *user department* or *applications area* developed its own *application orientated* file structure.

For example, Student Administration may have had a file which in loose COBOL notation would look like:

```
01  STUDENT-RECORD
    02  STUD-DETAILS
        03 REG-NO                    PIC 9(4)
```

03 INITIAL	PIC X
03 SURNAME	PIC X(10)
03 ADDRESS	PIC X(20)
03 D-O-B	PIC X(6)
03 D-O-R	PIC X(6)
02 COURSE-DETAILS OCCURS n TIMES	
03 COURSE-CODE	PIC X(7)
03 COURSE-NAME	PIC X(30)
03 RATING	PIC 9
03 RESULT	PIC X

Several things emerge from this declaration of a record structure.

1. It is a record *type* having many occurrences — those of ROBERTS, JUNG, etc. — and is therefore an example of the distinction made in 1.1.3.

2. Our convential file record is by no means self-explanatory; there is no indication that D-O-B and D-O-R are both dates, for example. We might hope that such a declaration would be accompanied somewhere by a file layout that may be more imformative. We might even hope for a file dictionary that told us all we needed to know about the data items — such as the range of permitted values in RATING, for example. In many installations we might well hope in vain!

3. Our sample data showed a relationship between STUDENT and STUDENTS AND COURSES:

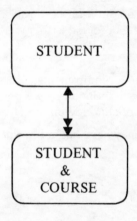

Fig. 1.10

Yet this relationship is nowhere explicity shown in our application orientated file. It is hidden away as a repeating group.

Furthermore the repeating group is trying to depict another relationship: that between COURSEs and STUDENTS AND COURSES, since COURSE-NAME and RATING are included in the repeating group. In the record structure the two *explicit* relationships shown in Fig. 1.8 become one *implicit* relationship expressed as an OCCURS clause, as shown in Fig. 1.11.

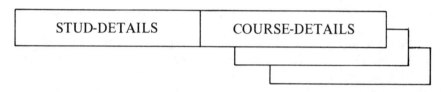

STUD-DETAILS	COURSE-DETAILS

Fig. 1.11

The consequence of this is *redundancy* or *duplication* of data. Even using our limited sample data several COURSE-NAMEs and RATINGs will be repeated. This, with a typical large volume file (Unihyp could easily have 10,000 students or more!) is extremely wasteful of storage space. However worse is still to come. Not only is this redundancy wasteful, it is also harmful. Consider what needs to be done if the COURSE-NAME of ENG 111 is changed from "BASIC SURVEYING" to "BASIC QUANTITY SURVEYING" (to alleviate continual student misunderstanding of what the course is about). The whole file needs to be read and the change effected many times. Yet it was only one simple change in a COURSE-NAME! The programs written to carry out such amendments will need to recognise this redundancy and read every record in the file: if they do not then we have the possibility of inconsistent values in our data items — one record says the name is one thing, another says that it is something else.

4. The privacy decisions taken by UniHyp become difficult to implement as access constraints with this sort of file structure and the associated software. Programs will either be denied access to the *whole* file or be permitted to have access to the *whole* file. It becomes very difficult to enforce decisions about particular occurrences of the STUDENT-RECORD.

17

5. In our point on redundancy, above, we mentioned the possible large numbers of STUDENT-RECORD occurrences. If the file had initially been stored as a serial magnetic tape file — perhaps in REG-NO sequence — then any access to one particular occurrence of a record is potentially very time consuming. On average half the file would need to be read. It becomes natural therefore to think in terms of changing the storage medium for the file; perhaps to a moving head disc or some such direct access device, coupled with an index sequential structure. However such a straightforward change in the way the data is *stored* and *accessed* (not in the logical nature of the data) becomes most unstraightforward when it needs to be carried out. At best all (COBOL) programs that reference the file will need their ENVIRONMENT and DATA DIVISIONs changed and the programs re-compiled. At worst the actual program logic will need to be changed. The "read next record, does it match the input transaction, ..." logic of processing serial files would need to be changed to accommodate direct access of the record required.

Yet more problems ensue if we look at what might be a typical situation. Of our (hypothetical) 10,000 STUDENT-RECORDs only a certain percentage will be accessed very frequently — those students, say, who are actively studying a course. If this percentage of active records — a *hit group* — is low then access to them will be inefficient possibly if they are stored with all the other (inactive) STUDENT-RECORDs. It might be desirable to store the active records on a high speed direct access device, whilst storing the inactive records on a slower speed serial access device such as a magnetic tape drive. All well and good: we want to store our records in a manner appropriate to the pattern of access. But look what we have to do: we have to create two separate files, say of STUDENT-ACTIVE records and STUDENT-INACTIVE records, each with their own set of programs to access and update them. If we want to run processes that look at *all* students we have the complication of co-ordinating programs running against two files. Yet the logic of the data stored on each file has not been changed, only the way it is stored!

Such a file approach exhibits what is known as *physical data dependence*: a change in the physical storage of data, or the physical access mechanisms to data, results in a need to change application programs.

This situation is bad enough in itself, but it is only half the the picture. Typically there will be *other* application orientated files developed to meet the various information processing needs. For example, Course

18

Administration at UniHyp might have its own application orientated file composed of records looking like:

```
01  COURSE-RECORD
    02  COURSE-DETAILS
        03 CRSE-CD              PIC X(7)
        03 CRSE-NAM             PIC X(35)
        03 RATING               PIC X
        03 D-O-I                PIC 9(4)
        03 FACODE               PIC X
    02  STUD-DETAILS OCCURS n TIMES
        03 REG-NO               PIC X(4)
        03 NAME                 PIC X(15)
```

Such a file suffers from all the specific problems outlined above for the Student Administration file. However, the existence of the *two* files creates further problems.

1. It is not obvious that the two files are essentially describing the same *things*. PIC clauses are different (are different values allowed?), data item names are different (is NAME a composite of INITIAL and SURNAME, or is it just SURNAME?), and is RATING coded in a different way?

2. Redundancy is now positively dangerous: a change in a COURSE-NAME (same as CRSE-NAM?) now has to be effected on *two* files. It is bad enough ensuring that the logic of a program reads all the way through a file making all the changes, but now we are faced with the problem of co-ordinating two application suites. There is the very real danger that an administrator will pick up print-outs from the two suites and find conflicting values for something that is the same thing! In short, where we had *intra-file* redundancy we now also have *inter-file* redundancy.

However, these application orientated files had one saving grace (it was supposed): they were run-time efficient. The data was structured exactly to meet the requirements of the application. This is true, to a certain extent, though as we have seen with the case of hit-groups sometimes they cannot even tailor themselves to meet their own needs.

1.2.2 Conventional file approach II

Such considerations as these led naturally to the idea of a *consolidated file approach*: have one file from which all the application suites can work from. A consolidated file for our example might look like:

```
01  MASTER-RECORD
    0 2 STUDENT-DETAIL
        03 REG-NO                      PIC 9(4)
        03 INITIAL                     PIC X
        03 SURNAME                     PIC X(10)
        03 ADDRESS                     PIC X(20)
        03 D-O-B                       PIC X(6)
        03 D-O-R                       PIC X(6)
    0 2 COURSE-DETAIL OCCURS n TIMES
        03 COURSE-CODE                 PIC X(7)
        03 COURSE-NAME                 PIC X(35)
        03 RATING                      PIC X
        03 D-O-I                       PIC 9(4)
        03 FACULTY                     PIC X
        03 RESULT                      PIC X
```

Such an approach, however, has certain problems that illustrate clearly that you cannot simply dump all the data resource together and expect to be able to easily fish out the parts that you require.

1. The consolidated file approach requires that one application takes primacy over others. In our example it is assumed that the needs of Course Administration are seen as subordinate to those of Student Administration, since STUDENTs are seen as superior to COURSEs (the OCCURing group). This may well reflect a natural state of affairs, but it will not always be the case. It entails certain consequences:

    i) data items are defined in one form for *all* applications: this can result in a structure that is either needlessly complex for some applications or fails to represent the depth of detail for others.

ii) *sorting* of files becomes important. For Course Administration to obtain the view of data that it requires, the file must be shuffled and sorted. This is a time-consuming operation and effectively loses the application dependent efficiency we had in the previous approach.

iii) the implementation of privacy decisions becomes difficult since we tend to have the all or nothing approach to access to the whole file. The usual result is that privacy decisions are implemented as embedded procedures in program or operating procedures.

2. The consolidated file also has an inadequate structure: it is incorrect and incorrectable. Not only are relationships muddled as repeating groups, but they are inadequately expressed. For example, we cannot easily express the fact that our COURSE COMP272 is one of UniHyp's COURSEs, since we have no STUDENTs currently taking the COURSE. This could be rectified by making COURSEs superior to STUDENTs, but we would then have the same problem with people like D.WHITE: they are not currently taking any COURSEs.

All the previous problems also still remain: we have redundancy, we have physical data dependence, *and* we now have an additional problem — logical data dependence.

3. Imagine that Student Administration recognises that a significant number of STUDENTs are registered for two degrees and that this information is now required on the file. The suggested file now has a structure with records like:

01 MASTER-RECORD

    02 STUDENT-DETAILS
       .
       .
       .
    02 DEGREE-DETAIL OCCURS n TIMES
       .
       .
       .
       03 COURSE-DETAIL OCCURS n TIMES

This change, needed by Student Administration, impacts upon the programs of Course Administration: they must be changed, not because *their* view of the data has changed, but because some *other* view of the data has changed. The file has *logical data dependence*: a change to the logical structure of the data results in a need to change application programs that do not need the new logical structure.

What is wrong, in essence, with these approaches is that an enormous effort has been put into the development of *problem orientated* ways of describing *processes* (e.g. the development of high level languages such as COBOL and PL/I), but no real effort has gone into *problem orientated* ways of describing *data*. As such the data description is essentially *bound* to the programs: it is only there that it is described and then in an implicit fashion. The binding of the data into the programs means the data is only available for use by those programs: it is logically and physically dependent. Nolan (Reference (1.1)) likens this situation to one where the money resource is a frozen asset, only being able to be used to buy certain restricted things.

The database approach is an attempt to solve these problems: to treat data as an organisational resource that can be used to provide an organisation with the information it needs.

1.3 THE DATABASE APPROACH AND ITS OBJECTIVES

The previous section has highlighted the need to *manage* and *administer* the data resource. If money were treated in the same way as were our sample data, UniHyp would rapidly become bankrupt. Indeed treating data in that manner does cause financial problems. Many data processing departments have found that with files that are physically and logically dependent on programs an enormous amount of effort is expended in the trivial *maintenance* of application program suites to the exclusion of any application development. This is not only a waste of money, but also results in job dissatisfaction amongst programmers and analysts — they move to seek interesting jobs in other companies and more money is wasted in recruiting highly paid and highly gifted replacements who will find the situation much as their predecessors did.

To go back to our analogy with the money resource, we need:

* an administration function — the *database administrator* — who is charged with analysing, defining, and designing data structures that truly exploit data as a resource.

* a set of software tools to assist the database administrator in his/her task — a *database management system* (DBMS) to support the use of a database system.

We shall not here explore the specific duties of the database administrator for this whole book is an essay on those duties. Nor shall we define a database system in terms of some ready rote definition. Rather, we shall define a database system in terms of *what* we require of it in the light of the preceding discussion; that is, its *objectives*.

The objectives of the database approach

1. **The introduction of controlled redundancy.** Note that we are not saying "the elimination of redundancy". As we shall see redundancy is sometimes needed and is necessary — this we refer to as *controlled* or *minimal redundancy*. What we wish to avoid is the harmful redundancy illustrated in the previous sections; that is the *resolution of data inconsistency problems*. If we look back to our two separate application orientated files in 1.2.1 we can see that the duplication of COURSE detail means that we have the possibility of a new COURSE being added to the Student Administration file, but not to the Course Administration file. Similar catastrophes exist for the amendment and deletion of data items. Controlled redundancy should not allow these possibilities.

2. **Sharing of data.** Not only is redundancy controlled, but it becomes possible to develop *new* applications to work against the centralised data resource. For example, it is possible that Finance at UniHyp will want to develop a set of new application programs that will make use of NAMEs and ADDRESSes of STUDENTs. These new application programs should be able to *use* and *share* the same data on STUDENTs that already exists and is used and shared by Student Administration and Course Administration.

3. **Validation rules and standards for data.** Data redundancy is not only wasteful, it can also be contradictory. The application orientated files may have different rules for the representation, value ranges, and validation routines (i.e. integrity constraints) for the *same* data items — all probably buried in the procedural logic of their application programs. Centralised control of the data resource should make such rules, ranges, and routines *explicit*, and allow the possibility of resolving and recognising differences.

4. **Access control decisions can be implemented.** Just as the financial resource is controlled so that only *authorised persons* can use it, so the data resource needs to be similarly controlled. A database system will provide the access control mechanisms to meet the organisation's (and society's) decisions on the privacy rights of individuals and groups.

5. **The ability to support differing views**. The supporting of many application views of the same data will not be a simple process. Student Administration will require a STUDENT orientated view, whilst Course Administration will require a COURSE orientated view. In addition, the database must be capable of providing a service that meets a variety of response times and priorities for application systems. That is, one where applications requiring a response time of a high order can be supported without degrading the performance of other applications too severely. This obviously makes the design of a particular database a complex process involving many trade-offs and compromises. This is probably one of the aims that has in practice been least achieved by current DBMSs, and any one working in the database area should be very wary of giving the impression (as some promotional publicity does) that a database can quite simply be all things to all men.

6. **Security of data**. Any centralised control of the data resource should protect the data from program corruption and/or hardware failure.

7. **The provision of data independence**. As we have seen conventional files tend to produce data dependence. A database should provide:

    i)   **physical data independence;** that is a change in the physical storage of data, or in the physical access mechanisms to data, should result in no need to change application programs.

    ii)   **logical data independence;** that is a change to the logical structure of the data (e.g. the addition of new records, data items, relationships, and so on) should result in no need to change existing applications programs.

Achievement of these objectives will *cost*. Complex software will be required to provide these facilities. The overall efficiency of application programs may suffer since their application views and access is now provided via the software of the DBMS. However, achievement of these objectives is considered to be worth the cost. At a recent conference of database administrators and other interested persons the question:

> "What percentage increase in run-time of application programs would you be be prepared to pay for the benefits of the database approach — the drastic drop in program maintenance,etc.?"
>
> (Reference (1.6))

A straw vote revealed that the majority of people were willing to go to 20%, and that a significant number would be willing to go to 50%!

This book is about designing a database that will give you the performance needed without anything like that increase in processing time!

It is significant, however, that no published work (at the time of writing) actually demonstrates in hard terms the benefit gained by using database: it seems largely to be an act of faith and trust in "intangible" benefits.

SUMMARY

We can summarise this chapter with two sets of diagrams. Figs. 1.12 and 1.13 illustrate the change invoked by treating data as an organisational resource. Figs. 1.14 and 1.15 illustrate the data processing change that is invoked by the use of a database : that it is a radical way of organising data that reverses our previous view of the relationship between programs and files.

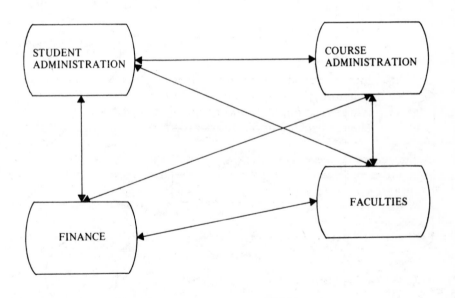

Fig. 1.12
Traditional View of Data as a Resource

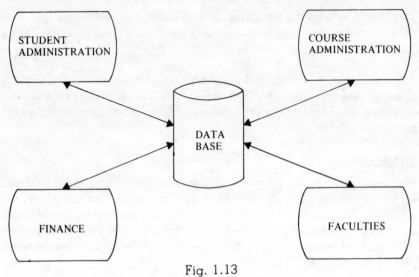

Fig. 1.13
Database View of Data as a Resource

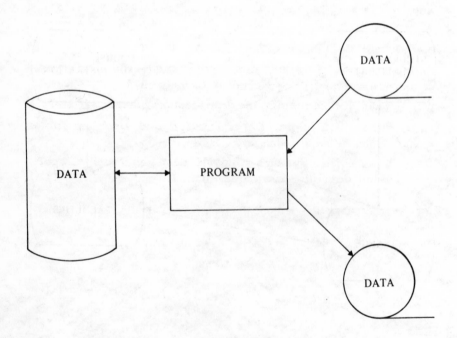

Fig. 1.14
Traditional View of Data and Programs

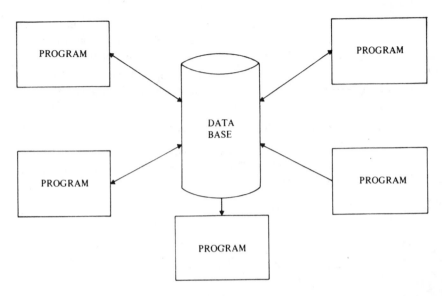

Fig. 1.15
Database View of Data and Programs

REFERENCES AND BIBLIOGRAPHY

(1.1)   Nolan, R.L. **Computer data bases: the future is now**, Harvard Business Review: September — October 1973.

(1.2)   Nolan, R.L. **Managing the data resource function**, West, 1974.

(1.3)   Fisher, D.L. **Data, Documentation and Decision Tables.** Comm. ACM,**9,** 1, January, 1966.

(1.4)   King, P.J.H. **Systems analysis documentation: computer-aided data dictionary definition**, Computer Journal, **12,** 1, Feb. 1969

(1.5)   Conway, R.W., Maxwell, W.L., and Morgan, H.L. **On the Implementation of Security Measures in Information Systems.** Comm. ACM, **15,** 4, April 1972.

(1.6)   Online **Database** conference, London, September, 1977. Straw vote taken during the paper **The alternative to database**, Biggar, C.

EXERCISES

1.1   For an organisation with which you are familiar, assess the impact of the loss of one main file, be it a computer file or a clerical file.

1.2 Could any of the problems outlined in section 1.2 have been avoided using other file structures, such as (say) inverted files? Would these structures have caused problems of their own?

1.3 Examine a program that processes a stored data structure and assess the impact on the program of changing the way the data structure is stored and accessed.

1.4 What new relationship has been introduced in the file structure depicted in 1.2.2, i.e.

      01 MASTER-RECORD
         .
         .

         02 STUDENT-DETAILS
            .
            .

         02 DEGREE-DETAILS OCCURS n TIMES
            .
            .

            .
           03 COURSE-DETAIL OCCURS n TIMES

Try and draw a diagram similar to that of Fig. 1.8 to express the new situation.

Chapter 2

THE ARCHITECTURE OF A DATABASE SYSTEM

"But the purpose here isn't exhaustively to analyze the motorcycle. It's to provide a starting point, an example of a mode of understanding of things which will become itself an object of analysis."
Robert M. Pirsig, Zen and the Art of Motorcycle Maintenance

Having outlined the aims of the database approach in the previous chapter we now look at a general model or *architecture* for a database system. We shall then be able to comprehend more fully the ways in which the aims of the database approach can be achieved, the approaches that are used in practice, and what the task of designing a database involves.

Fig. 2.1 illustrates a generalised architecture for a database system. Much work is currently going on in this area, both at a theoretical and at a practical level. An important set of proposals on architecture published in recent years has been those resulting from the ANSI/X3/SPARC work — see references (2.1) and (2.2). C. J. Date, reference (2.7), emphasises the importance of a clear architecture in comprehending database systems. The work of the various CODASYL committees in this area has also been extremely valuable (see Chapter 4). Therefore the architecture given in Fig. 2.1 is something of a simplified view — an outline of the state of the art, and it may be some time before agreed definitions of the architecture and its components are reached. For these reasons the architecture components are named in a neutral fashion using some of Date's terminology, with no particular bias to any one view. Equivalences are given where helpful.

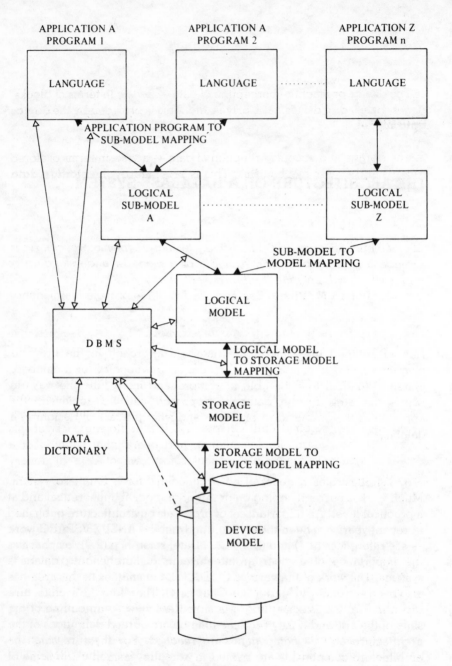

Fig. 2.1.
Generalised Architecture for a Database System

The essential feature of this architecture is that it provides four views or *perceptions* of data that were implicit in the discussion in Chapter 1. These four views are:

1. The device or machine perception of data — a view in terms of blocks, pages, bytes, disc drives, tape drives, etc. This is provided by the **device data model**.

2. The storage and access perception of data — a view in terms of stored records and access mechanisms. This is provided by the **storage data model**.

3. The organisational or global view of the data and its inherent logical characteristics. This is provided by the **logical data model**: a statement of *what* the data and its structure is, including access constraints and integrity constraints.

4. The application systems view of the data — a perception in terms of the constructs manipulated by high level languages: records, fields, etc. This is provided by the **logical data sub-models.** (It should be noted that some DBMSs allow the use of assembler languages with logical data sub-models.)

We shall describe this architecture by examining the key features and distinctions present. Discussion of the role of the data dictionary component is postponed until Chapter 12. It is sufficient to say at this stage that the design, implementation and operational running of a database system is impossible without some form of data dictionary component.

2.1 LOGICAL MODELS AND PHYSICAL MODELS

There is a *logical data model* which is a description of the organisation's operational data in a manner which is independent of the way that the data is stored and accessed or allocated to particular machine devices. It is a description of *what* the data is in terms of the *sort* of data constructs manipulated by high level languages, such as COBOL, PL/I and FORTRAN. However, its description will not be in terms of the data constructs of any *particular* high level language. The description will be written in a *logical data model definition language* that will be machine translatable — in particular it will be translatable by the DBMS. The ANSI/X3/SPARC equivalent for the logical data model is the *conceptual schema*, a phrase that will give us a little confusion when we come to discuss conceptual data models in Chapter 7. Sometimes the logical data model is termed simply a *schema;* a recognition of the work of CODASYL in the area of database architecture.

There is, on the other hand, a *storage data model* and a *device data model,* which for the moment we shall treat as one and call the *physical data model.* The physical data model defines the way in which the data will be stored, accessed and placed on physical devices.

Because this distinction between logical and physical is so crucial a few examples are given.

Example 1

Consider a person's name. Logically it may be:

'H. M. ROBINSON'
i.e. a string of literals.

Physically this would be represented by a machine as something like:

C84BD44BD9D6C2C9D5E2D6D5
i.e. a string of bytes on an IBM 360 machine

Or as

1100561150561221171021111116123117116
i.e. as a series of words in a Univac 1100 machine

Despite the different physical representations there is only one logical representation.

Example 2

Again using a person's name, let us imagine that it forms part of a record:

01 PERSON-RECORD
02 PERSON-NAME
02 PERSON-ADDRESS

and that each PERSON-RECORD is uniquely identified by the value of PERSON-NAME, e.g. our record declaration might be extended to read:

```
01  PERSON-RECORD;
    IDENTIFYING KEY IS PERSON-NAME;
02  PERSON-NAME
02  PERSON-ADDRESS
```

What this declaration says is *what* the logical structure of the record is and *what* part of the record (the 'key') uniquely identifies an occurrence of the record. It is a *logical data model definition* (in a limited sense) of the record.

How the PERSON-NAME identifier is used to access and store occurrences of PERSON-RECORDs is *not* part of the logical data model definition of the record. It may be achieved by a hashing technique, indexes, or serial search, but these are not logical considerations. If a hashing technique were used, and this was *changed,* for performance considerations to an index technique, the logical structure of the record *would not* have changed. The definition of how the record is accessed and stored is part of the physical data model definition (in fact, as we shall see, part of the storage data model definition).

Example 3

This example is not drawn from computing, but makes the distinction well. Consider a book. We then have the following:

Logical	**Physical**
Word	Printing characters
Sentence	Line
Chapter	Page
Book	Volume

Notice that in this example the relationship between a physical construct and a logical construct is clearly not one-to-one.

The logical data model is clearly *machine independent,* whilst in a very strong sense part of the physical data model is *machine dependent.* It is this separation between the two models that allows the possibility of *physical data independence.* If we change the way that the data is stored and accessed, or laid out on physical devices — in other words change the physical model — we should not have to change the logical model.

So far we have treated the *device data model* and the *storage data model* as being together the *physical model*. We must now make the separation clear.

The *device data model* is concerned with the way that data is allocated to various physical devices, such as discs and tapes, with blocking factors, words, and bytes, etc. Clearly it is *machine dependent:* example 1, above, was really making the distinction between the logical data model and the device data model. The language used for defining the device data model will not be a language peculiar to the DBMS; it will, for all intents and purposes, be part of the operating system language of the machine. Hence the partially dotted line from DBMS to DEVICE MODEL in Fig. 2.1

However, between the device model and the logical model lies the *storage model:* a description of *how* the logical data model is stored and accessed. It is a description of *how* logical data model constructs, in particular logical data model records, are represented as storage data model constructs, in particular storage data model records, so that the *performance* of the database can be tuned in an *optimal* fashion. Of course, storage model constructs do need to be allocated to devices, etc., but the storage data model will tend, like the logical data model, to be *machine independent.* Techniques such as the grouping or splitting of logical data model records into storage data model records, accessing them via an index or hashing algorithm, and so on, are clearly not specific to any one machine. The storage data model will be defined by a *storage data model definition language* that will be peculiar to the DBMS and will be translatable by the DBMS. Example 2, above, was really a distinction between the logical data model and the storage data model. The point can be made more clear by expanding the example. Suppose the PERSON-RECORD was declared as:

> 01 PERSON-RECORD;
> IDENTIFYING KEY IS PERSON-NAME;
> 02 PERSON-NAME
> 02 PERSON-ADDRESS
> 02 PERSON-DETAILS

and that the access pattern for this record was such that

* PERSON-NAME, PERSON-ADDRESS were required frequently and quickly,

34

*   PERSON-NAME, PERSON-DETAILS were required infrequently
with a fairly slow response.

We could then define two storage records, thus:

01 STORAGE-RECORD IS PERSON-BASIC;
LOCATED BY HASHING IDENTIFYING KEY
USING NAME-HASH;
02 PERSON-NAME
02 PERSON-ADDRESS

01 STORAGE-RECORD IS PERSON-EXTRA;
LOCATED BY INDEX SEQUENTIAL USING
IDENTIFYING KEY;
02 PERSON-NAME
02 PERSON-DETAILS

to reflect this access pattern. The fact that PERSON-BASIC was stored on
a high-speed disc, and that PERSON-NAME was coded in hexadecimal
bytes would be a property of the device data model, as would the fact that
PERSON-EXTRA was stored on a slower speed device.

The ANSI/X3/SPARC equivalent for the storage data model is the
internal schema. The reader is referred to reference (2.3) for further
details of a well defined storage data model definition language.

What is important for us concerning storage data models is that they are
precisely the things that need to be changed in a database system to
reflect a change in volumes of stored data, accessing patterns, and so on,
without having to change the logical data model (and, hence, possibly
programs). Clearly, if such models are generalised, we can discuss
general strategies and languages for making such changes.

2.2 LOGICAL MODELS AND LOGICAL SUB-MODELS

A *logical data sub-model* is a description of the restricted view taken by
an application program or group of application programs of the logical
data model. The sub-model takes a *parochial* view, whilst the logical
model takes a *global* view. The sub-model view must be *derivable* from
the logical model. For example, a logical data sub-model may involve
the omission of record types, field types, and record relationship types;

different data definition of data types; different sequencing of data types; and so on.

Logical data sub-models are important for two interrelated reasons:

*   they permit the *application orientated* views of data that were discussed in the previous Chapter; each application, such as Course Administration, would have a logical data sub-model defined for it.

*   they allow the possibility of *logical data independence* discussed in Chapter 1: a change to the logical data model in areas not involved in a particular application's logical data sub-model should result in no need to change the application programs using that logical data sub-model.

Because of this we can realise two important features:

*   the logical data model will be described in a *program independent* way: it has to support logical data sub-models for several high level programming languages. Therefore there will be only *one* language for defining the logical data model in a given database system. There will also effectively be only *one* logical data model for a given database system (although, as we shall see, we shall want to qualify this statement later).

*   logical data sub-models will be described in *program dependent* ways. Therefore there will be as many languages for defining logical data sub-models as there are high level programming languages in a database system. For example, there will be perhaps a PL/I logical data sub-model language, a COBOL logical data sub-model language and so on. These languages will *not* be the same as the relevant data description portions of the high level languages themselves. Rather, they will interface to them: employing similar constructs. The major differences will be, as we might expect, some explicit form of *relationship* description. There will effectively be *many* logical data-sub models in a database system — roughly as many as there are distinct applications.

The logical data sub-models will be defined in *logical data sub-model definition languages* that will be translatable by the DBMS.

The ANSI/X3/SPARC term for a logical data sub-model is an *external schema.*

2.3 A LANGUAGE TO MANIPULATE THE DATABASE

This discussion of the interface between high level languages and the database system leads us naturally to the problem of how application programs manipulate the database, and in particular the new constructs explicity describing *relationships* that we saw were lacking in languages, such as COBOL, that had developed around conventional file structures. In theory there are two possibilities:

(i) a special purpose language — in short all the development put into languages such as COBOL would be abandoned and a new generation of languages would be designed.

(ii) a *host* language approach — existing high level languages would remain but would have special purpose database commands embedded in them, possibly specific to the programming language concerned.

Not surprisingly, as the previous discussion has hinted, approach (ii) has largley been followed — at least for application programs written by application programmers. The extent of the 'embedding' has varied. For example, COBOL using the CODASYL approach has resulted in an effective extension to the COBOL language, whilst FORTRAN using the CODASYL approach has resulted in no significant extension of FORTRAN since the language 'extensions' are handled via a CALL interface — see reference (2.4). Approach (i) has been used, however, in developing general purpose *query languages* for use by the so-called *end-user* — that is, non-programming staff such as administrators, clerks and so on. It has been argued that for such users the logical sub-model approach to viewing the data is too restrictive and is too program orientated. Suggestions have been made that their view of data is embedded in the structure of the dialogue they have with the computer. Reference (2.5) gives one particular approach, but the area is under critical development and a clear consensus is unlikely to emerge for some time.

2.4 MAPPINGS

2.4.1 Logical data sub-model — logical data model

How complex this mapping is allowed to be determines the degree of flexibility that the database system has in defining application orientated views. Some database system approaches, for example, do not allow logical records to be combined to form logical sub-model records. To illustrate this let us consider our sample data from UniHyp, which is given again in type form as Fig. 2.2, showing the relationships.

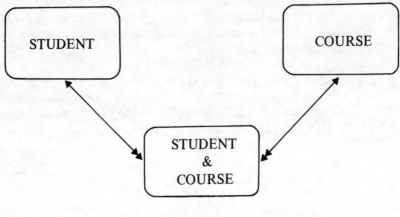

Fig. 2.2

Occurrences of each *box* relate directly to each *row* from the relevant table in Fig. 1.7. Let us assume that we have some form of logical data model that allows us to translate this directly to records and some form of relationship between records, as in Fig. 2.3.

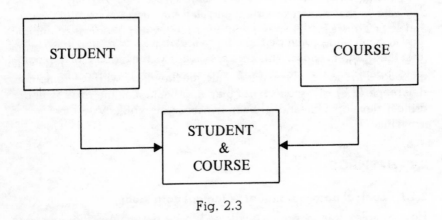

Fig. 2.3

Slightly different conventions are used to depict this to show that we are dealing with a logical data model.

Now, if we are to provide the logical data sub-model required by Student Administration, given as Fig. 2.4, we must form a single STUDENT-RECORD by taking various data items from all three of our logical data model records and combining them in a given way.

```
┌─────────────┐
│             │
│  STUDENT –  │
│  RECORD     │
│             │
└─────────────┘
```

Fig. 2.4

Note that we have re-introduced an element of redundancy here into the logical data sub-model that was absent in the logical data model. However, this is no longer the disaster that it was — we have only been making multiple copies of one thing that is stored once in the logical data model (conceptually at least — there may be multiple copies in the storage model for efficiency reasons).

If we cannot combine logical data model records in this fashion then clearly we cannot immediately satisfy the views required by the Student Administration and Course Administration departments. However, as we shall see later, this may not always be too much of a handicap.

Clearly, however, whatever the nature of the mapping it must be defined and at some stage converted into an executable set of routines and tables that the DBMS may use. This conversion allows the *binding* of the logical data model and the logical data sub-model with the program. That is, requests from a particular application program for one of its logical data sub-model record occurrences can be translated or mapped into requests for the necessary logical data model record(s). *When* this mapping or binding can be made clearly determines the degree of logical data independence made possible by the separation of the logical data model and the logical data sub-models. We have two extreme cases:

* the binding is made at every access or manipulation of the database by an application program. All the necessary tables and routines for carrying out the mapping need to be present. Such an approach may prove expensive in terms of software and processing time, but provides a high degree of logical data independence. A change to the logical data model that impacts

on a logical data sub-model will require a change to the mapping and not an associated change to the programs using the logical data sub-model.

* the binding is made in conjunction with the compilation of the application program. The necessary tables and routines need to be present only during the compilation process which now effectively binds program, logical data sub-model, and logical data model. Such an approach may prove cheaper in terms of software and processing time, but curtails logical data independence. A change to the logical data model that impacts on a logical data sub-model will require a change to the mapping and an associated re-compilation of programs using the logical data sub-model.

The state of the art is such that the latter method is used in many database system implementations.

2.4.2 Logical model — physical model

Again we would expect the mapping to be complex. Take, for example, the STUDENT logical data model record from Fig 2.3. We might wish, as discussed in Chapter 1, to store different occurrences of this record type in different ways to reflect the access pattern: frequently accessed occurrences as one type of storage record, infrequently accessed occurrences as another as illustrated in Fig. 2.5.

Or, it may be the case that within the STUDENT record we have a group of frequently accessed items, say REG-NO and NAME, and a group of infrequently accessed items, say ADDRESS, DATE-OF-BIRTH, and DATE-OF-REGISTRATION. We may therefore want to split the actual record type into two separate storage record types, as in Fig. 2.6

Or it may be that STUDENT and STUDENT & COURSE are accessed together so frequently that we wish to reflect this fact, as in Fig. 2.7.

The flexibility in the mapping will determine to a large extent the efficiency of the database system, and also the degree of physical data independence. If this sort of flexibility is not available, then the database designer is often forced to represent these accessing patterns in the logical data model, with the consequent penalty incurred should they change.

Whatever the nature of the mapping, it will need to be defined and binding will need to occur. A similar set of considerations apply here as did in Section 2.4.1.

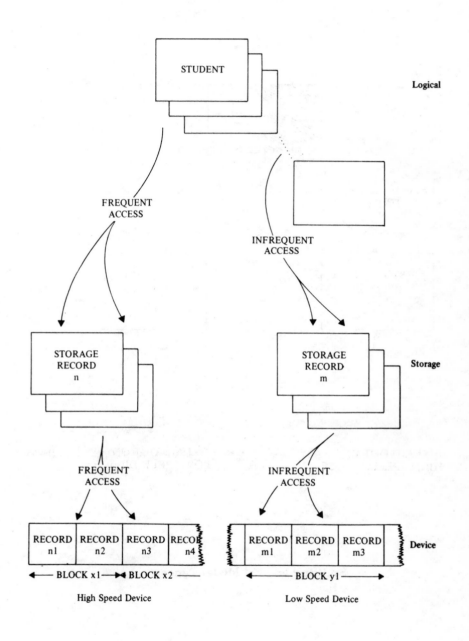

Fig. 2.5
Partitioning Logical Model Occurrences

41

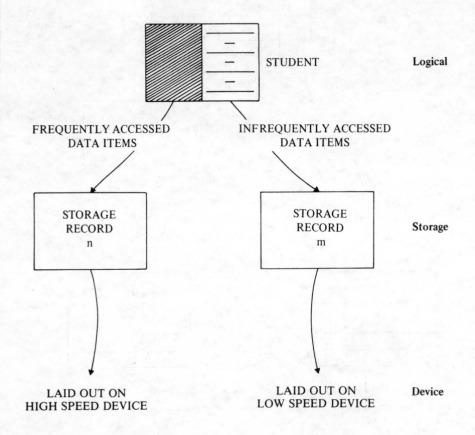

STUDENT   Logical

FREQUENTLY ACCESSED
DATA ITEMS

INFREQUENTLY ACCESSED
DATA ITEMS

STORAGE
RECORD
n

STORAGE
RECORD
m

Storage

LAID OUT ON
HIGH SPEED DEVICE

LAID OUT ON
LOW SPEED DEVICE

Device

Fig. 2.6
Splitting Logical Model Types

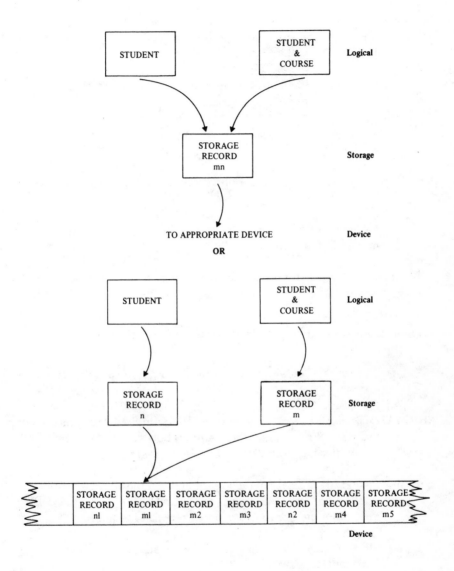

Fig. 2.7
Grouping Logical Model Types

43

2.5 THE ROLE OF THE DATABASE MANAGEMENT SYSTEM

The database management system (DBMS) is the software, used in conjunction with application programs, that generates, operates and maintains the database. The involvement it has with all the components of the architecture is shown in Fig. 2.1. It must have the facility to translate and comprehend at least four separate languages:

* the storage data model definition language that defines the storage data model.

* the logical data model definition language that defines the logical data model.

* the logical data sub-model definition language**s** that define the logical data sub-model**s**.

* the language — or more correctly — the partial language that manipulates the database.

It must also provide the facility to translate between the languages: to effect the mappings.

Simplistically, we can have the following sequence of events:

i) a program issues a request for a given *logical data sub-model record.*

ii) using the logical data sub-model definition, the logical data model definition, and the mapping between the two, the DBMS identifies the *logical data model record(s)* required.

iii) using the logical data model definition, the storage data model definition and the mapping between the two, the DBMS identifies the *storage data model record(s)* required.

iv) the storage data model records are retrieved from the appropriate device.

v) using the models and the mappings a *logical data sub-model record* is constructed and placed in the *workspace* of the calling program.

Notice that no real mention has been made of the device data model or the mapping between it and the storage data model. This is because our simplistic view is complicated by the fact that most machines have a well-tried resident piece of software, one of whose tasks is the manipulation of blocks and pages on physical devices, viz. the operating system. If operating systems and DBMSs had been developed together then it is possible that an integrated approach might have been adopted. However, most database systems use the DBMS as an *independent* system acting through an interface to the operating system as shown in Fig. 2.8.

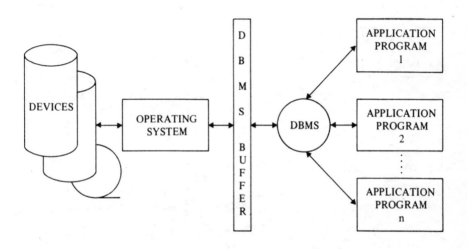

Fig. 2.8

Hence the DBMS comprehends very little of the device level view and "sees" the operating system as a device management system. The operating system effectively "sees" the DBMS as one large program that continuously passes requests to it for the access and storage of data at the device level.

We can now revise our simplistic account by giving a conceptual account of the operation of a database system, as in Fig. 2.9

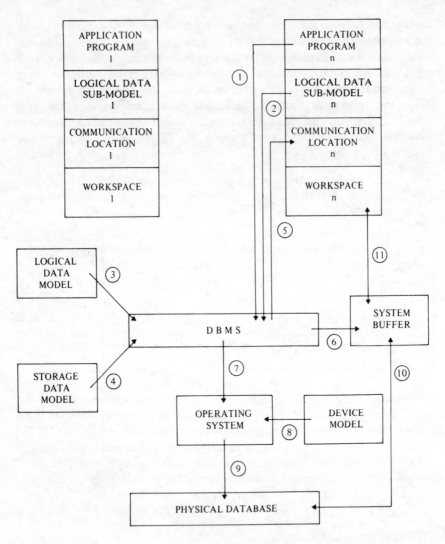

Fig. 2.9
Conceptual Operation of a Database System

* An application program requests a logical data sub-model record occurrence (1).

* The DBMS consults the appropriate logical data sub-model (2), the logical data model (3), and the storage model (4) to determine the storage record(s) required. The application

program request may be detected as being in violation of an access constraint (stated in the logical model, or in the logical sub-model), in which case an appropriate error indication will be made in the communications location (5) and the request will be aborted.

* The DBMS examines the system buffer to see if the physical units of data are already present (6).

* If they are not, then it issues a request to the operating system (7) for the storage records.

* The operating system consults the device model (8) and then locates and retrieves (9) the physical units of data and places them in the system buffer(10).

* The DBMS performs the necessary transformations to create the logical data sub-model record occurrence required, (4), (3), (2), and places the occurrence in the workspace of the application program (11), informing the application program of this via the communications locations (5).

* If no logical data sub-model occurrence actually existed in the database the DBMS informs the application program via the communications locations (5).

What is significant about this use of the operating system is that all the problems that operating systems have solved in certain areas are thrown back to the DBMS. If we are going to allow, as we surely are, *several* application programs to access the database concurrently then we shall have all the problems of concurrent usage to deal with within the DBMS, since as far as the operating system is concerned it is simply one (rather large) program that issues access and storage requests to it. We shall examine these problems and one way of solving them later in Chapter 4.

SUMMARY

A database system provides:

* a storage view of the data — the storage data model — and a . language for defining it.

* an organisational view of the data — the logical data model — and a language for defining it.

* application views of the data — the logical data sub-models — and languages for defining them.

* languages for manipulating the database.

software — the DBMS — that controls the connection and interrelation of these components and the interface to the operating system and the machine, or device level, view of data.

REFERENCES AND BIBLIOGRAPHY

(2.1)   **ANSI/X3/SPARC Study Group on Data Base Management Systems: Interim Report**. In FDT, the Bulletin of the ACM SIGMOD (Special Interest Group on the Management of Data) **7**, 2, 1975. An edited and more readable version of the Study Group's **Report** is contained in **The ANSI/X3/SPARC DBMS Framework**, edited by D. Tsichritizis and A. Klug, AFIPS Press, 1977.

(2.2)   Jardine D.A. (ed.), **The ANSI/SPARC DBMS Model**, North Holland, 1977.

(2.3)   CODASYL Data Description Language Committee **Journal of Development**, 1978.

(2.4)   Stacey, G.M. **A FORTRAN Interface to the CODASYL Data Base Task Group Specifications**, Computer Journal, **17**, 2, May, 1974.

(2.5)   **A progress Report on the Activities of the CODASYL End User Facility Task Group**, FDT, Bulletin of ACM SIGMOD, **8**, 1, 1976.

(2.6)   Nijssen, G.M. **A Gross Architecture for the Next Generation Database Management Systems**, in **Modelling in Data Base Management Systems**, ed. G. M. Nijssen, North Holland, 1976.

(2.7)   Date, C.J. **An Introduction to Database Systems**, Addison-Wesley, 1975

EXERCISES

2.1   In one sense, COBOL provides a rudimentary file management, access and storage system. Try to develop an architecture for COBOL in terms of the generalised architecture given in Fig. 2.1. Hint: for example, is the logical model distinct from the storage model?

2.2   This Chapter has concentrated on how the architecture
        supports the central objectives of the database approach: the
        provision of data independence and the ability to support
        conflicting needs. How does the architecture support the
        remaining objectives listed in Chapter 1?

Chapter 3

RELATIONAL DATABASE SYSTEMS

*"The words 'attribute' and 'relation' turn up so often in
the best discourse on the best of subjects . . ."*
Willard Van Orman Quine, From a Logical Point of View

For most of the rest of this Part of the book we shall concentrate on logical data models and logical data sub-models since it is here that the main emphasis of definition has been made and where the significant differences between the various approaches to database systems lie.

3.1 DATA AS TABLES: RELATIONS

We have already met a relational logical data model (or *relational schema* as it is sometimes called). The relational logical data model is based upon *tables* and we have a relational logical data model in the tables given in Chapter 1, which are reproduced here as Fig. 3.1.

3.1.1 A simple approach

The relational approach was largely pioneered by the work of E. F. Codd in the early 1970's and is very firmly based on sound mathematical ideas from set theory — hence *relations* (which should *not* be confused with *relationships*). Such a firm basis obviously gives it a strong appeal, and much of the theory that has been generated in the database area has stemmed from the relational approach, as we shall see in later chapters. However, its major appeal (and that preached by its advocates) is its simplicity: tables are a very simple and natural way of regarding data. We shall be pursuing this theme during the Chapter. References at the end of the Chapter give details of more rigorous treatments.

51

STUDENTS

REG. NO.	NAME	ADDRESS	DATE-OF-BIRTH	DATE-OF-REGISTRATION
9491	B. ROBERTS	9 INKERMAN ST.	8.6.58	1.10.77
3123	G. JUNG	26 SHAW ST.	19.11.59	2.10.78
7416	C. DAY	63 SPRING RD.	3.2.60	3.10.78
9372	D. THOMAS	14 CHURCH END	7.7.59	1.10.77
4739	D. WHITE	2 WARWICK AV.	21.1.61	1.10.79

COURSES

COURSE CODE	COURSE NAME	RATING	DATE-OF-INTRO	FACULTY
PHI 121	THE EARLY WITTGENSTEIN	1	1975	HUMANITIES
PHI 102	KANTIAN METAPHYSICS	2	1973	HUMANITIES
LIT 312	THE EXPATRIATES	2	1976	HUMANITIES
COMP141	COMPUTER ARCHITECTURE	1	1975	MATHEMATICS
COMP222	ADVANCED DATA STRUCTURES	2	1978	MATHEMATICS
CHEM301	MOLECULAR GENETICS	1	1979	SCIENCE
ENG 111	BASIC SURVEYING	1	1974	ENGINEERING
COMP272	CONCEPTUAL MODELS	2	1979	MATHEMATICS

STUDENTS AND COURSES

REG. NO.	COURSE CODE	RESULT
9491	PHI 121	PASS
9491	PHI 102	PASS
9491	LIT 312	PASS
9491	ENG 111	FAIL
3123	COMP141	PASS
3123	LIT 312	PASS
3123	ENG 111	FAIL
3123	PHI 102	PASS
7416	ENG 111	PASS
7416	CHEM301	–
7416	LIT 312	PASS
7416	COMP141	PASS
9372	PHI 121	FAIL
9372	PHI 102	FAIL
9372	ENG 111	PASS
9372	CHEM301	–

Fig. 3.1
Relational Tables

Before we begin, it is as well to remark that the relational approach does not use just *any* sort of table. The tables conform to a set of rules (that are an expression in 'table language' of what is effectively meant by a relation):

* Each box in a table contains one value — it is 'atomic'.
* Within a column the box values are all of the same kind.
* Each column has a distinct name.
* Each row is unique — there are no duplicates.
* The ordering of the rows and columns is not, for our purposes, significant.

Notice how the tables in Fig. 3.1 conform to these rules.

Two simple processes

To illustrate the simplicity of the relational approach consider two processes that need to be carried out at UniHyp.

Process 1

Course Administration wishes to know the REG. NO.s of the STUDENTs on a particular COURSE, say PHI 102.

This operation can be carried out intuitively by scanning down the STUDENTS AND COURSES tables looking for occurrences of 'PHI 102' in the COURSE CODE column and reading off the appropriate values in the REG. NO. column.

i.e. we get '9491', '3123', '9372'

Of course, the process required by Course Administration may not be quite this simple. They may require the NAMEs of all STUDENTs on a particular COURSE, say PHI 102.

The first part of the process would be as before: the STUDENTS AND COURSES table would be examined and would yield the REG. NOs. '9491', '3123', '9372'. The STUDENTS table would then be examined looking for each of the selected REG. NO. entries and the appropriate values in the NAME column would be read,

i.e. we get 'B.ROBERTS', 'G.JUNG', 'D.THOMAS'.

Things could, of course, get yet more complicated. The request could be for the NAMEs of all STUDENTs who are on a COURSE which is the responsibility of the MATHEMATICS FACULTY. We can formalise the steps in our operation into an algorithm, thus:

1. Take the COURSES table and search the column headed FACULTY for entries equal to 'MATHEMATICS'. For each of these entries read along the row selected and read the value in the COURSE CODE column. We get three values: 'COMP141', 'COMP222', and 'COMP272'.

2. Take the COURSE CODE values obtained in 1 and search the COURSE CODE column in the STUDENTS AND COURSES table for a matches on each of these values. We match in fact on COMP141 only and obtain two matches: '3123 COMP141 PASS', '7416 COMP 141 PASS'. For each match read along the selected row and find the entry in the REG. NO. column. We obtain '3123' and '7416'.

3. Take the REG. NOs. obtained and search the STUDENTS table by looking down the REG. NO. column for a match with the two values. When a match occurs read along the selected row and find the entry in the NAME column. We obtain our result of 'G.JUNG' and 'C.DAY'.

Process 2

Student Administration wishes to know what are the COURSE CODEs of the COURSESs studied by the STUDENT with REG. NO. of 9491.

We take the STUDENTS AND COURSES table and look down the REG. NO. column for a value of '9491'. We get four matches. For each match we read across the matched row and find the value in the COURSE CODE column.

i.e. we get 'PHI 121', 'PHI 102', 'LIT 312', 'ENG 111'

Matters could be more complex; the process could be to find the COURSE NAMEs of all the COURSES taken by B.ROBERTS.

We would take the STUDENTS table and search the NAME column for a match on 'B.ROBERTS', and read across to the value in the REG. NO. column, obtaining '9491'. We would then examine the STUDENTS AND COURSES table to obtain the four COURSE CODEs, as above. The

COURSES table would then be examined by searching the COURSE CODE column for matches on these four values. For each match we would read across to the COURSE NAME column and read the appropriate value, obtaining our result of 'THE EARLY WITTGENSTEIN', 'KANTIAN METAPHYSICS', 'THE EXPATRIATES', and 'BASIC SURVEYING'.

Finally, our process could be to retrieve the COURSE NAMEs of all COURSES studied by STUDENTS born later than 31.12.59. As before, we can formalise this thus:

1. Take the STUDENTS table and read the DATE-OF-BIRTH column for entries later than '31.12.59'. For each match read across to the REG. NO. column and read the appropriate entry. We obtain '7416' and '4739'.

2. Taking the two REG. NO. values obtained in 1, search the REG. NO. column of the STUDENTS AND COURSES table for matches on these values. For each match read across the row selected and obtain the values in the COURSE CODE column. We get 'ENG 111', 'CHEM301', 'LIT 312', and 'COMP141'.

3. Take the COURSE CODES obtained and search the COURSES table by looking down the COURSE CODE column for a match on each of the values. For each match read across the selected row and obtain the value in the COURSE NAME column. We obtain our result: 'BASIC SURVEYING', 'MOLECULAR GENETICS', 'THE EXPATRIATES', and 'COMPUTER ARCHITECTURE'.

3.1.2 Some observations

1. The processes in our two examples were *symmetric,* just as the problems were symmetric, i.e.

    'The *NAMEs* of all *STUDENTs* who are on a *COURSE* which is the responsibility of the MATHEMATICS FACULTY'.

    and

    'The COURSE *NAMEs* of all *COURSEs* studied by *STUDENTs* born later than 31.12.59'

2. The whole business was achieved by looking through the *rows* and *columns* of *tables.*

55

3. The fact that some STUDENTs were not taking COURSEs, and that some COURSEs were not yet taken by students did not hinder the processes: it merely resulted in a 'no match' situation.

4. We can see the way that the table approach has tackled our two one-to-many relationships of Fig. 1.8. It has been done by having matching values in *common columns*. To find the *rows* in the STUDENTS AND COURSES table related to *one* row in the STUDENTS table we use the fact that REG. NOs. appear in both tables and search the STUDENTS AND COURSES table REG. NO. column for values the same as in the REG. NO. column of the STUDENTS table. Precisely the same holds for finding the *rows* in the STUDENTS AND COURSES table that relate to *one* row in the COURSES table.

3.1.3 A simple extension

We can gain further insight into the simplicity of the relational approach by considering an example taken from the Courses area at UniHyp. It will be recalled from Chapter 1 that one relationship that was significant in UniHyp's data resource was that of *requisites* amongst courses: that a course may require that certain other courses need to be studied previously, and that study in a given course allowed progression to study in other courses.

We can illustrate such a situation with Fig. 3.2 which shows some occurrences of the relationship. The relationship is portrayed as an *hierarchy*, as it naturally might be, say, in an example taken from UniHyp's Prospectus. In order for a student to take Conceptual Models he/she must also have taken (successfully) Business Systems Analysis, Advanced Data Structures, and Structure and Design of Programming Languages. In order to take the latter, the student must have taken Basic Data Structures, Principles of Programming, and Compiling Techniques. And so on for other courses. Conversley, if a student has (successfully) taken Basic Data Structures it becomes possible for Advanced Data Structures and Compiling Techniques to be taken. If in addition, after taking Compiling Techniques, Principles of Programming has been taken, then the student can take the Structure and Design of Programming Languages. It is worth noticing two points:

1. The hierarchical method of displaying the relationship occurrences introduces redundancy, Basic Data Structures is duplicated several times.

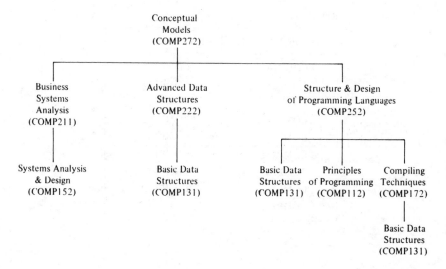

Fig. 3.2
Requisites at UniHyp

2. This type of situation is similar to the bill-of-materials problem often encountered in production control: the need to express what products are needed to make a particular product, and what products a particular product is used to make. In terms of a relationship **type** the situation is as in Fig. 3.3.

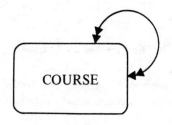

Fig. 3.3
A Many-to-Many Relationship Involving One Thing

Fig. 3.4 shows one way that a relational approach might handle the situation.

REQUISITES

MAJCOURSE CODE	MINCOURSE CODE
COMP272	COMP211
COMP272	COMP222
COMP272	COMP252
COMP211	COMP152
COMP222	COMP131
COMP252	COMP131
COMP252	COMP112
COMP252	COMP172
COMP172	COMP131

COURSES

COURSE CODE	COURSE NAME . . . .
COMP272	CONCEPTUAL MODELS
COMP211	BUSINESS SYSTEMS ANALYSIS
COMP222	ADVANCED DATA STRUCTURES
COMP252	STRUCTURE AND DESIGN OF PROGRAMMING LANGUAGES
COMP152	SYSTEMS ANALYSIS AND DESIGN
COMP131	BASIC DATA STRUCTURES
COMP112	PRINCIPLES OF PROGRAMMING
COMP172	COMPILING TECHNIQUES

Fig. 3.4
Requisites as Tables

First notice that we have *two* tables: one (REQUISITES) handles the actual relationship between courses, whilst the other (COURSES) holds all the necessary information about a course — in other words it is another example of the same COURSE table as in Fig. 3.1. This also eliminates our redundancy problems: we seem to have 'one fact in one place'. The techniques for ensuring such a situation are known as *normalisation* and were first developed in relational database theroy, but now have such widespread application that they are treated separately in Chapter 7.

Secondly see how easily the REQUISITES table handles the sort of questions that might be posed.

Question 1

'What courses must I study in order to take COMP272?'

Answer

The MAJCOURSE CODE column is searched for entries equal to 'COMP272'. For each match the corresponding value in the MINCOURSE CODE column is read: 'COMP211', 'COMP222', and 'COMP252'.

The process can be repeated to find out what course are required for any of these. Eventually we might come to examine what courses are needed for 'COMP131': the abscence of any entries in the MAJCOURSE CODE column tells us that there are no pre-requisites.

Question 2

'What courses can I study now that I have taken COMP131?'

Answer

The MINCOURSE CODE column is searched for entries equal to 'COMP131'. For each match the corresponding MAJCOURSE CODE values is read, giving 'COMP222', 'COMP252', and 'COMP172'. If I now wish to ensure that no other courses are required for each of these, I must repeat the process of Question 1, and I will find that I can take COMP172 and COMP222 without the necessity of taking any other pre-requisites.

3.1.4 Terminology

The previous examples have shown the power of employing a simple concept like that of tables to represent data and its relationships. However, as might be expected, something based on mathematical theory could not simply be described in terms of tables, rows and columns. There is a specialised set of terms to confuse the uninitiated.

A *table* is called a RELATION (not to be confused with a relationship).

A *row* is called a TUPLE, or sometimes an n-TUPLE, where n is the number of columns in the table (relation).

A *column* is called an ATTRIBUTE.

The *values* in a column are drawn from a DOMAIN. For instance, with the REQUISITES table (relation) we have two attributes — MAJCOURSE CODE and MINCOURSE CODE both having values drawn from the common domain of COURSE CODEs.

The *number of columns* (attributes) in a table (relation) is the DEGREE of the relation.

The *number of rows* (tuples) in a table (relation) is the CARDINALITY of the relation.

This terminology is illustrated in Fig. 3.5.

Relations may be informally defined by giving a name to the relation and the names of its attributes, thus:

COURSES (COURSE CODE, COURSE NAME, RATING, DATE-OF-INTRO, FACULTY)

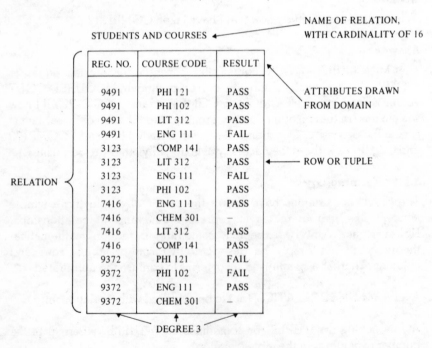

Fig. 3.5
Relational Terminology

RELATION STUDENTS- AND-COURSES	(REG. NO.	DOMAIN REG. NO.,
	COURSE CODE	DOMAIN COURSE CODE,
	RESULT	DOMAIN RESULT)

Several things are worth noting here.

1. The declaration of DOMAINs allows us to define formats and standards for the data items in the relations. Despite the different syntax it is not essentially different in *what* it is saying to facilities in other database systems, such as CODASYL. However, *where* it is saying it is different: the declarations are not associated with any particular relation — they are statements about the data as a whole. As we shall see, this forms a small beginning for a data dictionary, a beginning of data about data and the interesting point is that it is included in the relational schema definition.

2. The declaration of domains *separate* from attributes allows us to explicity say that DATE-OF-BIRTH and DATE-OF-REGISTRATION are the same sort of thing, but in this application are different from DATE-OF-INTRODUCTION.

3. The definition given is not in any standard syntax — simply because no such standard exists. The syntax used here is based on that employed by C. J. Date in Reference (3.9). In practice when such a standard is developed there will be a greater need for punctuation and consistent forms for names of relations, attributes and domains — notice that this has informally been done in the case of writing STUDENTS AND COURSES as STUDENTS-AND-COURSES. Correspondingly there will be default options that do not require the declaration of a DOMAIN name following an ATTRIBUTE declaration where the two names are the same.

3.2 THE MANIPULATION OF RELATIONS

The algorithms given in section 3.1.1 illustrate well the intuitive approach to manipulating relations. Our manipulation is done with a conceptual pair of scissors and a conceptual pot of glue. We cut up our tables and stick the pieces together again to form new relations — the only rule being that we can only stick glue over common columns, and that it only sticks on common values.

Such algorithms need to be formally described in terms of a programming language, or, more properly, in terms of the partial programming language that will be hosted in an existing high level language. Part of the appeal of the relational approach is the sorts of (partial) programming languages that are possible.

3.2.1 A tuple-based language

Like many new developments the relational approach is in one sense a new twist to an old idea. One can regard relations as *files* in the conventional data processing sense, with the provisos mentioned in 3.1.1. Tuples then become *records,* attributes become *data item* or *field types* (with corresponding *occurrences* of the values permitted), the degree of the relation becomes the *number* of *data item types* in the *record,* and the cardinality becomes the *number* of *records* in the *file.*

For example, our relation COURSES may be regarded as a file consisting only of occurrences of the following record type:

    01 COURSES-RECORD
        02 COURSE-CODE
        02 COURSE-NAME
        02 RATING
        02 DATE-OF-INTRO
        02 FACULTY

It is therefore possible to define a partial language that manipulates relations (files) at the tuple (record) level — rather as COBOL or PL/I does. Algorithms described in such a language would, like COBOL or PL/I, contain a specification of *what* processing needs to be done, *as well as* a description of *how* it is to be carried out: that is, it is highly *procedural.*

Such an approach to the manipulation of relations has not, in fact, been developed significantly since there are two other possibilities that are more attractive.

3.2.2 Languages based on relational algebra

Since relations are mathematical constructs we can use mathematical approaches to specify our manipulation. One approach is to base such a language on *relational algebra.* For example, we could describe the process of retrieving the NAMEs of all STUDENTS who are on a COURSE which is the responsibility of the MATHEMATICS FACULTY in a language based on relational algebra language thus (using a syntax and style based on that described in Reference (3.9)):

1. SELECT *COURSES* WHERE FACULTY = 'MATHEMATICS' GIVING *R1*

2. JOIN *R1* AND *STUDENTS-AND-COURSES* OVER COURSE CODE GIVING *R2*

3. JOIN *R2* AND *STUDENTS* OVER REG. NO. GIVING *R3*

4. PROJECT *R3* OVER NAME GIVING *ANSWER*

The relations being operated on have been *italicised*: R1, R2, R3 are temporary, "working", relations and ANSWER is a relation of degree 1 cardinality 2, the tuples being 'G.JUNG' and 'C.DAY'.

This book is not centered on database processing, and we will not enter into a discursive account of relational algebra, but it is important to see the sort of thing that is happening here.

Step 1 effectively cuts out from the COURSES relation the tuples that have a value of 'MATHEMATICS' for the FACULTY attribute. R1 therefore consists of three tuples:

'COMP141, COMPUTER ARCHITECTURE, 1, 1975, MATHEMATICS'.

'COMP222, ADVANCED DATA STRUCTURES, 2, 1978, MATHEMATICS'.

'COMP272, CONCEPTUAL MODELS, 2, 1979, MATHEMATICS'.

Step 2 effectively sticks, and therefore selects, these tuples onto those tuples in the STUDENTS-AND-COURSES relation that have the *same* COURSE CODE values. R2 therefore has two tuples:

'3123, COMP141, PASS, COMPUTER ARCHITECTURE, 1, 1975, MATHEMATICS'.

'7416, COMP141, PASS, COMPUTER ARCHITECTURE, 1, 1975, MATHEMATICS'.

Step 3 effectively sticks our extended and selected R2 tuples to tuples in the STUDENTS relation where the REG. NO. value is the same. Two such tuples are identified giving for our R3 relation:

'3123, G.JUNG, 26 SHAW ST., 19.11.59, 2.10.78, COMP141, PASS, COMPUTER ARCHITECTURE, 1, 1975, MATHEMATICS'.

'7416, C.DAY, 63 SPRING RD., 3.2.60, 3.10.78, COMP141, PASS, COMPUTER ARCHITECTURE, 1, 1975, MATHEMATICS'.

Step 4 effectively masks out all the attributes in R3 except those that interest us, giving the two unary tuples of ANSWER.

What is happening is that we have a language that is at a higher *level* than the tuple-based language and is less *procedurally orientated* than the tuple-based language. Operations are defined on *relations,* not on the *tuples* that make up the relations. There is some form of *processing independence:* a separation of *what* needs to be done from *how* it is done. This separation is not complete because we could have written:

1. JOIN *STUDENTS* AND *STUDENTS-AND-COURSES* OVER REG. NO. GIVING *R1a.*

2. JOIN *R1a* AND *COURSES* OVER COURSE CODE GIVING *R2a.*

3. SELECT *R2a* WHERE FACULTY = 'MATHEMATICS' GIVING *R3a.*

4. PROJECT *R3a* OVER NAME GIVING *ANSWER.*

and still have achieved the same result.

3.2.3 Languages based on relational calculus

A more exciting approach is that based on a relational calculus, which is in turn based on the first-order predicate calculus of mathematical logic. E. F. Codd (Ref. (3.3)) has proposed such a language — "data sub-language ALPHA" — which exhibits a high degree of processing independence. There is a strong separation of *what* processing needs to be done from *how* it is practically performed. For example our process of 3.2.2 could be described in a relational calculus as:

RANGE STUDENTS-AND-COURSES SC

RANGE COURSES C

GET W (STUDENTS.NAME): $\exists$SC(SC.REG.NO. = STUDENTS.REG.NO.
$\qquad\qquad\qquad\land\exists$C(C.COURSE CODE = SC.COURSE CODE
$\qquad\qquad\qquad\land$C.FACULTY = 'MATHEMATICS'))

What these statements do essentially is as follows:

1. The RANGE statements provide us with a shorthand way of referring to our relations (although they are needed for other reasons).

2. GET W (STUDENTS.NAME) — this states that we want in the workspace is a relation of degree one consisting of NAMEs from the STUDENTS relation.

3. : ∃SC. . . . etc. — this specifies the selection criteria for these NAMEs. We will only select those whose REG. NO. exists in both STUDENTS and SC, and then we will only select those where the COURSE CODE in SC is the same as the COURSE CODE in C with a value in the FACULTY attribute of 'MATHEMATICS'.

The expression specifies the *intent* of the process leaving the implementation (and optimisation) to software that may possibly operate in some form of a tuple-based language.

These examples of relational algebra and relational calculus are given not because they are vitally necessary to the analysis and design of a system using database (*practically,* at the moment they are not — but this situation is liable to change in the future), but because they illustrate something frequently overlooked in computer science: *common themes.*

Much of this book so far has emphasised the need to separate out a description of *what* the data structure is, from a description of *how* it is accessed and stored. This emphasis will continue in the Parts on Analysis, Design and Implementation. Here we have a similar emphasis developed in the area of programming languages. What *is* practically important to database analysts and designers is to realise that the distinctions and techniques that they use have been made or are being made in other areas of computer science. This produces a vital area of common ground between specialists. The database analyst and designer should be aware when talking of design techniques, data independence, etc. to systems analysts and programmers that they have very similar concerns, albeit phrased in different terminology. It is important to recognise this similarity, and not to perpetuate a gulf in understanding (and consequent rejection) that may jeopardise the successful use of a database system in an organisation. Reference (3.4) details one eminent authority's views on the independence issue in the specification of programming languages.

However, the reader should not dismiss relational calculus as something that programmers practically may never use: Reference (3.5) suggests some realistic extensions to COBOL to incorporate a relational calculus based partial language.

3.3 MAPPINGS

As was pointed out in Section 2.4.1, the complexity of the mapping between logical data models and logical data sub-models is of some importance in determining the degree of flexibility that a database system has in defining differing application orientated views.

3.3.1 The relational sub-models

Fig. 3.6 shows that the relational logical data sub-model (or relational sub-schema) is made up of relations. This need not necessarily be the case: it is possible for the logical sub-model to provide other structures. For example, conventional files could easily be defined (following the suggestions of 3.2.1) based on an underlying relational schema. A similar approach is possible for hierarchies or CODASYL-type structures. Indeed, it is likely that full-scale commercial implementations of the relational approach will support such other views. However, for clarity, in this chapter we shall restrict ourselves to regarding the relational sub-model as being composed of relations.

3.3.2 The mapping

Example 1

The view required by Student Administration at UniHyp could be provided by the following three relations:

RELATION STDNTS (REG.NO., NAME, ADDRESS, DATE-OF-BIRTH, DATE-OF-REGISTRATION)

RELATION CRSES (COURSE CODE,COURSE NAME,RATING)

RELATION SDNTS-AND-CRSES (REG.NO., COURSE CODE, RESULT)

The mapping could then be defined *using* either languages based on relational calculus or relational algebra. For example, using algebra:

MAPPING

    STUDENTS IS STDNTS;

    PROJECT COURSES OVER COURSE CODE,COURSE NAME, RATING GIVING CRSES;

    STUDENTS-AND-COURSES IS SDNTS-AND-CRSES;

Example 2

Suppose that Course Administration at UniHyp required a view of the data involving the addresses of students on courses, to support some statistical research. Such a view could be defined by a relation thus:

RELATION STUDADDRESS (REG. NO.,COURSE CODE,ADDRESS)

The mapping could then be defined as:

MAPPING
> PROJECT(JOIN STUDENTS-AND-COURSES AND COURSES
> > OVER REG.NO.)
> > OVER REG.NO.,COURSE CODE,ADDRESS
> GIVING STUDADDRESS;

Which is a more elegant way of saying:

JOIN STUDENTS - AND - COURSES AND COURSES OVER REG. NO. GIVING R1
PROJECT R1 OVER REG. NO., COURSE CODE, ADDRESS GIVING STUDADDRESS;

Notice that here we have *combined* logical model objects to form logical sub-model objects. Our mapping is not restricted to being a simple sub-set.

3.4 IMPLEMENTATION

No large-scale commercial implementation of the relational approach is available at the time of writing. This is largley because of the problem of efficiently implementing relational structures at the storage and device levels. The JOIN operation, for example, requires (conceptually, at least) that all the many values of a particular attribute be found. This can, of course, result in lengthy searches on backing store. However, some promising experimental systems and small to medium-scale commercial systems have been developed, and it is likely that a large-scale commercially available system available will be produced in the near future, possibly by IBM.

Because of this lack of any widely accepted commercial system it should be realised that the architecture diagram of Fig. 3.6 is essentially incomplete. No accepted relational approach to the storage data model exists and the situation is similar in the data dictionary area.

Reference (3.6) details one of the more successful experimental systems, and it should be noted that ADABAS (see Chapter 5) has certain relational properties, and that the MAGNUM relational system of Tymshare is currently enjoying some commercial success, as is the RAPPORT system of Logica.

SUMMARY

The relational approach to logical data models is simple and natural. However, it is not widely used but will be increasingly important in future work.

REFERENCES AND BIBLIOGRAPHY

(3.1)   Codd E.F., **A Relational Model of Data for Large Shared Data Banks**, Comm. ACM, **13,** 6, June 1970. The seminal paper by Codd that largley initiated the widespread interest in the relational approach.

(3.2)   Date C.J., **Relational Database Concepts**, Datamation, **22,** 4, April 1976. An excellent introduction to the principles of the relational approach.

(3.3)   Codd E.F., **A Data Base Sublanguage Founded on the Relational Calculus**, Proc. 1971 ACM SIGFIDET Workshop on Data Description, Access, and Control.

(3.4)   Dijkstra E.W., **On the BLUE Language submitted to The DoD**, in ACM SIGPLAN Notices, **13,** 10, October 1978.

(3.5)   Dee E., Hilder W., King P., and Taylor E., **Syntax for a COBOL-Based Data Manipulation Language**, Report of BCS Advanced Programming Group Database Working Party, BCS, October 1973.

(3.6)   Todd S.J.P., **The Peterlee Relational Test Vehicle — A System Overview**, IBM Systems Journal, **15,**4, 1976.

(3.7)   Hitchcock P., **User Extensions to the Peterlee Relational Test Vehicle**, in **Systems for Large Data Bases**, ed. P. C. Lockemann and E. J. Neuhold, North Holland, 1977.

(3.8)   Astrahan M.M., Blasgen M.W., Chamberlain D.D., Eswaran K.P., Gray J.N., Griffiths P.P., King W.F., Lorie R.A., McJones

P.R., Mehl J.W., Putzlou G.R., Traiger I.L., Wade B.W., and Watson V., **System R: A Relational Approach to Data Base Management**, ACM Transactions on Database Systems, **1**, 2, June, 1976.

(3.9)   Date C.J., **An Introduction to Database Systems**, 2nd. edition, Addison-Wesley, 1977.

EXERCISES

3.1   Define a relational schema for the tables of Fig. 3.4 in a similar manner to the example given in section 3.1.5.

3.2   One of the key features claimed for the relational approach is the degree of logical data independence provided. Assess this claim by considering what needs to be done to the relational schema defined in section 3.1.5 to add the information about *requisites* given in the tables of Fig. 3.4. What is the effect on the algorithms defined in section 3.1.1?

3.3   Rewrite the four algebra statements given in section 3.2.2 as one statement using the embedded bracketed notation used for the MAPPING definition of Example 2 in section 3.3.2.

3.4   Example 1 in section 3.3.2 provides the view required by Student Administration as three relations. An alternative is to define a relation STUD-ADMIN-VIEW (REG. NO., NAME, ADDRESS, DATE-OF-BIRTH, DATE-OF-REGISTRATION, COURSE CODE, COURSE NAME, RATING, RESULT). If this relation obeys the same rules for tables as we gave in section 3.1.1 write down a set of occurrences of the rows of the table STUD-ADMIN-VIEW.

3.5   Define the MAPPING for STUD-ADMIN-VIEW.

Chapter 4

CODASYL DATABASE SYSTEMS

"Such a schema is supplied with the tables as the rule for its use".
Ludwig Wittgenstein, Philosophical Investigations

4.1 THE ROLE OF CODASYL

CODASYL is an acronym for **C**onference **o**n **Da**ta **Sy**stems **L**anguages and maintains many standing committees that address various problems of concern to the data processing community. The following is an extract from the CODASYL Data Description Language Committee **Journal of Development,** 1978.

"A product of CODASYL is not the property of any individual, company, or organisation or any group of individuals, companies or, organisations.

No warranty, expressed or implied, is made by any contributor or by any CODASYL committee as to the accuracy and functioning of any system developed as a result of this product.

Moreover, no responsibility is assumed by any contributor or by any committee in connection therewith.

This product neither states the opinion of, nor implies concurrence of, the sponsoring institutions".

CODASYL is perhaps best known as the body which conceived, in 1959, the COBOL language and has been responsible for its continuing development.

In 1965, in response to the sort of problems outlined in Chapter 1, CODASYL formed a List Processing Task Force which became, in 1967, the Data Base Task Group (DBTG) of the Programming Language Committee. This Group produced two Reports, one in 1969 followed by a more widely circulated one in 1971. At the end of 1971 the DBTG became a CODASYL committee in its own right: the Data Description Language Committee producing its own **Journal of Development.** A **Journal** was published in 1973 followed by one in 1978. In 1973 the Data Base Language Task Group **Draft COBOL Facility** was published, later to be incorporated in the Programming Language Committee **COBOL Journal of Development,** published in 1975 and 1978. In 1976 a CODASYL **FORTRAN Data Base Facility** was published, incorporated into a **Journal of Development** published in 1977. In 1973 the Data Base Administration Working Group was formed as a joint Group of the Data Description Language Committee and the British Computer Society. In 1975 this Group produced a **Report,** developments of which were incorporated as an Appendix in the Data Description Language Committee **Journal of Development** for 1978. There are other CODASYL Committees and Groups active in the database field which have not been mentioned here: one has been referred to (reference (2.5)) in an earlier Chapter.

The quotation and potted history given above have been included not because they are interesting, which they are in their own right, but because they graphically illustrate several key features which are vital to an understanding of the CODASYL database approach.

1. CODASYL is essentially committee run: committees and groups are made up of representatives from various institutions such as manufacturers, software houses, users, academics, consultancies, and so on — any interested party in fact. As with all committees, sub-committees and groups there is a problem of control. The DBTG **Reports** of 1969 and 1971 gave a fairly coherent and consistent account of CODASYL's proposals in the database area. Since that date the work of the DBTG has spawned many committees and groups looking at various aspects within the database framework. It is now no longer possible to turn to one single document giving an account of the CODASYL proposals, various **Journals of Development** and **Reports** need to be examined, and even then minor inconsistencies will be found between, say, assumptions and facilities in the **COBOL Journal of Development** and the **FORTRAN Journal of Development.** This is a natural and understandable situation, but it is one that potentially makes for confusion.

2. CODASYL does not produce DBMSs: you cannot go to CODASYL and buy a DBMS in the same way that you can go to, say, IBM and buy a DBMS such as their Information Management System (IMS).

All CODASYL does is to produce specifications for certain aspects of the DBMS architecture. How, and whether, these specifications are implemented is left entirely to other people — the computer manufacturers, software houses, etc. Notable implementations of the CODASYL work are Sperry Univac's DMS-1100, Honeywell's IDS, and Cullinane Corporation's IDMS (both ICL and Sperry Univac have rights to develop IDMS for their own range of computers).

3. CODASYL does not have a complete specification of all aspects of database system architecture. In the past it has concentrated on:

    *   the logical data model
    *   the logical data sub-model for COBOL
    *   the data manipulation language for COBOL

    Recently, it has worked on:
    *   the storage data model
    *   the logical data sub-model for FORTRAN
    *   the data manipulation language for FORTRAN

    Currently, it is working on such areas as:
    *   language facilities for the re-organisation of databases
    *   control facilities required by the database administrator

    Outstandingly, it has not worked on the area of data dictionaries, although it has maintained strong connections with one group, the British Computer Society Data Dictionary Systems Working Party, active in this field.

4. The CODASYL specifications are an evolving concept. The work published in 1969, 1971 and 1973 by the DBTG and its successor, the Data Description Language Committee (DDLC) show a stepwise evolution. However, the DDLC, **Journal of Development** published in 1978 shows a more radical change.

4.1.1 A version of CODASYL

All this poses a problem for students (and authors!) concerned with the CODASYL approach. CODASYL proposals are necessarily several years ahead of any implementation made of them. Current implementations of the CODASYL proposals are largely based on the DBTG **Report** of 1971 and the (fairly trivial) extensions made to it in the DDLC **Journal of Development** of 1973. Yet these proposals differ in a non-trivial way from the latest CODASYL proposals, in particular those embodied in the DDLC **Journal of Development** of 1978. Which version do we study?

Whilst it would be academically interesting to examine the latest proposals in detail it would not serve much useful purpose here: nobody has got around yet to implementing them commercially and is unlikely to do so in the immediate future. We shall therefore concentrate on a version of CODASYL centered around the **DDLC Journal of Development of 1973,** with occasional sallies forth into the later work, simply because it is this version, as implemented, that database analysts and designers are faced with in practice. However, reference will be made to the later work, where necessary,as in many cases it provides illumination on the nature of CODASYL specifications.

4.1.2   The architecture of a CODASYL database system

Fig. 4.1 shows the architecture of a CODASYL database system in terms of the generalised architecture developed in Chapter 2. The key features are now listed.

1. The CODASYL term for the logical data model is a *schema,* which is defined by means of the schema **D**ata **D**escription **L**anguage (DDL).

2. The CODASYL term for the logical data sub-model is the *subschema,* which is defined by means of a subschema data description language.

3. The CODASYL term for the storage data model is the *storage schema,* which is defined by means of the **D**ata **S**torage **D**escription **L**anguage (DSDL). This component of the architecture is not present in the version of CODASYL that we are examining in detail. Strictly speaking the DSDL is not yet an official CODASYL proposal since its specification was included as a draft in an appendix to the DDLC **Journal of Development,** 1978.

4. The CODASYL approach to the manipulation of the database is a host language approach, a host language having extensions known as a **d**ata **m**anipulation **l**anguage (DML). DML commands deliver subschema objects into the workspace of the application program, which in CODASYL is known as the **U**ser **W**ork **A**rea(UWA).

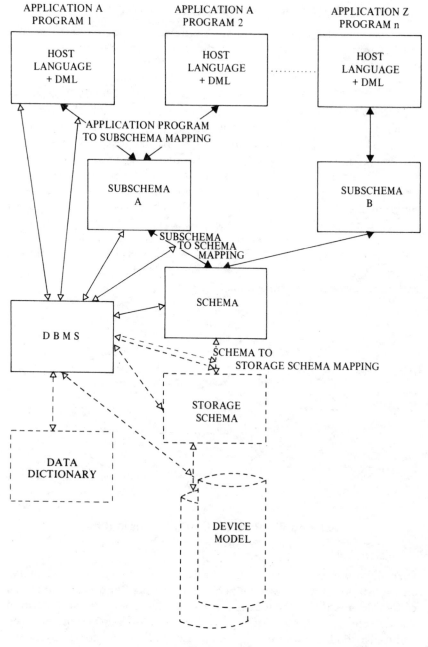

Fig. 4.1
Architecture of a Codasyl Database System

4.2 THE SCHEMA DATA DESCRIPTION LANGUAGE

The basic constructs used to define a schema are *records* and *sets*. We shall examine these in detail below, but a general appreciation is helpful at this stage.

A *record* is essentially the same as a record in the COBOL sense — indeed CODASYL has been criticised for being too COBOL orientated in its approach to database systems. A *set* is the means by which relationships between records are represented in CODASYL. Essentially it allows for the explicit representation of one-to-many relationships only. Using these two constructs we can give a diagrammatic expression to a CODASYL schema with a *schema diagram*, sometimes called a *Bachman diagram* after C. W. Bachman who first drew such diagrams and played a leading part in the development of CODASYL. A schema diagram for a schema incorporating the sample data of UniHyp that we introduced in Chapter 1 is given as Fig. 4.2 *Records* are depicted as rectangular boxes whilst *sets* are depicted by arrowed lines connecting the record boxes, the arrow depicting the direction of the one-to-manyness.

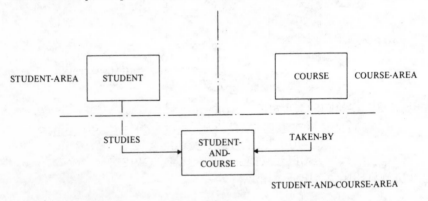

fig. 4.2
Schema diagram for UniHyp sample data

Formally a schema is expressed in terms of the schema DDL, the syntax and semantics of which are defined in the various **Reports** and **Journals of Development.** The reader is referred to the references at the end of the Chapter for such a rigorous definition. We shall explore the key features of the DDL for the task of database analysis and design by means of our UniHyp example. A definition of the schema diagram of Fig. 4.2 in DDL is now given below.

SCHEMA NAME IS OPERATIONAL-STUDENT-COURSE;
ACCESS-CONTROL LOCK IS 'PYHINU'.

AREA NAME IS STUDENT-AREA;
ACCESS-CONTROL LOCK IS STUDENT-BOX.
AREA NAME IS COURSE-AREA;
ACCESS-CONTROL LOCK IS COURSE-BOX.
AREA NAME IS STUDENT-AND-COURSE-AREA;
ACCESS-CONTROL LOCK IS PROCEDURE CHECK-AUTHORITY.

RECORD NAME IS STUDENT;
    LOCATION MODE IS CALC REG-INDEX USING REG-NO IN
        STUDENT
        DUPLICATES ARE NOT ALLOWED;
    WITHIN STUDENT-AREA;
    ON STORE CALL STUDENT-STORE-CHECK.
    02 REG-NO;   PIC 9(4).
    02 STUDENT-NAME;   PIC X(12).
    02 ADDRESS;   PIC X(20).
    02 DATE-OF-BIRTH;   PIC 9(6).
    02 DATE-OF-REGISTRATION;   PIC 9(6).

RECORD NAME IS COURSE;
    LOCATION MODE IS CALC COURSE-CODE-HASH USING
        COURSE-CODE IN COURSE
        DUPLICATES ARE NOT ALLOWED;
    WITHIN COURSE-AREA.
    02 COURSE-CODE;   PIC X(7).
    02 COURSE-NAME;   PIC A(30).
    02 RATING;   PIC 9;
        CHECK IS VALUE 1 THRU 4.
    02 DATE-OF-INTRODUCTION;   PIC 9999.
    02 FACULTY;   PIC A(12).

RECORD NAME IS STUDENT-AND-COURSE;
    LOCATION MODE IS VIA STUDIES SET;
    WITHIN STUDENT-AND-COURSE-AREA.
    02 REG-NO;   PIC 9(4).

```
    02  COURSE-CODE;                              PIC X(7).
    02  RESULT;                                   PIC A(4);
            CHECK IS VALUE 'PASS', 'FAIL';
            ACCESS-CONTROL LOCK IS RESULT-BOX.

SET NAME IS STUDIES;
    OWNER IS STUDENT;
    ORDER IS PERMANENT INSERTION IS FIRST.
    MEMBER IS STUDENT-AND-COURSE FIXED AUTOMATIC;
    SET SELECTION IS THRU STUDIES OWNER IDENTIFIED BY CALC-
                            KEY.

SET NAME IS TAKEN-BY;
    OWNER IS COURSE;
    ORDER IS PERMANENT SORTED BY DEFINED KEYS DUPLICATES
                            ARE NOT ALLOWED;
    MEMBER IS STUDENT-AND-COURSE FIXED AUTOMATIC;
    KEY IS ASCENDING COURSE-CODE, REG-NO IN STUDENT-AND-
                            COURSE;
    SET SELECTION IS THRU TAKEN-BY OWNER IDENTIFIED BY
                            CURRENT OF SET.
```

As we can see from this example, a DDL described schema consists of four entry types which serve to:

*   Identify the schema — the Schema Entry — of which there is only one occurrence.
*   Define the areas — the Area Entry — of which there may be many occurrences.
*   Define the records — the Record Entry — of which there may be many occurrences.
*   Define the sets — the Set Entry — of which there may be many occurrences.

4.2.1   The Schema Entry

The schema entry achieves three things:

1. It names the schema: this can be very important when several databases and schema versions are involved. The example schema is named OPERATIONAL-STUDENT-COURSE.

80

2. It optionally specifies a database procedure to be performed when the database administrator is manipulating the schema. The example schema does not contain such a specification.

3. It optionally specifies access-control locks for protecting the manipulation of the schema. Access-control locks are the basic mechanism of CODASYL for implementing privacy decisions. An access-control lock requires a matching *key* to be supplied by a program before the lock will 'open' and allow access to the protected objects. The lock may be either:

   * a literal — as in this case, being 'PYHINU'.
   * lock-name.
   * a procedure.

We shall give examples of the other two techniques later.

4.2.2 The Area Entry

The concept of an area is somewhat muddled in our version of CODASYL (and remains so to a certain extent in the later versions). It seems to have two distinct and potentially incompatible functions:

   * a named sub-division of addressable storage space, relating to a disc pack, a cylinder, etc. In other words, it is a high-level statement that is partly the mapping to a storage schema, partly the storage schema, and partly the mapping to the device model.
   * a named logical sub-division of the schema for the purpose of recovery, access control and integrity.

In our example we have three named areas — STUDENT-AREA, COURSE-AREA and STUDENT-AND-COURSE-AREA — which have been shown on our schema diagram by means of broken lines partitioning the diagram. For each area we have defined an ACCESS-CONTROL LOCK. In the first two cases a lock-name is given: STUDENT-BOX, COURSE-BOX are the names of data items which contain as their values the lock values that any key must match. In the case of the final entry occurrence a procedure has been specified. Any program that wishes to access the data in STUDENT-AND-COURSES-AREA must provide appropriate parameters to the procedure CHECK-AUTHORITY. This procedure will return one of two values: lock open or lock closed. For example a password could be supplied which would then be checked against a table of allowable passwords.

4.2.3 The Record Entry

Substantially the three record entry occurrences in our example look like record declarations in the DATA DIVISION of a COBOL program. The chief difference between a COBOL record declaration and a schema record declaration is in the specification of a LOCATION MODE: a statement of the way in which the DBMS should store and locate[1] the record. There are four MODEs.

1. DIRECT: each record occurrence in the database is given a unique *logical* identifier called the *database key*. Simplifying somewhat a LOCATION MODE of DIRECT means that:

    —   on storing a record occurrence an application program will provide this database key,

    —   on accessing a record occurrence an application program will supply the database key. As we shall see this *logical* address has been transformed into a *physical* address by many implementations, and this causes problems. There are no DIRECT LOCATION MODEs in our example.

2. CALC: the named CALC procedure will take the named CALC-key and use this to store and access record occurrences. What the CALC procedure is CODASYL does not specify: all it must do is to take a logical application data item — a record key — and use this to determine some database key. Thus the CALC procedure may be some form of randomising algorithm or an index. In the case of all procedures in CODASYL the database administrator must specify the procedure: they are not CODASYL supplied (although they are frequently implementor supplied). In our example two CALC LOCATION MODEs have been specified in the schema: REG-INDEX for STUDENT and COURSE-CODE-HASH for COURSE.

3. VIA: the record will be stored and located by means of its set relationship to another record. It then becomes necessary to specify in the schema (in a Set Entry) how such an occurrence of the named

---

[1]More correctly, it specifies the main way in which an application program will use the DBMS in locating a record. An application program can, however, locate records in ways other than that specified by the LOCATION MODE. For example, a record may always be located by a serial search using a series of FIND NEXT WITHIN AREA commands in the DML.

set relationship will be identified by the DBMS. In our example the LOCATION MODE of the STUDENT-AND-COURSE record is declared to be VIA the STUDIES set relationship.

4. SYSTEM: the DBMS uses an implementor defined method for storing and accessing the record occurrences. No LOCATION MODE of SYSTEM is included in this example.

Some other features of the Record Entry shown in our example are:

*   ON STORE CALL STUDENT-STORE-CHECK: this specifies for the STUDENT record that when occurrences are stored in the database the storage will be checked by a database administrator defined procedure called STUDENT-STORE-CHECK. If necessary an error status can be returned to the Communication Location of the application program to indicate an error in storage. More powerful validation facilities are defined at the data item level for RATING and RESULT. Note that allowable values are specified.

*   RESULT has its own ACCESS-CONTROL LOCK (a lock-name). Access control is not limited to AREAs but can be carried down to a fine level, including locks on sets.

Some other features of the Record Entry *not* shown in our example, but which can be of use in the design of schemas are as follows.

*   Clearly we have some duplication of data items in the schema: REG-NO and COURSE-CODE appear in STUDENT and COURSE respectively as well as in STUDENT-AND-COURSE. This redundancy was also present in our relational schema, but there it was positively needed to express the relationships between the relations. This is no longer needed in the CODASYL schema since this task is now performed by the set construct. However, it might still be desirable to have REG-NO and COURSE-CODE present in the STUDENT-AND-COURSE record; for one thing their presence acts as an identifying key for sequencing the records within the ORDER defined for the TAKEN-BY set. The connection between these data items and the corresponding data items in STUDENT and COURSE could have been expressed and controlled by

02 REG-NO;   PIC 9(4);
                    IS VIRTUAL AND SOURCE IS REG-NO OF
                              OWNER OF STUDIES SET.

02 COURSE-CODE;   PIC X(7);
>   IS VIRTUAL AND SOURCE IS COURSE-CODE OF
                 OWNER OF TAKEN-BY SET.

declarations for REG-NO and COURSE-CODE in STUDENT-AND-COURSE. What this means simply is that the data items are 'virtual' and are not physically stored in the stored representation of the STUDENT-AND-COURSE record, but appear to any programmer requesting a STUDENT-AND-COURSE record as if they did. The DBMS effectively copies down the appropriate value from the set owners whenever required.

* An extra data item that might be required in a COURSE record is the total number of students studying the course. This field might be defined as

02 TOTAL-NUMBER-OF-STUDENTS;   PIC 9(9);

However, the value of this field for any given COURSE record is clearly the number of members in its TAKEN-BY set occurrence. There is, then, an element of *derived* redundancy present here. The connection between the two can be expressed by an appropriate clause in DDL:

02 TOTAL-NUMBER-OF-STUDENTS;   PIC 9(9);
>   IS ACTUAL RESULT OF COUNT-THE-MEMBERS
ON ALL MEMBERS OF TAKEN-BY.

Here the data item actually exists in the stored representation of COURSE but is updated as a result of applying the database administrator specified procedure COUNT-THE-MEMBERS to the members of the TAKEN-BY set. This procedure is executed whenever a change to the number of STUDENT-AND-COURSE members in a TAKEN-BY set occurrence takes place, as a result of insertions and deletions. If the data item is declared to be VIRTUAL, instead of ACTUAL, then the procedure is executed only when a request for the data item is made.

The ACTUAL facility may also be used with the SOURCE option. This allows some form of control over storage redundancy.

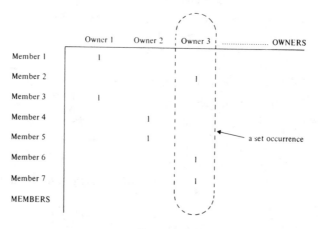

Fig. 4.4
Set Depiction as Sparse Arrays

Alternatively, we can depict sets as a circular list as in Fig. 4.5. With both these depictions it should be remembered that they do not intend to represent an implementation view.

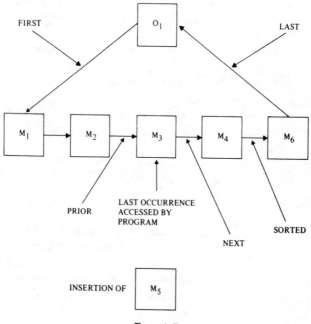

Fig. 4.5
Set Depiction as Circular Lists

For each set entry occurrence an ORDER must be specified stating where, logically, the DBMS is to insert a new member occurrence. The possibilities are:

FIRST: immediately following the owner

LAST: immediately before the owner

NEXT: immediately following the last accessed record in the set

PRIOR: immediately before the last accessed record in the set

IMMATERIAL: at the convenience of the DBMS

SORTED: to preserve some declared ordering on the members.

In our example schema two sets are declared, STUDIES and TAKEN-BY, with a set ORDER of FIRST declared for STUDIES and an ORDER of SORTED by ASCENDING COURSE-CODE, REG-NO for TAKEN-BY. Fig. 4.5 illustrates the meaning of the various ORDER options.

In our example schema each set entry occurrence has the words FIXED AUTOMATIC declared after the name of the member. This clause can be viewed as an attempt to define the nature of the relationship between the two record types in the set. AUTOMATIC refers to an option that can be taken when a member record is first stored in the database. If AUTOMATIC is declared, then when the member record is stored it will be inserted automatically into the appropriate set occurrence by the DBMS without the need for any explicit insert statement from the application program. The alternative option is to define the member as MANUAL, in which case when it is first stored in the database it will not be inserted automatically into a set occurrence: an explicit command will be required from the application program.

In our example AUTOMATIC is clearly needed, since a STUDENT-AND-COURSE record has to be related to a COURSE and to a STUDENT by the logic of the application.

FIXED refers to an option that can be taken to describe what is allowed to happen to the member record *once* it is inserted into an occurrence of the set. FIXED means that the member cannot be removed from that *particular* set occurrence *at all*, save by deleting it from the database. The alternative options are MANDATORY and OPTIONAL. If MANDATORY is declared then the member record occurrence can be removed from that particular set occurrence, but only to an occurrence of the *same* set type. If OPTIONAL is declared then the member record occurrence can be removed from the set occurrence entirely and remain unconnected to the set type. It should be emphasised that *insert* and *remove* are being used to denote connection and disconnection from *sets* only, and not from the database.

In our example both entries have FIXED declared since, especially, once a RESULT is allocated it is always for *a* particular STUDENT on *a* particular COURSE.

The final clause in the Set Entry that needs to be mentioned is the SET SELECTION clause. There are many formats that this can take, and only the simplest forms have been given here. However, it is important to realise *why* the set selection clause is required. Basically it is required for two reasons within the schema declaration:

1. The LOCATION MODE of VIA SET requires that the DBMS be capable of identifying a particular occurrence of the set defined.

2. The AUTOMATIC option for membership in a set also requires the DBMS to be able to identify a particular occurrence of the defined set into which it will insert the member record occurrence.

If an application program stores a new STUDENT-AND-COURSE record in the database described by our sample schema, a STUDIES set occurrence will need to be identified for reasons 1 and 2, above, and a TAKEN-BY set occurrence will need to be identified for reason 2, above. A STUDIES set occurrence will be selected THRU STUDIES OWNER IDENTIFIED BY CALC-KEY. This means that the application program will provide a value of REG-NO for the CALC procedure REG-INDEX to use to identify a STUDENT record occurrence. This STUDENT record occurrence will be the owner of a STUDIES set occurrence. Thus the DBMS can identify the required STUDIES set occurrence. In the case of the TAKEN-BY set the selection is THRU TAKEN-BY OWNER IDENTIFIED BY CURRENT OF SET. Here the DBMS will use the current of set type currency indicator (see section 4.4.1) to identify the required TAKEN-BY occurrence. This current of set type indicator will be the database key of the owner or of a member of the last occurrence of TAKEN-BY accessed by the application program. Therefore, as with the STUDIES set, the application program provides the DBMS with the information needed to allow the required set occurrence to be selected.

More complicated versions exist, for example consider the case where our example schema is extended to include two new record types —

COURSEWORK and EXAM — and one new set type — COMPLETED — from Fig. 4.3. The SET SELECTION clause for COMPETED could then read:

SET SELECTION FOR COMPLETED IS THRU STUDIES OWNER

    IDENTIFIED BY CALC-KEY

    THEN THRU COMPLETED WHERE OWNER

    IDENTIFIED BY REG-NO, COURSE-CODE IN STUDENT-AND-
                             COURSE;

The meaning of this is that the DBMS will be able to identify an occurrence of the COMPLETED set by first identifying an occurrence of the STUDIES set *and* then using this to identify an occurrence of the COMPLETED set. The occurrence of the STUDIES set will be identified by the application program identifying the owning STUDENT record occurrence. It will do this by providing a value for the CALC-KEY REG-NO. This occurrence of the STUDIES set will identify many member STUDENT-AND-COURSE records who are also owners of COMPLETED set occurrences. Which STUDENT-AND-COURSE record is selected (and hence which COMPLETED set occurrence) will be determined by the application program supplying a value for the REG-NO and the COURSE-CODE in STUDENT-AND-COURSE. Notice that this requires REG-NOs and COURSE-CODEs to be unique within STUDIES occurrences. This should be ensured by the addition of a special clause — DUPLICATES ARE NOT ALLOWED — to the member clause in the set entry for the STUDIES set.

4.3 SUBSCHEMA DATA DESCRIPTION LANGUAGES

Recalling our discussion in Chapter 2 on a generalised architecture we would expect there to be several subschema facilities defined by several subschema DDL s to meet the needs of several high level languages. In fact we find at the time of writing only two:

a COBOL subschema facility

a FORTRAN subschema facility

This is, however, a fairly natural situation to expect given the predominance of COBOL and FORTRAN. Outside the CODASYL specifications, several implementors of the CODASYL proposals have gone ahead and defined their own high-level language subschema facilities. PL/I, APL and even BASIC interfaces to CODASYL schemas have been defined.

Given all this we shall concentrate on the COBOL subschema facility simply because this is the most widely used and most thoroughly worked out.

4.3.1 The nature of a CODASYL subschema

In theory there is nothing in the CODASYL approach that prevents the mapping between schema and subschema from being as flexible as required in Chapter 2. Indeed the CODASYL specifications have indicated that the nature of the mapping would have this flexibility. However, to date, this flexible mapping has not been specified in any detail nor implemented in practice. Therefore what we are now going to examine is a very restricted notion of the schema-subschema mapping that should in future years be made considerably more flexible.

Generally, however, the subschema provides a measure of logical data independence and a level of access control by specifically excluding parts of the database from application programs.

Specifically, the subschema can omit the following:

* the declaration of one or more record types
* the declaration of one or more data items from within a record type
* the declaration of one or more set types
* the declaration of specific member record types from a set
* the declaration of one or more areas

The omission would seem to need to be consistent, i.e. the omission of an area precludes the retention of the record types and set types peculiar to that area. The subschema is a simple sub-set of the schema. Some minor details of change are, however, allowed:

* aliases, or private names, can be defined for areas, sets, records and data items.
* data items may be given different data types.
* the ordering of data items within a record declaration may be changed.

* different SET SELECTION clauses may be defined.
* access control locks may be changed.

As we shall see the omission of schema objects in a subschema is *implicit* from the declaration of the subschema. This, coupled with the specification of the minor changes, means that effectively the mapping from schema to subschema is contained in the definition of the subschema.

4.3.2 The COBOL subschema

We shall illustrate the COBOL subschema facility by means of a subschema defined on the example schema used already. Suppose that Course Administration at UniHyp is interested in statistics on the success rate of students on courses. A suite of application programs is developed to meet these needs. The view of the schema that they require is data about COURSEs records and data about STUDENT-AND-COURSEs records. Fig. 4.6 gives the subschema diagram for this view. This subschema can be defined in COBOL subschema DDL as follows.

TITLE DIVISION.
SS COURSE-STATISTICS WITHIN OPERATIONAL-STUDENT-COURSE.

MAPPING DIVISION.

ALIAS SECTION.
AD = = TAKEN-BY = = SET-NAME BECOMES C-SC.
AD = ⇌ COURSE = = RECORD-NAME BECOMES C.
AD = = STUDENT-AND-COURSE = = RECORD-NAME BECOMES S-C.

STRUCTURE DIVISION.

REALM SECTION.
RD COURSE-AREA.
RD STUDENT-AND-COURSE-AREA.

SET SECTION
SD C-SC.

RECORD SECTION.
01 C.
      02 COURSE-CODE   PIC X(7).
      02 RATING   PIC 9.
      02 DATE-OF-INTRODUCTION   PIC 9999.

01 S-C.
      02 RESULT   PIC A(4).

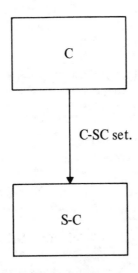

Fig. 4.6
Subschema diagram

As we can see the subschema here is even more COBOL-like than the schema — as we would expect. The subschema consists of three Divisions: a Title Division, a Mapping Division and a Structure Division.

The Title Division names the subschema and the schema on which it is based — in our example it is the COURSE-STATISTICS subschema based on the OPERATIONAL-STUDENT-COURSE schema.

The Mapping Division specifies the relationship between the subschema and the schema. We have one Section — the Alias Section — where one set and two records are re-named to meet the particular programming standards of the application.

The Structure Division defines the logical structure of the subschema. Within the Structure Division the Realm Section defines, naively, the schema AREAS used. The change of name is necessary since AREA is a reserved word in COBOL. More correctly a REALM is not quite the same as an AREA. Firstly, it does not have the storage connotations of AREA, and secondly a REALM does not necessarily have to relate directly to an AREA since it can contain sub-sets of the records in one or more AREAs. In our example, however, the two REALMs are directly associated with the two corresponding AREAs in the schema.

The SET SECTION names the sets included in the subschema. In our example only one set is defined. Notice that it is referred to by the private name defined for it in the ALIAS SECTION.

The RECORD SECTION defines the records and the data items included in the subschema. Notice that several data items have been omitted from the subschema record declarations.

4.3.3   The FORTRAN subschema

Suppose Student Administration has a suite of FORTRAN programs that merely require
REG-NO, STUDENT-NAME and DATE-OF-BIRTH as the one record type that they process. Such a subschema view could be defined as:

SUBSCHEMA STUDS, SCHEMA OPERATIONAL-STUDENT-AND-
COURSE

      ALIAS (REALM) STUDSA = 'STUDENT-AREA'
      ALIAS (RECORD) STUD = 'STUDENT'
      ALIAS REGNO = 'STUDENT.REG-NO'
      ALIAS NAME = 'STUDENT.STUDENT-NAME'
      ALIAS DOB = 'STUDENT.DATE-OF-BIRTH'

      REALM STUDSA

      RECORD STUD (WITHIN STUDSA)
            CHARACTER REGNO * 4, NAME * 12, DOB * 6
END

All this example really shows is the renaming necessary for the FORTRAN subschema due to the length and character restrictions of

FORTRAN names. The schema area STUDENT-AREA is renamed STUDSA, the schema record STUDENT is renamed STUD, and the three data items required from that record are renamed appropriately.

More subtle variations are possible: subschema access control locks could have been declared. It is interesting that such locks do not override locks declared in the schema: in the case of the COBOL subschema the reverse is the case!

4.4 DATA MANIPULATION LANGUAGES

As we saw in the early part of this Chapter the CODASYL approach to the issue of a language to manipulate the database is a *host language* approach. The special database commands are called a **D**ata **M**anipulation **L**anguage (DML) and there will be a DML for each high-level language facility. Therefore at the moment we have a COBOL subschema DML and a FORTRAN subschema DML. The two are different, but not essentially so: we can therefore concentrate on the COBOL subschema DML without a great loss in generality.

One significant feature that must be appreciated about any CODASYL DML and about the CODASYL approach in general is that the manipulation of the database is *highly procedural* and is *record occurrence based.* A program follows explicit paths from one record to the next in search of the required data. The term 'navigation of the database' has been used, by C. W. Bachman, to characterise this process. This fact explains much of the apparent difference between the CODASYL approach and the relational approach. The descriptive power of the two approaches is roughly the same. They differ in that the manipulation of a relational database, as we have seen, is highly *non-procedural,* whilst that of a CODASYL database is highly *procedural.* Because of this we have the complexity of the schema DDL compared to the apparent simplicity of a relational schema definition. Much of the schema DDL that we have examined has been concerned with the selection of record occurrences and set occurrences. This difference between the two approaches should be borne in mind when any comparison is made, as should the fact that any implementation at a storage level of a relational database would probably not differ from that of a CODASYL database, since ultimately they both are constrained by the nature of current software and hardware. Indeed, what we are likely to see in the future is storage schemas, or similar constructions, that are capable of supporting both CODASYL databases and relational databases.

4.4.1 COBOL subschema DML

To fully appreciate the DML commands we must gain some understanding of a crucial CODASYL concept called *currency.*

A CODASYL database is a complex of record occurrences related in sets to other record occurrences: there are many paths a program can take using these sets. The situation is much more complex than that involved in reading, say, a sequential file. It is clearly important that a program has some means of recording and knowing where it is in the database. This is the basic idea behind currency: it records where a program is in the database by recording the unique logical address, i.e. the database key.

Currency works on the notion of a *run-unit* which for our purposes we can regard simply as being the execution of an application program running against the database; that is, an occurrence of a program — the next time the program runs it will be a different run-unit. For each run-unit the DBMS maintains the following *currency indicators:*

* REALM — for each realm accessed the most recently accessed record by the run-unit in that realm is known as the *current of realm.*

* RECORD TYPE — for each record type accessed the most recently accessed occurrence of that record type is known as the *current of record.*

* SET TYPE — for each set type accessed the most recently accessed occurrence of the set is known as the *current of set type.* Sets do not have database keys, of course, so an occurrence of a set type is uniquely identified by the member or owner that has been accessed. That record is known as the *current of set.*

* ANY RECORD TYPE — the most recently accessed record occurrence is known as the *current of run-unit.*

Thus we can see that currency locates where a program has got to in its exploration of the database. Currency can in certain circumstances be suppressed — i.e. a new occurrence of a record type can be accessed without updating the currency indicators. However, this need not concern us here, except to note that the programmer is effectively saying — 'I am really *here,* but I am just going to look over *there'.*

The DML commands, then, are:

FIND — locates an existing record occurrence and makes it the current of run-unit, updating other currency indicators as necessary.

GET — retrieves the current of run-unit. Therefore we access a record by FINDing it and then GETting it.

MODIFY — updates the current of run-unit.

CONNECT — inserts the current of run-unit into named set occurrences.

DISCONNECT — removes the current of run-unit from named set occurrences, but note that it does not delete the record occurrence.

ERASE — deletes the current of run-unit from the database.

STORE — creates a new record occurrence in the database.

The new record occurrence will AUTOMATICally be CONNECTed into the set occurrences for which it has been declared to be an AUTOMATIC member.

EXAMPLE

Using the subschema of our example imagine that we need to print out the totals for pass and fail on course 'PHI 121' 'The Early Wittgenstein'. The following is a portion of the necessary code showing the use of DML commands.

```
    MOVE 'PHI 121' TO COURSE-CODE IN C.
    FIND ANY C.
    IF C-SC IS EMPTY GO TO NO-TAKERS.

AGAIN.

    FIND NEXT S-C RECORD WITHIN C-SC.
    IF ERROR-STATUS = end-of-set GO TO FINISH.
    GET S-C.
```

    (perform the necessary COBOL processing)
    GO TO AGAIN.

NO-TAKERS.

    (display suitable message)

FINISH.

    (display suitable message)

MOVE 'PHI 121' TO COURSE-CODE IN C initialises the calc key COURSE-CODE for the CALC procedure COURSE-CODE-HASH to operate and thus FIND a C occurrence. A test is then performed on a data base condition that is maintained by the DBMS. The data base condition used is the MEMBER CONDITION, which may be tested on a selected set occurrence to see whether any member records are present. Given that there are members, each member is accessed with a FIND and GET command. A check is made to ascertain when the end of the set has been reached. This check is made by reference to the value of a DBMS maintained ERROR-STATUS register. In this particular case whilst the end of set is not reached the register will be set to zero. When the end of set is reached the register will be set to a specific four digit value to indicate this fact. Generally speaking the ERROR-STATUS register would be checked following all significant DML commands. This has not been done in the above example for sake of clarity. It is intersting to note that COBOL DML does not have an AT END OF SET clause as one would expect from the normal spirit of COBOL file processing.

This code would be embedded in the normal procedure division of a COBOL program and would look like any other COBOL program save for an addition to the data division — a SUBSCHEMA SECTION. In our case the start of the program would read, for the DATA DIVISION thus:

DATA DIVISION.
SUBSCHEMA SECTION.
DB COURSE-STATISTICS WITHIN OPERATIONAL-STUDENT-COURSE.
FILE SECTION.
followed by normal COBOL entries.

Note that it is only necessary to define the subschema once to the DBMS: COBOL programs using it then reference it in the above fashion. Note also that a program may use only one subschema.

4.5 THE DATA STORAGE DESCRIPTION LANGUAGE

In the light of what was said concerning storage data models and logical data models in Chapter 2 the reader may have formed the opinion that certain aspects of the CODASYL schema described in this Chapter do not really pertain to a logical data model. In particular the following features that we have described can be said to be more properly the business of a storage data model.

1. The database key concept: even as a unique non-physical address it can be said to properly belong to the storage data model. As it is, it has largely been seen by implementors as being a form of physical address.

2. The *location mode* clauses, which are concerned with *how* a record will be stored and accessed.

3. The ACTUAL/VIRTUAL feature of the SOURCE and RESULT clauses.

CODASYL has now recognised such (and other) deficiencies and they have been removed from the schema DDL specified in the DDLC **Journal of Development,** 1978. There removal has been accompanied by the inclusion, as an Appendix, of a draft proposal for a *Storage Schema* produced by the Data Base Administration Working Group. This storage schema is described by means of a **D**ata **S**torage **D**escription **L**anguage (DSDL).

The DSDL is a complex language, as it must be in order to give the database administrator the fine control needed over storage and access to the database. We shall not describe the DSDL in any detail save to point out its major constructs. There is not, at the time of writing a working implementation of the DSDL commercially available.

The major constructs of a storage schema described in DSDL are:
1) the *storage record*
2) the *mapping*
3) the *index*

The storage record as defined in the draft DSDL specification is 'a variable length addressable container for data and pointers associated with a single schema record'. The association referred to is basically a 1:n relationship: a schema record may be represented by several storage records in an manner similar to the example discussed in Chapter 2, Fig. 2.6. The capacity to combine schema records into storage records, in a manner similar to that discussed in Chapter 2, Fig. 2.7, is not supported.

This association, or mapping, between schema records and storage records is defined by means of the Mapping Description Entry in the draft DSDL specification. The Mapping Description Entry allows the definition of how a schema record is mapped onto storage records. The mapping need not always be 1:n — in the simplest case a schema record will be supported by one storage record. Where the mapping is 1:n, the storage records supporting the schema record may overlap in the sense that they duplicate schema data items. The DBMS is in a position to control and maintain this duplication.

An index as defined in the draft DSDL specification is 'a structure which supports access paths to storage records'. It consists of a sequence of elements each of which contains a pointer and, where specified, a key.

It will be noted that no mention is made of a separate storage set construct. Instead the method of representing the set association is defined in the storage record declaration as being by means of pointers held in storage records (that is a storage implementation of Fig. 4.5, essentially), or by means of indexes to represent the set.

The LOCATION MODE clause of the schema DDL has been replaced by a PLACEMENT clause in the storage record declaration. Three placement strategies are allowed:

RANDOM —	enabling quick location of a given record occurrence when data item values (i.e. the record key) have been given.
SEQUENTIAL —	enabling reasonably fast access by key but optimised to allow for the processing of records in some defined key sequence.
CLUSTERED —	records are grouped together according to their set membership. This allows the optimisation of access to records in set groups by grouping storage records on the same, or adjacent, pages.

A page may be thought of as being analogous to a block: the unit of physical transfer between the database and the DBMS system buffers.

The reader is referred to the Draft DSDL for further details. It should be mentioned that it is only a *draft* and is not a CODASYL specification. However, it is worth remarking that certain features of the DSDL, such as the CLUSTERED placement, have been used by implementors. Clearly the acceptance of a storage schema definition and its availability from implementors would provide a database system with considerable physical data independence.

As well as removing several constructs more correctly concerned with storage the 1978 **Journal of Development** also introduced greater structuring capability into the schema DDL. Particularly, the notion of a *recursive* set was introduced that would allow the SUPERVISES recursive set of Fig. 4.3 to be an allowable construction directly in DDL.

4.6 IMPLEMENTATION

Many successful implementations of the CODASYL proposals are now commercially available. Most of these are based around the specifications of the DDLC **Journal of Development** of 1973 with minor extensions. Notable products are Sperry Univac's DMS 1100, Honeywell's IDS-II, Cullinane's IDMS, DEC's DBMS-10, Rank Xerox's EDMS and PRIME'S CODASYL product.

The schema DDLs of these products and the operation of the DBMS all follow the general pattern of the CODASYL specifications. They do, however differ in several respects. Notably the schema DDLs usually include far more detail concerning the mapping to storage. This is a consequence of the fact that the CODASYL proposals on which they were based made no detailed reference to this feature of the architecture other than the unspecified Device Media Control Language. Implementors have therefore had to tackle the question in the best way that they saw fit.

For example, in DMS 1100 the unit of physical storage is a *page* which we can equate for our purposes with the notion of a conventional *block*. Typically several schema records will be stored on one page. As a consequence our example AREA entries in DMS 1100 schema DDL would read perhaps (depending on the storage we had available):

AREA NAME IS STUDENT-AREA;

ACCESS CONTROL LOCK IS STUDENT-BOX;
 ALLOCATE 1000 PAGES;
 PAGES ARE 112 WORDS.

and so on.

This means that STUDENT records will be stored on 112 word pages, and that 1000 such pages are allocated for their storage.

The relative address of each page will go to make up the database key of each record, its position within the page providing the remainder. Thus a logical concept has been implemented as a storage feature. This is not so terrible a mistake as it sounds since initial CODASYL ideas on the matter were very muddled.

Another problem that implementations of the CODASYL proposals faced was that caused by concurrent usage of the database. Most DBMSs allow many run-units to access the database at the same time. This brings problems of data sharing beyond the control of the operating system, since the operating system sees only the DBMS, not the individual run-units.

Typical problems are:

i) **The Lost Update**

Run-unit A FINDs and GETs record X

Run-unit B FINDs and GETs record X

Run-unit A MODIFYs record X

Run-unit B MODIFYs record X

The result is that run-unit A's update is lost.

ii) **The out-of-date retrieval**

Run-unit A FINDs and GETs record X for update.

Run-unit B FINDs and GETs record X for retrieval.

Run-unit A MODIFYs record X.

The result is that run-unit B gets an out-dated retrieval.

Such problems as these were recognised by the early versions of CODASYL and specifications were defined for a monitored mode based on a notifying protocol. Unfortunately these proposals had certain inherent inconsistencies. Several implementations, including DMS 1100, went for a different solution based on *locking*. It is notable that proposals based on these ideas have now become incorporated into the latest CODASYL specifications.

For example, the DMS 1100 solution is the *page lock* (not to be confused with the ACCESS-CONTROL LOCK). The page lock is the exclusive right to access a page and is set for a run-unit when:

a) a FIND command is issued which selects a new current of run-unit — the lock is then temporary and is removed on the next FIND or STORE command from the run-unit.

b) a STORE, MODIFY, INSERT, REMOVE or DELETE[1] command is issued by a run-unit — the lock is then permanent for the duration of the run-unit (but see below).

Hence our two problems would be solved by the page lock correctly sequencing the commands.

i) Run-unit A FINDs and GETs record X
Run-unit A MODIFYs record X and finishes.
Run-unit B FINDs and GETs record X
Run-unit B MODIFYs record X and finishes.

ii) Run-unit A FINDs and GETs record X
Run-unit A MODIFYs record X and finishes.
Run-unit B FINDs and GETs record X.

There are some more subtle problems that any system for dealing with concurrent usage must solve. For example we could have the following situation. Run-unit A GETs record Z, inspects the record and then wants to FIND and GET record X to check some condition before updating record Z. Thus the page lock on Z is deleted and another run-unit could alter record Z, making any alteration run-unit A may subsequently carry out invalid.

The solution adopted by DMS 1100 is to have a special DML command KEEP which places a permanent page lock. Thus run-unit A would KEEP record Z prior to examining record X.

---

[1] INSERT, REMOVE, and DELETE are the same as CONNECT, DISCONNECT, and ERASE, respectively.

There is also the more traditional problem of the **deadly embrace.**

Run-unit A GETs and KEEPs record X
Run-unit B GETs and KEEPs record Y
Run-unit A attempts to GET record Y
Run-unit B attempts to GET record X.

The solution adopted here is to first *detect* that a deadly embrace has occurred and then to *rollback* one of the offending run-units, presumably the one with the lowest priority. Rollback refers to a process which reverses the effects that a run-unit has had on the database. We postpone discussion of *how* this is done to later Chapters.

Page locks obviously degrade performance in the database: large portions of the database could be locked. The solution within DMS 1100 is a FREE command that can be issued when a program is satisfied that it does not need the locks that it has set so far — it releases all locks set for the run-unit up to that point. Thus we can think of run-units as being composed of *success-units* — the processing between FREEs.

Notice that the *granularity* of the locks discussed here is at the *page* level. The new CODASYL proposals incorporating such a locking scheme have a granularity at the *record* level.

SUMMARY

The CODASYL database system approach:

* is an evolving concept, but many implementations have centered around the work produced up to about 1973.

* has as its logical data model a *schema* that consists of *records* and *sets* partitioned amongst *areas.*

* has as its logical data sub-model a *subschema* that consists of selected records and sets from the schema partitioned amongst *realms.*

* has as its manipulation language a *DML* hosted in a high-level language. The DML is a record-at-a-time language.

* has removed various storage constructs from its work up to 1973 into a *storage schema* described in terms of *storage records* and *indexes.*

* has been implemented in several successful commercial systems. These commercial systems have been based on the work up to

1973 and therefore have had to develop their own techniques for dealing with the mapping to storage.

REFERENCES AND BIBLIOGRAPHY

(4.1)   CODASYL **Data Base Task Group Report,** April, 1971.

(4.2)   CODASYL **DDLC Journal of Development,** 1973.

(4.3)   CODASYL **DDLC Journal of Development,** 1978.

(4.4)   CODASYL **COBOL Data Base Facility Proposal,** 1973.

(4.5)   CODASYL PLC **COBOL Journal of Development,** 1975.

(4.6)   CODASYL PLC **COBOL Journal of Development,** 1978.

(4.7)   CODASYL **FORTRAN Data Base Facility, Journal of Development,** 1977.

(4.8)   BCS/CODASYL **Data Base Administration Working Group Report,** 1975.

(4.9)   Brown, A.P.G. **Progress of the CODASYL Data Base Specifications,** Online Database Conference, London, 1977. Proceedings published by Online Conferences Limited, Uxbridge, England.

(4.10) **DMS 1100 System Support Functions Manual,** Sperry Univac.

(4.11) **DMS 1100 Schema Definition Manual,** Sperry Univac.

(4.12) Manola, F.A. **The CODASYL Data Description Language: Status and Activities, April 1976,** in **The ANSI/SPARC DBMS Model,** ed. D. A. Jardine, North Holland, 1977.

(4.13) Engles, R.W. **Currency and Concurrency in the Cobol Data Base Facility,** in **Modelling in Data Base Management Systems,** ed. G. M. Nijssen, North Holland, 1976.

(4.14) Manhood, D.W. (ed.), **Storage level control of a CODASYL data base: Part I,** Computer Bulletin, September, 1980. A fine account of post-1978 developments in the DSDL, including an example storage schema.

EXERCISES

4.1   Devise a schema diagram to illustrate all possible combinations of the membership clause. Remember that for insertion we have AUTOMATIC and MANUAL, and for removal we have FIXED, MANDATORY and OPTIONAL.

4.2   Devise a schema diagram that models the *requisites* example given in Fig. 3.4 of Chapter 3. Remember that we can think of a *relation* as being a record *type* and *relationships* between relations as being shown by attributes from common *domains.*

4.3   Describe the schema diagram from Exercise 4.2 in terms of the schema DDL.

4.4   Is there anything corresponding to a *domain* in CODASYL? Why might such a concept be important? Consider the case of the various name and date fields in the example schema and the situation where they are not so helpfully named.

4.5   Study References (4.2), (4.3) and (4.9). Do you consider that there are any remaining clauses in the schema DDL that do not properly belong to a logical data model?

4.6   If the mapping between schema and subschema were more complex how would you expect it to be defined? Where would the mapping definition be placed?

4.7   What are the advantages of a concurrent usage locking scheme having a granularity at the record level rather than at the page level?

IMS's Solution

IMS offers a variety of solutions to such problems where the redundancy is seen not to be required for reasons of efficiency. One such solution, known as *virtual pairing*, is shown in Fig. 5.6. The root nodes of the two hierarchies are retained, but the STUDENT AND COURSE data is held only in one hierarchy. A system of pointers between the two hierarchies exists and is maintained by IMS. IMS can use these pointers to provide either of the hierarchical views shown in Fig. 5.3 to an application program. The application program is unaware of the existence and use of the pointers in this transformation. The reader may care to compare the pointer system with the pointer systems for implementing CODASYL sets described in Chapter 10: they are remarkably similar storage structures.

5.1.3 IMS and database architecture

The following is a set of equivalences for the generalised architecture in terms of IMS. Necessarily, this is something of a simplification.

Logical data model: the logical data model in IMS is, confusingly, a collection of what are termed *physical databases.* A physical database is, in fact, a hierarchy type, such as given in Fig. 5.3, and consists of an ordered collection of occurrences of the hierarchy type. Again confusingly, the hierarchy type is termed a *physical database record type,* whilst the hierarchy occurrences are *physical record occurrences.* What perhaps we would more naturally term records, that is the nodes, are termed *segments* in IMS. The physical database record type is defined by means of a *database description,* which certainly does contain elements of the mapping to storage — hence there is some justification for the predicate *physical.*

Logical data sub-model: the logical data sub-model in IMS is a collection of what are termed *logical database record types.* A logical database record type is simply a hierarchy and consists of an ordered collection of the hierarchy occurrences — the *logical database record occurrences.* The logical database record type is a *sub-hierarchy* of one physical database record type: that is, a logical database record type may omit any segment from the physical database record type on which it is defined, together with all its children. Thus we have a similar mapping capability to that present in CODASYL. The logical database record is defined, along with its mapping to a physical database record, in a *program communication block.* The collection of program communication blocks (i.e. the collection of logical database record types — the data sub-model) is defined by means of a *program specification block.*

This account is complicated by the fact that the system of pointers between hierarchies described above allows the definition of what amounts to *virtual* physical databases. As far as we are concerned, we can regard a virtual physical database as being the same as any other physical database. That is, logical database records may be defined from it.

A language to manipulate the database: IMS employs a host language approach — the special database commands being expressed in a language known as DL/I which can be embedded in PL/1, COBOL or assembler, save that the embedding is done as ordinary subroutine calls. The unit of retrieval in DL/I is really the segment, and any 'navigation' that the program has to do is within the context of a hierarchy. Therefore in a sense the task of programming in an IMS database is simpler than for the corresponding situation in a CODASYL database.

Storage data model: IMS does not have a machine independent storage model in the sense of our generalised architecture (or in the sense of the later CODASYL work on a storage schema for that matter). Rather, physical placement utilises standard IBM access methods, such as ISAM and VSAM, although one special IMS technique, OSAM, has been developed.

Data dictionary: a data dictionary facility is available with IMS, and is known as, simply, Data Dictionary. It should be pointed out however that it does not provide anything like the range of facilities discussed in Chapter 12. As one would sensibly expect the Data Dictionary is itself a database system, structured around five IMS physical database record types.

In summary, the modelling element chosen by IMS — the hierarachy — can cause problems. These problems can be overcome by the use of pointers between physical database records, but the price of this can be costly:

* a significant amount of storage space can be used solely for pointers and control fields,
* a significant amount of CPU time can be used purely for the execution of internal IMS routines,
* the task of database design is complex for an IMS database system resulting in a complex structure that is not amenable to reorganisation and change in an easy fashion.

Correspondingly however, the view seen by the application programmer is a fairly simple one, not involving any significant 'navigation' of the database. It is interesting to note that the main thrust of IBM's objections to the CODASYL DBTG Proposals of 1971 was directed to the complexity, as they saw it, of the DML.

5.2 INVERTED FILE APPROACHES

Inverted file structures have traditionally been seen as an extension to conventional file structures that can go some way to expressing the relationships between data items in a more explicit or efficient manner. It is not therefore surprising to find several commercially available database systems that base their approach around the utilisation of inverted structures for data organisation. We shall examine one of these systems — the Adapatable Data Base System or ADABAS developed by Software AG of the Federal German Republic.

5.2.1 Basic element: a file

The basic data modelling element in ADABAS is a *file* composed of *record* occurrences which in turn are composed of *fields*. For a given file record occurrences may be of one or more record types. Simplistically, relationships between (the records in) different files are expressed by means of *coupling indexes* that relate records by means of bidirectional pointers. The system requires the records being related to have what is known as a *common descriptor* (a declared status for a record field): thus in ADABAS there are some strong similarities with the relational approach (although the ADABAS 'tables' — i.e. the record types — can break the rules that we set out for relational tables in Chapter 3). Access to records other than via a relationship can be achieved in ADABAS by means of *inverted indexes* which are of a fairly conventional nature.

5.2.2 ADABAS database structure

An ADABAS database system has two major structural components: Data Storage and Associator.

Data Storage contains the application data. This is held in a compressed form — eliminating empty (null) fields, leading zeroes, trailing blanks, and so on — that is transparent to application programs. It has been claimed that anything up to some 50% of storage space can be saved using this technique.

The Associator has four sub-components:

1. The **Field Description Tables** that define the fields for all the record types in an ADABAS database system.

2. The **Association Network** which contains the coupling indexes and the inverted indexes for representing the relationships between records and the accessing of records respectively. Internally all records are referenced by a symbolic Internal Sequence Number (ISN) that is similar in many respects to the CODASYL notion of a database key. We can illustrate the use of ISNs and some of the features of ADABAS generally by considering the way that our sample data on students and courses would be represented. First we make one assumption: we assume that data about the results of students on courses is not required; therefore we have to model a many-to-many relationship. Fig. 5.7 shows how ADABAS would define this situation. Notice that one of the files must carry the common descriptor field as a repeating field. In our case we have chosen to do this by repeating COURSE-CODE for the STUDENT file, but, alternatively, we could have repeated REG-NO.s for the COURSE file. Notice that the coupling indexes created invert this repitition. This is obviously a more complex case than a one-to-many relationship. In that case one of the coupling indexes contains only two ISNs per entry to represent the one-to-one aspect of the one-to-many relationship (it is one-to-many in one direction, but one-to-one in the other, see Chapter 7).

3. The **Address Converter** which maintains the correspondence between Internal Sequence Numbers and physical addresses. Logical records in ADABAS are grouped into blocks of data for physical storage. The Address Converter allows a block to be located; it can then be searched for the desired logical record.

4. **Storage Management Tables** which manage storage space in the Associator and Data Storage. The management is dynamic, in the sense that storage space no longer in use, say after a record deletion, is made available, and should a file exceed the storage space allocated to it then more is allocated from unused storage.

5.2.3 ADABAS and database architecture

The following is a set of equivalences for the generalised architecture in terms of ADABAS. Again, this is something of a simplification.

Logical data model: the logical data model in ADABAS can be thought of as being the Field Description Tables *plus* the Association Network;

Fig. 5.7
STUDENTs and COURSEs

STUDENTs File

102 9491 B.ROBERTS 9 INKERMAN ST. 8.6.58 1.10.77 PHI 121
PHI 102 LIT 312 ENG 111

 99 3123 G.JUNG 26 SHAW ST. 19.11.59 2.10.78 COMP141
LIT 312 ENG 111 PHI 102

317 7416 C. DAY 63 SPRING RD. 3.2.60 30.10.78 ENG 111 CHEM301
LIT 312 COMP141

etc.

ISN   DATA   COURSE-CODE

COURSEs File

  3   PHI 121 THE EARLY WITTGENSTEIN 1 1975 HUMANITIES

113   PHI 102 KANTIAN METAPHYSICS 2 1973 HUMANITIES

419   LIT 312 THE EXPATRIATES 2 1976 HUMANITIES

 77   COMP141 COMPUTER ARCHITECTURE 1 1975 MATHEMATICS

789   CHEM301 MOLECULAR GENETICS 1 1979 SCIENCE

756   ENG111 BASIC SURVEYING 1 1974 ENGINEERING

etc.

ISN   DATA

STUDENT Coupling Index				**COURSE Coupling Index**			
STUDENT ISN	COURSE ISNs			COURSE ISN	STUDENT ISNs		
102	3 113 419 756			3	102		
99	77 419 756 113			113	102 99		
317	756 789 419 77			419	102 99 317		
				77	99 317		
				789	317		
				756	102 99 317		

that is, data plus the data relationships. This separation of relationships from data has much to be said for it in terms of providing flexibility and data independence. Notice that there are aspects of the storage data model present here: the Association Network not only defines relationships, but also says how they will be implemented as indexes. Notice also that there is a similarity with the relational approach: records that are to be connected by a relationship must have a common descriptor field.

Logical data sub-model: in ADABAS the logical data sub-model is not defined as a separate entity, rather it is defined by the application program. In common with many approaches, the application program may define this logical data sub-model to be only a sub-set of the logical data model. In a similar fashion to the CODASYL subschema facility, the ADABAS logical data sub-model may change the format of data items within a record, and resequence them if required. It is of interest to note that the binding of this simple mapping between logical data model and logical data sub-model occurs on program execution which clearly aids the level of logical (and physical) data independence. Since the logical data sub-model is program declared there is an obvious connection with sub-model facilities and application program languages. Facilities are available for high level languages such as COBOL, FORTRAN and PL/I, and query language facilities are also available.

A language to manipulate the database: ADABAS employs a host language approach — the special database commands being embedded in the host language as subroutine calls. The database commands are procedural in nature, although the use of inverted indexes does allow the specification of logical searches against a set of selection criteria. In this case the Association Network is used by the command to employ the most effective search procedure. Thus ADABAS exhibits some separation of processing statement and processing implementation.

Storage data model: this element of the generalised database architecture is fulfilled by two ADABAS components: the Address Converter and the Association Network. Thus we can see that the separation of the logical data model from the storage data model is not complete since the Association Network fulfils aspects of both elements. The Storage Management Tables also fulfil part of the storage data model function, although it would be more accurate to say that they define the mapping to the physical database. Notice also in this context that there is no storage data model record concept in ADABAS analogous to that

118

proposed in CODASYL: logical records are simply grouped into blocks. There is therefore a limit on the tuning that can be conducted on an ADABAS database.

Data dictionary: ADABAS provides its own data dictionary facility, which appears to give adequate structuring for the documentation and relationships of files and programs (see Chapter 12).

In summary, ADABAS presents a simple but surprisingly effective database system. Once designed, an ADABAS database is fairly convenient to specify and implement. The product has been successfully used by many organisations that require such a straightforward, basic approach.

5.3 NETWORK APPROACHES

Network approaches to database systems usually employ the use of a linked list structure to express the relationship existing between records. We have already examined, in one sense, a network approach; namely CODASYL. The 1973 **Journal of Development** defines a *set* as being a certain type of logical association between an owner record type and member record type. One can, as was done in Chapter 4, depict such an association as a circular linked list. Indeed, many CODASYL *implementations* have treated the set concept as forms of circular linked lists. However, strictly speaking, these are aspects of the storage data model of such implementations, and it is worthwhile noting that the draft CODASYL storage schema proposals make use of **indexes** as well as lists to represent sets.

Other network approaches than these CODASYL implementations are available. The one that is now examined as an example is TOTAL, a database system developed by Cincom Systems Inc. of Ohio, U.S.A. TOTAL has many characteristics in common with the CODASYL approach and as an aid to understanding these similarities will be emphasised.

5.3.1 Basic elements: master files and variable files

The basic data modelling element in TOTAL consists of two types of file: master files and variable files (or Master Data Sets and Variable Entry Data Sets in the terminology of TOTAL). These two file types permit the modelling at the logical level of a one-to-many relationship.

A master file contains what are known as master records that are non-volatile and homogeneous. This requirement that they be relatively

119

stable and predictable expresses, in TOTAL terminology, facts that are true because 'you are in business'. They can be regarded as simply being owner records in a manner analogous to CODASYL. A variable file contains volatile variable records, and expresses, in TOTAL terminology, facts that are true because 'you *do* business'. They may be regarded as simply being member records analogous to CODASYL. Master records (owner records) are related to variable records (member records) by a bi-directional linked list that is similar (but different in certain important features) to CODASYL implementations of the set concept. This linked list facility is termed the 'linkage path' feature in TOTAL.

This modelling technique can be illustrated by using the sample data on students and courses. This could be represented as in Fig. 5.8.

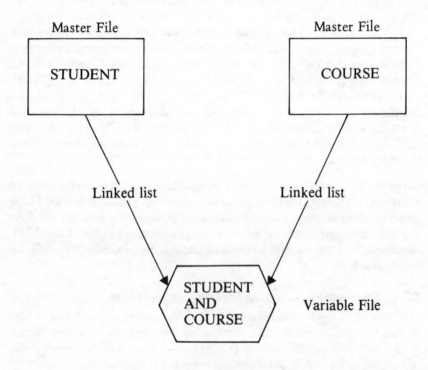

Fig. 5.8
Students and Courses in TOTAL

There are two master files: a STUDENT master file and a COURSE master file. There is one variable file: the STUDENT AND COURSE variable file. Two linkage paths are used to express the two one-to-many relationships, hence there are two linked list types. An occurrence of one of these linked lists is shown as Fig. 5.9.

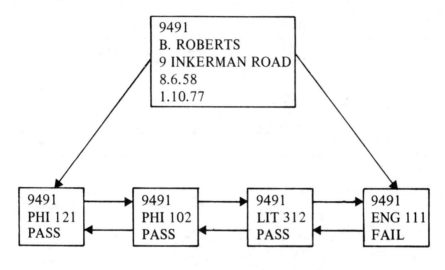

Fig. 5.9

Note that neither the one-to-many aspect (owner to member) nor the many-to-one aspect (members to owner) of the relationship is directly represented in TOTAL. In the former case the linked list has to be traversed to locate a particular member, whilst in the latter the REG-NO. key in the member can be used to access the owner directly. All variable file records must contain the key of the owning master file record. Access to owners directly is supported by a hashing procedure. The ability to locate member records directly is not supported in TOTAL.

Whilst being able to handle relationships such as those portrayed in Fig. 5.8 directly, TOTAL cannot directly deal with hierarchies, e.g. it cannot directly model the structure of Fig. 5.2. It can indirectly handle the situation with link or dummy master files, as Fig. 5.9 illustrates.

Thus the limitation that a variable file cannot also be a master file is overcome by means of a special link master file. A link master file record owns just one occurrence within the variable Big Boss File. A record within the link master file also owns many occurrences in the Middle Boss variable file, thus indirectly relating a Big Boss record to many Middle Boss records. This process can be continued down the hierarchy as necessary.

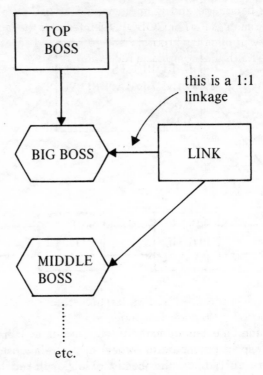

Fig. 5.9 ??

5.3.2 TOTAL database structure

A TOTAL database (a group of files needed by a set of application suites) is defined by means of a Data Base Definition Language (DBDL).

The DBDL allows the definition of:

(a) the master and variable files

(b) their physical representation and layout on the physical data model — records being grouped in a conventional manner into blocks

No explicit definition is made of relationships; it is implicitly achieved by stating the key fields on which the linkages will be built to maintain the linked list.

The manipulation language provided by TOTAL is known as the Data Manipulation Language and is implemented as call statements from a host language such as PL/I or COBOL. Of interest is the fact that the unit of access for an application program is what is termed an 'element' — one or more of the fields that comprise a record.

5.3.3 TOTAL and database architecture

The following is a set of equivalences for the generalised architecture in terms of TOTAL. This is *very* much a simplification since TOTAL has effectively, collapsed many of the generalised architecture components into its own limited architecture.

Logical data model: the logical data model in TOTAL is the set of master and variable files described in the DBDL. Note, however, that the logical data model is conflated with the physical data model since the DBDL also states the layout of the physical database.

Logical data sub-model: as in ADABAS the logical data sub-model is not defined as a separate entity, but is defined by the application program. Since the unit of access for the application program is an element a degree of logical data independence is provided — logical record types can be extended in their definition in the DBDL without the need to change existing programs. The mapping between model and sub-model is a simple sub-set: the definition of new files or linkages requires re-definition (and re-creation) of the affected files.

A language to manipulate the database: as mentioned previously, a Data Manipulation Language is provided and is implemented as call statements from the host language. The DML is navigational in the sense that linkage paths need to be specified.

Storage data model: TOTAL has no component that can be said to correspond directly to this element of the generalised architecture, other than the hashing scheme provided for direct access.

Data dictionary: a variety of data dictionary systems are available for use with a TOTAL database system. For example, Cincom provide a Data Dictionary but (at the time of writing) this is only available on certain machine implementations of TOTAL, notably IBM 360s and 370s. Lexicon, of Arthur Andersen and Co., and Data Catalogue, of the Synergetics Corporation, are also available for use with a TOTAL database system. None of these data dictionary systems adequately cover the range of facilities discussed in Chapter 12. In particular, they exclude any significant recognition of the conceptual view of data.

SUMMARY

TOTAL is a relatively simple database system — more so than ADABAS, for example. As a consequence it has proved very popular for small applications. It is available for implementation on a wide range of machines, and there are over 2,000 TOTAL installations in the world. Being a simple database system, however, the level of data independence provided is not high and the logical and physical data structures available are comparatively inflexible. As a consequence there is little opportunity for tuning the database response to new or better understood processing patterns.

REFERENCES AND BIBLIOGRAPHY

(5.1)   **Selection of Database Software,** National Computing Centre, 1977.

(5.2)   **Database Systems,** Infotech State of the Art Report, 1975.

(5.3)   **Database Implementation Experience,** proceedings of BCS seminar, Open University, October, 1976.

(5.4)   Davis, B. **Data Base Management Systems: User Experience in the U.S.A.,** National Computing Centre, 1975.

(5.5)   Date, C.J. **An Introduction to Database Systems,** 2nd edition, Addison Wesley, 1977.

(5.6)   Lefkovits, D. **File Structures for On-line Systems,** Spartan Books, 1969.

EXERCISES

5.1   How could the *requisites* example in Fig. 3.4 of Chapter 3 be modelled using IMS?

5.2   Using the logical data model given in Fig. 5.5 write down (informal) algorithms that have segments as the unit of access for the following two process taken from section 3.1.2 of Chapter 3:

> (i) Find the NAMEs of all STUDENTs who are on a COURSE which is the responsibility of the MATHEMATICS FACULTY.
>
> (ii) Find the COURSE NAMEs of all COURSEs studied by STUDENTs born later than 31.12.59.

5. What can be said about the two algorithms of Exercise 5.2 in contrast to the equivalent algorithms for a relational implementation. (Hint: look at section 3.1.2 of Chapter 3!).

5.4 Compare the ISN of ADABAS with the database key of CODASYL.

5.5 How would the *requisites* example in Fig. 3.4 of Chapter 3 be modelled using TOTAL?

ANALYSIS

The aim of this Part of the book is to define the analysis required prior to attempting any design of a database system. It attempts to show that the analysis required is not radically different in kind to that which *should* traditionally be practised by systems analysts, *but* that it differs, for very good reasons, in providing a formal framework for the conduct and expression of the analysis exercise.

Chapter 7

CONCEPTUAL MODELS

"A few words are worth a thousand pictures".
J. K. Galbraith

"I never read, I just look at pictures".
Andy Warhol

7.1 DATA MODELS AND PROCESSING MODELS

In Chapter 6 the need for a conceptual model of an organisation's data processing system was established. This conceptual model is composed of a data model and a process model, a distinction which is somewhat arbitrary since both are closely interrelated and a full comprehension of one is dependent on an understanding of the other. However, without embarking on an Arian controversy, we can depict the conceptual data model as in Fig. 7.1

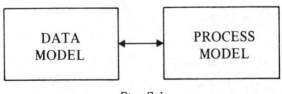

Fig. 7.1

What does need to be established is the *sort* of thing that is being produced when we define a conceptual model. The conceptual model is a *model* and the relation it bears to reality is a complex one. It is therefore important to understand its logical status. This can best be done by considering it as some form of *map*.

Looking at the railway map given as Fig. 7.2 we can appreciate the nature of this relation. Railway lines are not actually *straight* as the diagram portrays, they are not spaced as the map would indicate in terms

147

of distance from one another, and the stations are certainly not shaped the way the map portrays them. Yet it is a perfectly adequate map for the *use* made of it: getting from A to B on the CountyShire branch line as a passenger. We do not ask questions like 'Is Brownbury station shaped like that?' because we all understand the logical status of the map. So it is with conceptual models: they are a particular abstraction of an organisational reality for a particular use — that of analysing and designing data and processing structures. There are *other* abstractions of organisational reality, just as there are other models (for other uses) of the CountyShire branch line. For example, a surveyor's map (where the relation to reality is a different one) or a train timetable and so on. Conceptual models are trying to model aspects of an organisation for a particular purpose; they are not essays in descriptive metaphysics.

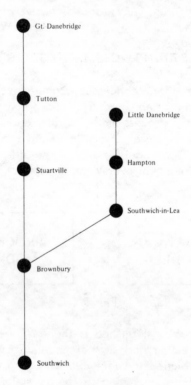

Fig. 7.2
CountyShire Branch Line

This can be illustrated by examining the importance and use of the conceptual data model.

148

7.1.1 The importance of the conceptual data model

Organisations *implicity* have a data structure, and the application orientated data processing systems process the data within this data structure to provide operating information for the various parts of the organisation. These data processing systems are constrained in their use and representation of the data structure in two significant ways:

* by the technology, both hardware and software, that they use,

* by the fact that they are necessarily taking a parochial view of the data structure.

Any design process is normally characterised by being a series of *trade-offs* and *compromises* due to constraints against an ideal design. Therefore, specifically, if we are to design efficient, flexible, secure (notice the range of predicates) logical data structures we must be aware of the ideal we are compromising against. Hence the need for a conceptual view of data.

The conceptual view of data is the *explicit* fundamental structure of an organisation's data resource. It is the data structure that expresses the organisation's data and its relationships in a manner devoid of any implementation constraints as to how this operational data may be viewed by various application systems or stored on files or physical media. Given the understanding of the logical status of the conceptual data model, we can see that it does not make sense to ask if a conceptual data model is *right* or *correct*, however we can say that a *useful* or *good* conceptual data model will:

* provide a long term model against which to evaluate and understand an organisation's data needs. This will be particularly important if the organisation is dynamic and evolving.

* provide a basis on which to comprehend the multiplicity of schemas, records and data items of the various parochial application views.

* provide a basis for a design technique for efficient, effective database design.

7.1.2 What the conceptual data model is and what it is not

A significant recent development in database architecture has been the work of the ANSI/X3/SPARC Group on Database Management Systems.

149

In their reports (Reference (2.1), (2.2)) they have proposed a three level view of data:

external schema

conceptual schema

internal schema

The conceptual data model is *not* the same as the ANSI conceptual schema. The purpose of the ANSI conceptual schema is not completely clear from the published work to date. However, one function that it clearly has is to insulate the external schemas from changes in the internal schemas. It must provide, therefore, constructs that can support external schemas of differing approaches — relational, CODASYL, hierarchical, etc. These constructs have to be of an implementation nature. Thus it does not coincide with the conceptual data model. Furthermore, the conceptual data model incorporates *all* an organisation's operational data and thus differs from the conceptual schema since the latter is within the context of data on a database.

Another significant development in the database area has been the work of the British Computer Society Data Dictionary Systems Working Party (Reference (7.6)). The *notion* of a conceptual data model employed in this Chapter *is* essentially the same as the notion of a conceptual data model as proposed by the Working Party.

7.2   ENTITIES, ATTRIBUTES AND RELATIONSHIPS

Given what has been previously said it is a matter of concern that the manner of representation of the conceptual view of data be as natural a one as possible. There are several candidate formalisms for representing the conceptual view, none of which is without its problems, none of which is universally accepted. The one that will now be described *is* widely used, *is* widely accepted, *but* is criticised. The chief criticism that may be levelled is that it forms part of an architecture that has been too influenced by a concern for a *design methodology.* Correspondingly, this may be the reason for its wide acceptance since this methodology largely *works.*

The conceptual data model can be described in a formalism that employs three constructs — entities, attributes, and relationships — together with a set of rules defining a canonical form for expressing a combination of these constructs. We now define the three constructs leaving the definition of the set of rules until a later section. It should be noted here that Chapter 12 will show that we may incorporate a fourth construct, but this need not concern us at the present point.

7.2.1 Entity

An entity is an object or concept meaningful to the organisation about which there is a need to record data.

Examples:

* at UniHyp — STUDENT, STAFF, DEGREE, COURSE, FACULTY . . .

* in a distribution organisation — VEHICLE, DEPOT, PLANNED LOAD, ORDER . . .

* in an engineering organisation — PLAN, PART, ASSEMBLY, SUPPLIER, CONTRACT.

Entities may be diagrammatically portrayed thus:

STUDENT   DEPOT

Note the use of round-edged or 'soft' boxes: this distinguishes a diagrammatic representation of an entity from its logical counterpart in a schema diagram. However, this is just a depiction of an entity, other information will need to be recorded (just where, and how, that information will be recorded will be examined in Chapters 8 and 12):

— a description of the entity, for example, that a PLANNED LOAD consists of the goods that a VEHICLE is anticipated to deliver in a given day, within the constraints set by legal and union requirements.

— any other names by which the entity may be known, for example, that CUSTOMER ORDER is another name for ORDER.

— the names of the attributes which compose the entity, including those that uniquely identify an occurrence of the entity, for example that STUDENT has attributes NAME, ADDRESS, etc. and is uniquely identified by the attribute REGISTRATION NUMBER.

— the number of occurrences of the entity, for example, that there are 10,000 occurrences of the entity type STUDENT.

— the individuals/groups who are allowed to create, modify, delete, retrieve , or count entity occurrences, i.e. some record of *privacy rights.*

7.2.2 Attribute

An attribute is a property or characteristic of an entity about which there is a need to record data.

Examples:

* at UniHyp — NAME, ADDRESS (of STUDENT, STAFF), FACULTY NAME (of FACULTY) COURSE CODE, COURSE NAME, RATING (of COURSE) . . .

* in a distribution organisation — TOTAL MILES SINCE LAST SERVICE (of VEHICLE), LOAD TONNAGE (of PLANNED LOAD), ORDER NUMBER (of ORDER).

* in an engineering organisation — PART DESCRIPTION (of PART), SUPPLIER ADDRESS (of SUPPLIER), CONTRACT PRICE (of CONTRACT).

Attributes are not normally depicted on a data model diagram , since it results in an unwieldy picture for most purposes in practice. We can show them in a notation similar to that employed for relations, thus: Entity-name (attribute-name-1, attribute-name-2, . . . , attribute-name-n) with the attributes that uniquely identify the occurrence of an entity underlined.

As with entities other information will need to be recorded in some fashion:

— a description of the attribute, e.g. some definition of RATING.

— any other names by which the attribute is known, e.g. RATING is also known as COURSE RATING and RATING NUMBER.

— the entities that the attribute describes, e.g. ADDRESS describes both STUDENT and STAFF.

- the individuals/groups who are allowed to create, modify, delete, retrieve, or count attribute values.

- the source of the attribute value within the organisation, e.g. REGISTRATION NUMBER originates within Student Administration.

- the use made by the organisation of the attribute, e.g. REGISTRATION NUMBER uniquely identifies a student.

- the format of the attribute, e.g. ADDRESS is an alphanumeric string, consisting of 2 to 7 lines, the whole string being 10 to 200 characters in length.

- the values an attribute can take, e.g. MARITAL STATUS (an attribute of STUDENT at UniHyp) has values widowed, married, divorced, separated, single.

- the measurement units of an attribute, e.g. COURSE FEE (an attribute of COURSE at UniHyp) is measured in pounds and pence sterling.

It as at the attribute level that the independence of the conceptual view from any implementation view is most readily apparent. ADDRESS, for example, is simply an alphanumeric string with no character limitations or size constraints. The decision to restrict it to, say, the characters 0-9, space, A-Z, and some line-terminator symbol is a decision taken at the logical level. Of course, at the conceptual level we need to record (somehow) the variation in address formats so that the decisions taken at the logical level can be informed and responsive decisions. Again, COURSE FEE is simply a value in pounds and pence. The decision to represent it as, say, a binary value in pence is a decision at the storage level.

Furthermore, it can be seen here that what counts as an attribute or an entity does depend on the organisation that is being modelled. For example, MARITAL STATUS is an attribute, so it would seem, of the entity STUDENT when modelling UniHyp. But, if we were modelling the data resource of, say, a computer-dating bureau then MARITAL STATUS might well be an entity in its own right. ADDRESS is an attribute of STUDENT at UniHyp, but to a postal organisation it, again, might well be an entity. Thus there is no universal list of entities and attributes, which is precisely the conclusion that an understanding of the logical status of conceptual models leads to, anyway.

7.2.3 Relationship

A relationship is an association between entities that is operationally significant to the organisation.

Examples:

* at UniHyp — STUDENTs *TAKE* COURSEs, FACULTYs *HAVE* STAFF, . . .

* in a distribution organisation — DEPOTs *MAINTAIN* VEHICLES, PLANNED LOADs *CONSIST OF* ORDERS, . . .

* in an engineering organisation — ASSEMBLYs *HAVE* PARTs, STAFF *WORK ON* CONTRACTs.

Graphically, relationships can be depicted by a line connecting the entity types, thus:

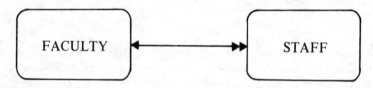

Relationships can be categorised in several ways.

DEGREE

There are three types here, and they have been described already in Chapter 1. Here we merely outline them, and note that, as we shall see, our canonical form does nothing to enforce one, and expressly cannot handle another. Hence, again, this formalism is by no means completely satisfactory — although here it is perhaps better to say that the canonical form is inadequate.

    (i)   1:1, for example:

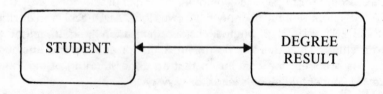

(ii)   1:n, for example:

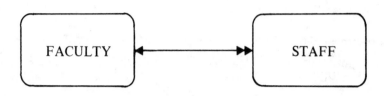

(iii)   m:n, for example

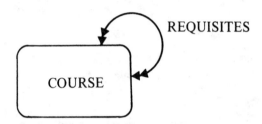

Two points are worth noting here:

1.   The example of an m:n relationship emphasises the point that a relationship does not have to be between *two* entity types.

2.   Different notations are sometimes employed to show the degree of a relationship. Two common other ones are:

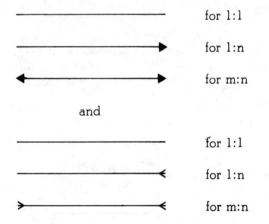

————————————————	for 1:1
————————————————➤	for 1:n
◀———————————————➤	for m:n

and

————————————————	for 1:1
————————————————<	for 1:n
>————————————————<	for m:n

The choice of the particular notation used in this book was dictated by three requirements that none of the two notations above seem to adequately fulfil together:

*   the notation should be distinct from any employed in depicting a logical data model,

    and

*   the notation should emphasise that the 'many' in a 1:n relationship are related to a 'one', as well as the 'one' being related to the 'many'; hence the backward arrow,

    and

*   the notation should be capable of distinguishing a relationship *type* from a relationship *occurrence*.

EXISTENCE

The rules by which a relationship occurrence of a given type may come into existence need to be defined. Pictorially three broad categorisations can be made.

1. Mandatory

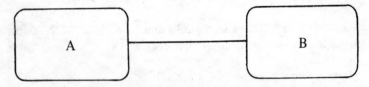

Occurrences of entity type A are always related to occurrences of entity type B through the relationship, and entity type B occurrences are always related to entity type A occurrences through the relationship, e.g.

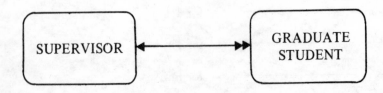

That is, given the rules concerning registration for a higher degree at UniHyp, a Graduate Student must have a Supervisor *and* a Supervisor has to be supervising at least one Graduate Student.

2. Contingent

Occurrences of entity type A are always related to occurrences of entity type B through the relationship, but occurrences of entity type B need not necessarily be related to occurrences of entity type A through the relationship. e.g. the FACULTY: STAFF relationship depicted earlier is really contingent thus:

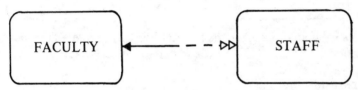

since all Faculties have Staff, but not all Staff belong to a Faculty.

3. Optional

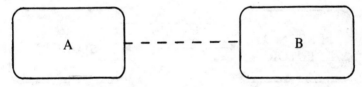

Occurrences of entity type A *may* be related to occurrences of entity type B through the relationship, and vice versa, e.g.

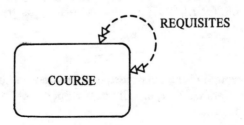

A course *may* have several other Courses as pre-requisites, and study of a Course *may* permit study at a later date of many other Courses.

PERMANENCE

The rules governing what may happen to a relationship once it has been created need to be defined. Three broad categorisations can be made, which are not normally depicted pictorially.

1. **Fixed**

Once an occurrence of the relationship is created the entity occurrences are *always* related together by *that* occurrence of the relationship, e.g.

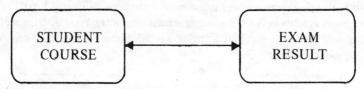

Once a particular occurrence of EXAM RESULT is related to a particular occurence of STUDENT COURSE that association is *fixed.*

2. **Transferable**

Once an occurrence of the relationship is created one of the entities at least musy always participate in *an* occurrence of the relationship (but not necessarily the original occurrence). e.g.

A STUDENT entity occurrence must always participate in an occurrence of the TUTORS relationship, but may be transferred from TUTORS occurrence to TUTORS occurrence. Depending on the organisational definition of PERSONAL TUTOR, the same may be true of that entity type.

3. **Transient**

Once an occurrence of the relationship is created one of the entities at least may be removed from all occurrences of the relationship completely, e.g.

158

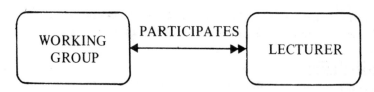

WORKING GROUP — PARTICIPATES → LECTURER

A LECTURER occurrence may be related in an occurrence of PARTICIPATES to a WORKING GROUP, but can be removed from the relationship type PARTICIPATES completely, i.e. be associated with no WORKING GROUPs.

Two points need to be made about these categorisations.

(i)   The categorisations on permanence are not disjoint since they relate to entities participating in the relationship. For example, STUDENT may be TRANSFERABLE in the TUTORS relationship, whilst PERSONAL TUTOR may be TRANSIENT.

(ii) The categorisations on existence *and* permanence are not disjoint, obviously. However, the examples given above for permanence all portray the relationships as being MANDATORY in their existence for the sake of simplicity.

EXCLUSIVITY

Participation in one relationship may exclude participation in another relationship. This is depicted thus:

e.g.

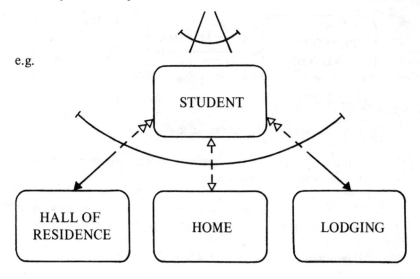

A Student may be living in *either* a Hall of Residence *or* at home *or* in lodgings, but only in one of these at any one time.

INCLUSIVITY

Participation in one relationship may include participation in another relationship. This is depicted thus:

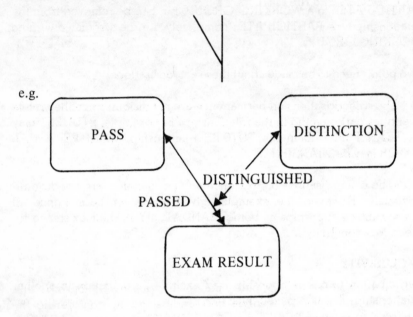

e.g.

An EXAM RESULT participating in the DISTINGUISHED relationship is included in the PASSED relationship, but not vice versa.

As with the two other constructs this, and other information, will need to be recorded in some fashion for each relationship:

— a description of the relationship, e.g. a definition of TUTORS.

— the entities related in the relationship.

— the degree, existence, permanence, exclusivity or inclusivity of the relationship as necessary.

— the individuals/groups who are allowed to create, modify, delete, retrieve, or count relationships.

— the number of occurrences of the relationship.

7.3 DATA MODEL DIAGRAMS

The pictorial representation of entities and relationships allows a *data model diagram* to be drawn to depict, in summary fashion, a given conceptual data model. Several examples are now given, in which all relationships, for simplicity, are shown as being MANDATORY.

7.3.1 Doctors and Nurses

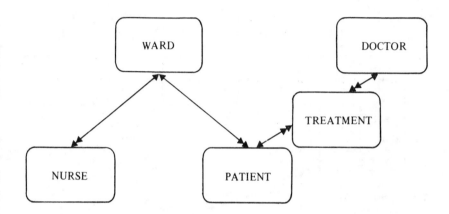

A WARD has many PATIENTs who are cared for by the NURSEs on the WARD: thus the two 1:n relationships relating these entities. The TREATMENT entity and its participation in two 1:n relationships with DOCTOR and PATIENT can be best understood by considering the relationship between DOCTOR and PATIENT. This is m:n — a DOCTOR will treat many PATIENTs *and* a PATIENT will be treated by many DOCTORs (one for his ear infection, one for his kidney failure, etc. representing medical specialisation). However, there is some data that needs to be recorded about this m:n relationship: the TREATMENT a particular DOCTOR prescribes for a particular PATIENT. Hence the TREATMENT *intersection* entity, which will have attributes such as the medication prescribed or the surgery to be performed, and so on.

7.3.2 Agricultural Research

Within the Science Faculty at UniHyp a group of agricultural researchers are responsible for investigating the milk producing capacities of various breeds of cattle. For each breed several herds are kept, and within each herd a detailed record is kept of the mating of bulls with cows and of the offspring produced. There is, within a herd, a natural hierarchy amongst the animals that is of interest to the

161

researchers. For each cow a record is kept of daily milk production. The climatic conditions for each day — such as rainfall and temperature — are carefully monitored and recorded.

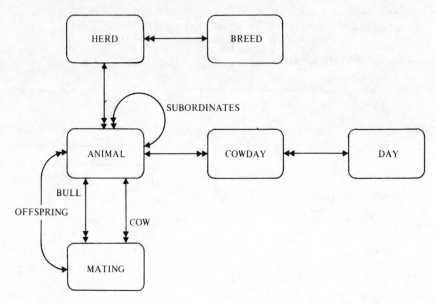

The data model diagram given above models the data required by the researchers. The entities and attributes involved could be defined thus:

BREED   (<u>Breed Name</u>, Date of Origin of Breed, Country of Origin)

HERD   (<u>Herd No.</u>, Date Started, No. of Animals)

ANIMAL   (<u>Animal No.</u>, Date of Birth, Sex)

MATING   (<u>Bull Animal No.</u>, <u>Cow Animal No.</u>, Date of Mating)

COWDAY   (<u>Animal No.</u>, <u>Date</u>, Milk Yield)

DAY   (<u>Date</u>, Temperature, Rainfall)

Several points are worth noting about this example:

1.   The use of *composite keys* in MATING and COWDAY.

2.   The *involuted* relationship SUBORDINATES on the entity ANIMAL.

3. The relationships between ANIMAL and MATING. These can best be understood by considering a more naive diagram:

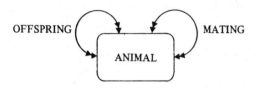

The MATING relationship is m:n since one bull will mate with many cows, and one cow will mate with many bulls. As has been seen in the previous example, a m:n relationship can be replaced by two 1:n relationships at the conceptual level where there is meaningful intersection data, thus:

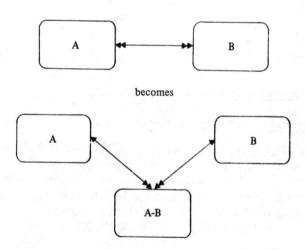

If entity A and entity B are identical, i.e. the m:n relationship is involuted, then precisely the same technique applies, viz.

163

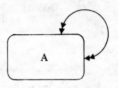

becomes

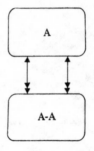

This technique has been applied to the ANIMAL entity and the MATING relationship since there is meaningful intersection data — such as the Date of the Mating. The resolution produces two entities — ANIMAL and MATING — and two 1:n relationships — BULL and COW. The BULL relationship gives the MATINGs a particular bull has participated in whilst the COW relationship gives the MATINGs a particular cow has participated in. Note that a MATING occurrence is related to just one ANIMAL through the BULL relationship, and just one ANIMAL through the COW relationship, which reflects the biological facts of the matter. The BULL and COW relationships are, in fact mutually exclusive on ANIMAL. This resolution allows us to represent the m:n OFFSPRING relationship for what it is — a 1:n relationship between a MATING (which involves two ANIMALS) and other ANIMALS.

164

* patient names and G.P. names are not unique
* hospital names are unique
* consultants have just one phone-no. — that of their 'home base'

Step 1

We begin by eliminating repeating groups.

PATIENT-1 (<u>NHS No.</u>, Name, G.P. No., G. P. Name, G. P. Address)

and

APPOINTMENT (NHS No., Appointment-Date, Appointment-Time, Consultant-Name, Consultant-Phone-No., Hospital, Hospital-Address)

i.e.

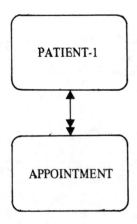

What normal form APPOINTMENT is in depends on the identifying key. We could have:

(a)   <u>NHS No.</u>, <u>Appointment Date</u>

   or

(b)   <u>Consultant Name</u>, <u>Appointment-Date</u>, <u>Appointment-Time</u>

that is, we have two candidate keys.

We will explore both possibilities, first looking at (a).

177

Step 2α

We eliminate non-full dependence on the identifying key. We have PATIENT-1, and APPOINTMENT with a key of <u>NHS No.</u>, <u>Appointment-Date</u>. With both these entities there are no non-full dependencies on the identifying keys to eliminate. They are both already in 2NF.

Step 3α

We now eliminate transitive dependencies.

For PATIENT-1 we have

<u>NHS No.</u>   Name   G. P. No.   G. P. Name   G. P. Address

i.e. G. P. Name and G. P. Address are transitively dependent on NHS No. via G. P. No.

We therefore split PATIENT-1 into:

PATIENT-2 (<u>NHS No.</u>, Name, G. P. No.)

        and

G. P. (<u>G. P. No.</u>, G. P. Name, G. P. Address)

and these two entities are both in 3NF in our "weak" definition of section 7.4.4.

For APPOINTMENT we have:

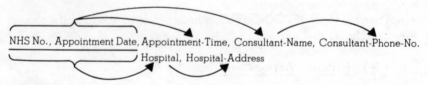

<u>NHS No., Appointment Date,</u> Appointment-Time, Consultant-Name, Consultant-Phone-No.
Hospital, Hospital-Address

i.e. Consultant-Phone-No. is transitively dependent on the identifying key via Consultant-Name

        and

Hospital-Address is transitively dependent on the identifying key via Hospital.

We therefore split APPOINTMENT into:

APPOINTMENT-1 (NHS No., Appointment-Date, Appointment-Time, Consultant-Name, Hospital)

CONSULTANT (Consultant-Name, Consultant-Phone-No.)

HOSPITAL (Hospital, Hospital-Address)

and these three new entities are all in "weak" 3NF. The Step 3a data model diagram is now:

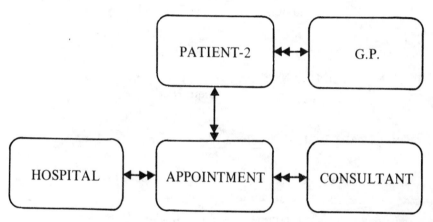

Step 4a

We now check that each entity is in S3NF by ensuring that every determinant is a candidate key.

PATIENT-2:   the only candidate key is NHS No. and this is the only determinant.

G.P.:   the only candidate key is G.P. No. and this is the only determinant.

HOSPITAL: the only candidate key is Hospital and this is the only determinant.

CONSULTANT: the only candidate key is Consultant-Name and this is the only determinant.

APPOINTMENT-1:   we   have   two   candidate   keys   —
NHS No., Appointment-Date

and

Consultant-Name, Appointment-Date,
Appointment-Time

we have determinants of —

the two candidate keys above,

plus

Consultant-Name, Appointment-Date which
together determine Hospital.

Therefore all our entities, except APPOINTMENT-1 are in S3NF. We can
cast APPOINTMENT-1 into two entities in S3NF thus:

PATIENT-APPOINTMENT (<u>NHS No.</u>, <u>Appointment-Date</u>, Appointment-
Time, Consultant-Name)

and

CONSULTANT-VISIT (<u>Consultant-Name</u>, <u>Appointment-Date</u>,
Hospital)

Our final (a) version data model diagram now looks like:

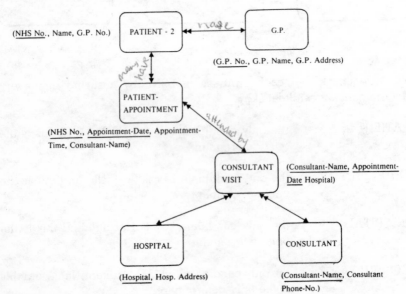

180

The resolution of the functional dependencies that has taken place between this diagram and the one for "weak" 3NF can best be expressed by saying that we now overtly identify the fact that consultants visit hospitals.

Note that PATIENT-APPOINTMENT has two candidate keys: that given, plus Consultant-Name, Appointment-Date, Appointment-Time. These are the only determinants.

We now return to our APPOINTMENT entity produced by Step 1 and explore the other possible candidate key to show that we obtain the same final set of entities in S3NF.

Step 2b

We eliminate non-full dependence on the identifying key.

We have PATIENT-1

and

APPOINTMENT with a key of Consultant-Name, Appointment-Date, Appointment-Time

We ignore PATIENT-1: its treatment is exactly the same as in steps (a). APPOINTMENT is clearly in 1NF, but is not in 2NF since we have the following non-full dependencies on the identifying key:

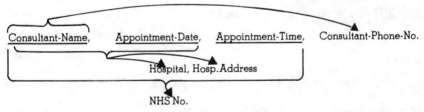

i . e .Consultant-Phone-No. is functionally dependent on Consultant-Name only,

and

Hospital, Hospital Address are functionally dependent on Consultant-Name, Appointment-Date,

and

NHS No. only is functionally dependent on the whole key.

We can eliminate these non-full dependencies with the following entities.

PATIENT-APPOINTMENT   (<u>Consultant-Name</u>,   <u>Appointment-Date</u>,
                        <u>Appointment-Time</u>, NHS No.)

CONSULTANT-HOSP. (<u>Consultant-Name</u>, <u>Appointment-Date</u>,
Hospital, Hospital-Address)

CONSULTANT (<u>Consultant</u>, Consultant-Phone-No.)

Step 3b

We now eliminate transitive dependencies. We have only two:

— that in PATIENT-1 as detailed before,

— Hospital Address is transitively dependent on the composite key
<u>Consultant Name</u>, <u>Appointment-Date</u> via Hospital.

We therefore transform CONSULTANT-HOSP into two entities:

CONSULTANT-VISIT (<u>Consultant-Name</u>, <u>Appointment-Date</u>,
Hospital)

and

HOSPITAL (<u>Hospital</u>, Hospital- Address)

Step 4b

We now check that every determinant is also a candidate key.

With the exception of PATIENT-APPOINTMENT all our entities have
only one candidate key and this is the only determinant.

For PATIENT-APPOINTMENT we have two candidate keys; that given
plus

<u>NHS No.</u>, <u>Appointment Date</u>

These are the only determinants.

Therefore our "weak" 3NF model is also in S3NF.

Summary

This example has demonstrated three things:

*   that S3NF is stronger than 3NF, in the sense that entities in 3NF are not necessarily in S3NF,

*   that S3NF is needed in certain situations to obtain a full understanding of the data model: without it approach (a) would have fallen short,

*   that there are several routes to take to arrive at the same set of entities in S3NF. There are unfortunately no rules as to which is the easiest route.

7.4.5 Further Normal Forms

The pre-occupation of relational theory, from which normalisation has been derived, with identifiers and with the insistence that things be normalised (i.e. 'boxes' are atomic) has led Fagin (Ref. (7.3)) and Zaniolou to propose a Fourth Normal Form. In a somewhat similar vein Delobel (Ref. (7.4)) has proposed a First Order Hierarchic Decomposition. Discussion of these are beyond the scope of this book. However, it may be remarked that it is the author's opinion that these extensions — important as they are to relational theory — are of limited practical use for the immediate task of the analysis and design of database systems since they offer solutions that are more readily achieved by good data analysis (see Chapter 8). In one sense, they are formulations of the inadequacies of the particular version of a normalisation process based on an initial First Normal Form. The reader is, however, referred to Fagin's paper.

7.5 EVENTS AND OPERATIONS

So far, this Chapter has examined in some detail the aspect of conceptual modelling that is covered by a conceptual data model. Attention must now be focussed on the aspect covered by the conceptual process model. This aspect of conceptual modelling is not so central to our theme as is data modelling; nevertheless, as we shall see, an understanding of it is necessary in order to conduct the analysis needed for effective data design. The process model can be defined using two constructs: *events* and *operations*. The latter construct is sometimes termed a *function*.

7.5.1 Events

Events are the stimuli of an organisation; they are the "triggers" which initiate processes. For example, an event could be

*   the birth of a baby

* the receipt of an application form for admission to UniHyp
* completion of a course at UniHyp by a student

Again, as with conceptual data models, notice that the relation with reality is a complex one.

7.5.2 Operations

Operations are the tasks that must be performed as a direct result of an event. For example, corresponding to the events given above, we could have the following operations:

* register the birth
* record the application
* assess the overall course performance by the student

7.5.3 Relationship between events and operations.

To appreciate fully the nature of events and operations we need to examine the relationship between them.

(a) Operations may be initiated by events.

e.g.   the birth of a baby will initiate operations such as

— registration of the birth
— application for child benefit

(b) Operations can cause events.

e.g.   the operation of completing the application form for admission at UniHyp will, together with the operation of posting the application form, cause the event of the receipt of an application form.

(c) Operations can be broken down into more elementary operations.

e.g.   the operation of registration of death can be broken down into

— obtaining the Death Certificate
— visiting the Registrar of Births, Marriages, and Deaths
— completing the necessary forms
— and so on . . .

(d) Operations can lead to other operations.

e.g.   date stamping of the application form (initiated by the event of its receipt) can lead to

- checking for completion of all necessary parts of the form
- checking for satisfactory educational qualifications
- and so on . . .

This inter-relation between events and operations can best be displayed as a **data model diagram,** as in Fig. 7.9. Note that it is a model about a model, or a **meta-model,** a theme that will be returned to in Chapter 12.

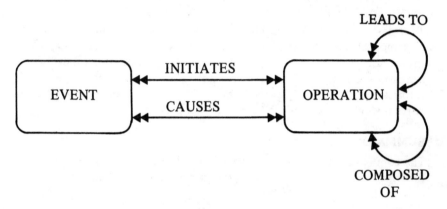

Fig 7.9
Events and Operations

7.5.4 Documenting events and operations.

Just as a diagram did not suffice for the conceptual data model, so with the conceptual process model there will be a need to document further details.

For events:

- the conditions which cause the event to occur, e.g. receipt of an application form is the result of a student completing and submitting an application form.

- when an event occurs, e.g. applications are received at the rate of 1,000 a month in the three months leading up to the start of the academic year.

- what operations the event initiates, e.g. receipt of an application form initiates the operations of date stamping the application form, checking for completion, and so on.

For operations:

— the event(s) that trigger the operation.

— the processing that the operation performs.

— the data that the operation needs: this point will be enlarged on in the following Chapter.

— the event(s) caused by the operation, if any.

— the elementary operations into which the operation can be decomposed.

This last point raises certain analogies with normalisation, which decomposes large groupings of data types into smaller, more elementary groupings in one sense. There is not any formal counterpart to normalisation for events and operations, although a recent paper by K. Robinson (Ref. (7.8)) suggests that a form of program decomposition has certain similarities with the normalisation process.

SUMMARY

The conceptual model of an organisation's data processing system can be thought of as consisting of two interacting models: a data model and a process model.

The conceptual data model can be described in terms of entities, attributes, and relationships, with a set of rules — normalisation — for their combination.

The conceptual process model can be described in terms of events and operations.

An important link between the two models, for our purposes, is the data needed by the processing performed by the operations.

REFERENCES

(7.1) Codd E.F., **A Relational Model of Data for Large Shared Databanks,** Comm. ACM, **13,** 6, June, 1970.

(7.2) Codd E.F., **Further Normalisation of the Relational Model,** in **Data Base Systems,** ed. R. Rustin, Courant Computer Science Symposium 6, Prentice-Hall, 1972.

(7.3) Fagin R., **Multivalued Dependencies and a new Normal Form for Relational Databases,** ACM Transactions on Database Systems (TODS), **2,** 3, September, 1977.

(7.4) Delobel C., **Normalisation and Hierarchical Dependencies in the Relational Data Model,** ACM TODS, **3,** 3, September, 1978

(7.5) **Data Analysis for Information Systems Design,** proceedings of British Computer Society conference, Loughborough, June 1978. All the papers are worth attention, but in particular those of C. Warner and M. Newton, and I.R. Palmer are relevant to this Chapter.

(7.6) **British Computer Society Data Dictionary Systems Working Party Report,** in ACM SIGMOD **Record, 9,** 4, December, 1977 and **Database** (Journal of ACM SIGBDP), **9,** 2, Fall 1977. Clearly this is directed specifically to data dictionaries, but it contains much that is relevant to an understanding of the conceptual model.

(7.7) Kent W., **Limitations of Record-Orientated Information Models,** ACM TODS, **4,** 1, March 1979. An excellent statement of some of the problems associated with data models based on the entity notion.

(7.8) Robinson K.A., **An Entity/Event Data Modelling Method,** Computer Journal, **22,** 3, August, 1979.

(7.9) Chen P.P.S., **The Entity-Relationship Model — Towards a Unified View of Data,** ACM TODS, **1,** 1, March 1976.

(7.10) Kent W., **New Criteria for the Conceptual Model,** in **Systems for Large Data Bases,** ed. P.C. Lockemann and E.J. Neuhold, North Holland, 1977.

EXERCISES

7.1 Classify the relationships shown in Fig. 7.6 as to their *existence* and *permanence.*

7.2 The following pairs of entities obviously enjoy a m:n relationship (convince yourself!). Suggest non-key attributes that would allow the m:n relationship to be replaced by two l:n relationships and an intersection entity.

  (a) Commodity:Supermarket

(b) Student:Exam

(c) Lecturer:Course

7.3   Under what conditions would the identifying key of the MATING entity of section 7.3.2 be inadequate? How would you change the key?

7.4   The following entity TREATMENT is defined as (Patient-No., Patient-Name, Drug-Name, Dosage, Prescribing-Doctor-Name), and has occurrences such as:

      (1234, Jones, Valium, 1 mg., Eugen)
      (1234, Jones, Warfarin, 5 mg., Platt)
      (9197, Smith, Valium, 1 mg., Eugen)
      (9197, Smith, Penicillin, 10 mg., Eugen)
      (1911, Robinson, Atavin, 1 mg., Platt)

Given that:
*   Drug-Names are unique
*   Prescribing-Doctor-Names are unique
*   Patient-Names are not unique, but Patient Nos. are unique,

transform the entity, according to the *strict* rules of normalisation, into a set of entities in S3NF. What do you find unsatisfactory about such a process in this case?

7.5   Write down the activities associated with the process of opening a bank account. Classify these activities into events and operations.

Chapter 8

DATA ANALYSIS

". . . of adults who are not the world's guests but its hosts".
John Updike, Couples

"Things are only real after one has learned to agree on their realness".
Carlos Castaneda, Tales of Power

Having described the conceptual model in general and the conceptual data model in particular in the previous Chapter, the task that must now be faced is one of defining a method for determining the conceptual data model for an organisation — the task of data analysis. The conclusion of Chapter 6 was that we could portray data analysis as in Fig. 8.1

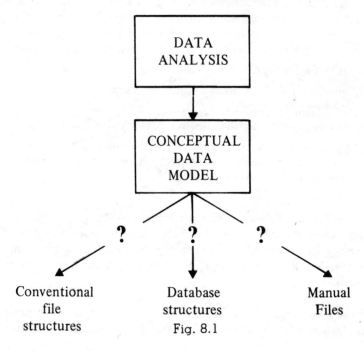

Fig. 8.1

As will be seen this is something of an over-simplification, but it does emphasise some significant features of data analysis. The conceptual data model, as has been discussed, is implementation-free. It exhibits what can be termed *conceptual data independence*. That is, a change in the way the data is modelled at the logical level should not require a change in the way the data is modelled at the conceptual level. Therefore, it follows that *useful* data analysis (producing a *useful* conceptual data model) will be a *permanent* investment. It should not need to be repeated when:

— an implementation of a particular database system approach is enhanced, e.g. a move from an implementation of CODASYL '73 to an implementation of CODASYL '78.

— a change is made from one particular database system approach to another, e.g. a move from a hierarchical approach to a relational approach.

— a change from conventional file structures to database structures.

Notice that the predicate *useful* is used for a data model rather than *correct*. This is a consequence of the logical status of a model. Models are not right or wrong, correct or incorrect. They are either useful or not useful in a given context. Within the context of a conceptual data model some of the criteria for a *useful* model will be that any such model:

— exhibits conceptual data independence

— provides a basis from which to comprehend the various implementation views

— provides a basis for the effective design of logical data structures

— provides a long term model of an organisation's data needs. A useful data model, in this respect, will spring no surprises on us when the organisation evolves.

Notice that the middle two criteria are somewhat at conflict with the first and last. The model is being used as a tool for pure analysis *and* as a tool for the *move* to implementation structures. It is *this* type of criticism that can be levelled at the formalisms of conceptual modelling — that their aims conflict.

Fig. 8.1, as we remarked, represents an over-simplification. It portrays data analysis as a full-frontal one-off exercise: data analysis is conducted in a global fashion producing in one effort the global conceptual data model. Such an approach is not practically possible for the majority of organisations since it does not take account of several crucial factors.

1. A massive investment would be needed for such a frontal approach. The resources required for data analysis of a significant aspect of an organisation's data needs can typically be measured in man-months.

2. It is by no means clear *how* such a global exercise could be conducted. The conceptual data model is implementation-free; it is not application orientated. But just *where* do we get such an implementation-free, application independent view from?

3. Whilst it is certainly true that data analysis *can* be conducted *merely* to gain a more fundamental understanding of an organisation's data resource, it is unlikely to be performed *just* for that reason. In practice it will be performed as a precursor to database and/or conventional file design. As such it needs to be recognised that few organisations sensibly convert to database structures or computer files en masse. Typically they commence by tackling manageable areas and evolve towards a total conversion.

Any account of data analysis must incorporate these factors.

8.1 DATA MODELS AND DATA SUB-MODELS

The solution to the problems outlined above lies in the phrase 'data *needs* of an organisation'. The way that a coherent and systematic analysis of these needs can be performed is by considering the *processes* carried out by the organisation. In other words, the interaction portrayed in Fig. 7.1 between the conceptual data model and the conceptual process model needs to be examined.

8.1.1 Functional areas

The aspect requiring examination is embedded in the notion of a *conceptual data sub-model*: the conceptual view of the data needs of a set of *activities* (i.e. events and operations) within an organisation. Sensibly, the set of activities will relate to what is termed a *functional area* within an organisation. For example, at UniHyp, functional areas might be:

* Admissions — all the activities connected with applications for admission to UniHyp as a student.

* Course Registration — all the activities connected with the registration of students on particular courses.

* Course Assessment — all the activities connected with assessing the success or otherwise of students on particular courses.

* Graduation — all the activities connected with the assessment and award of one of UniHyp's formal qualifications.

Unless an organisation has been deliberately structured along functional lines, these functional areas will not relate directly to divisions or departments. For example, at UniHyp, the Course Registration function will be carried out partly by Student Administration and partly by Course Administration.

This association of a conceptual data sub-model with a localised functional area has lead to the alternative terms *local sub-model* and *functional sub-model*.

8.1.2 Relationship between local models and the global model

The term conceptual data sub-model obviously echoes notions of logical data sub-models. Certainly the relationship between the model and sub-model at the conceptual level will be at least as complex as that required between model and sub-model at the logical level in the generalised architecture. Certainly it will not be the relationship of a simple subset. However, the relationship will be potentially *more complex* than that described in the generalised architecture. A conceptual data sub-model will be *contained* in the conceptual data model rather than derived from it. For example,

* entities in a sub-model may be represented as relationships in the model,

* attributes in a sub-model may be represented as entities in the model,

* the degree and nature of a relationship in the sub-model may differ from its degree and nature in the model.

* attributes of one entity in the sub-model may be represented as attributes of a different entity in the model.

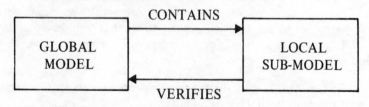

Fig 8.2
Interaction of Global Model and Local Models

Before turning to consider this methodology in detail an example is given to illustrate the way that the outline methodology will work in practice. The Admissions functional area of UniHyp is considered.

Stage 1

The obvious entity types are APPLICANT and DEGREE.

Stage 2

The obvious relationship type is the 1:n relationship between DEGREE and APPLICANT. Together these two stages reflect the fact that applicants apply for admission to study for a degree. Therefore the outline data model looks like:

Stage 3

Place offering on a degree is a process that deletes applicants by turning them into students (if they accept the offer).

Stage 4

Place offering on a degree introduces the idea of *student*. It must then be decided whether this is an entity or an attribute. If it is an entity, the question arises as to whether it is the same entity as APPLICANT. Assuming it is a new entity the outline data model now looks like:

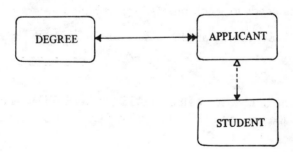

Stage 5

Consideration of how APPLICANT:STUDENT relationship occurrences are created leads to the processes of *interviewing* and *assessment of educational qualifications.* This will lead to a refinement of the outline data model of:

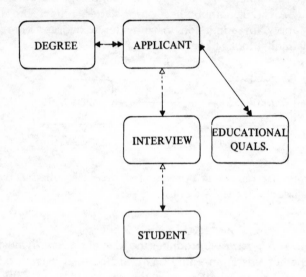

with INTERVIEW having attributes such as DATE-OF-INTERVIEW.

Stage 6

Consideration of how the attribute DATE-OF-INTERVIEW is initially set will lead to the process of *interview allocation.*

Stage 7

Interview allocation involves interviews by STAFF from one of the FACULTYs offering the DEGREE, refining the model to look like:

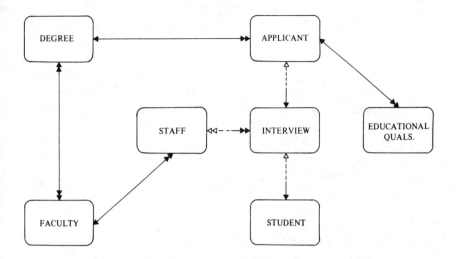

and so on; by continuing the iterations eventually all the data needs *and* processing requirements of the functional area will be determined as a consequence of the analysis of their interaction.

Although the word *process* has been used, note how the methodology naturally leads to a consideration of processes as requiring analysis themselves — into events and operations.

This outline methodology is now examined in more detail and the following specific problems addressed:—

1. What is the raw material on which this methodology operates: what are the sources for data analysis and functional analysis?

2. How are the 'obvious' entity types and relationship types ascertained: how may an outline data model be drawn up?

3. How are the data needs for each process identified?

4. What determines whether a data need is expressed as an entity, an attribute, or a relationship?

8.2.2 Sources for data analysis and functional analysis.

The raw materials of the two inter-twined aspects of conceptual analysis are the traditional sources used by any good piece of systems analysis, viz:

(a) Input documents.

(b) Output documents.

(c) Existing computer files. It is frequently the case that data analysis is conducted in order to design a database system that will replace a set of conventional files. In such a case, the definitions of the files (if such documentation exists) will form a valuable source of information. However, the remarks of Chapter 7 on the implementation-free nature of the conceptual data model will need to be borne in mind: conventional file structures are *implementation* models and it will be the analyst's task to differentiate between the conceptual and the implementation features.

(d) Existing manual files. Similar remarks pertain here as in (c) above. In particular it should be realised that manual files *do not* represent an implementation-free view simply because they are not computer files. Frequently they contain many features which are present solely as a result of implementation considerations.

(e) Existing computer programs — remembering that these will be process implementations.

(f) Job descriptions.

(g) Existing reports and documents. These will range from reports of previous investigations to quasi-legal documents in the case of certain organisations, defining the rule-orientated behaviour of the organisation. At UniHyp, for example, there will exist various regulations and codes defining as exactly as possible what counts as registering for a degree, gaining academic credit for a course, graduating with a degree, and so on.

(h) Interviews with persons in the functional area to ascertain what they do — one of the traditional techniques of systems analysis.

With all these sources the analyst will need to be aware that what is said to be the case and what actually is the case may be two quite different matters. The task is to come to some resolution as to what is needed to happen.

8.2.3 Determining outline data models

At the outset it should be stated that this is largely an intuitive process and as such has unsatisfactory aspects. However, refinement by the later stages of the methodology ameliorates this reliance on intuition. Some guidelines can be given that all try to recognise that *what* is being determined are the *significant* data objects used by the functional area.

for entities

* in reports, documents, interviews, etc. they tend to be the key *nouns* or *noun phrases*,

  e.g. *"Students* study for *degrees"*

* consider what the functional area *does*,
  e.g. Admissions deals with *applicants* for *places* to study for a *degree*.

* consider what the functional area *handles*,
  e.g. Course Registration handles the allocation of *students* to *places* on *courses* within their *degree*.

for relationships

* in reports, documents, interviews, etc. they tend to be the key *verbs* or *verb phrases*,
  e.g. "A course will *have* a number of pieces of assessed coursework *associated* with it . . . . ."

* in manual or computer files they tend to be represented by repeating entries or fields,
  e.g. `03 STUDENT-COURSEWORK OCCURS . . . . ."` within a STUDENT-RECORD.

* each entity type can be taken and paired with each other entity type by means of a matrix,

  e.g.

	STUDENT	STAFF	COURSE	FACULTY ...
STUDENT	✓ ?			
STAFF				
COURSE	✓✓			
FACULTY				

and each association of entity types can be considered for its operational significance to the organisation. Thus an association exists between STUDENT and COURSE, and this is operationally significant — students

199

take courses. An association exists between STUDENT and STUDENT — some students are, say, married to each other. This, however, may not be considered to be operationally significant.

Such a technique as this is liable to generate redundant relationships. For example:

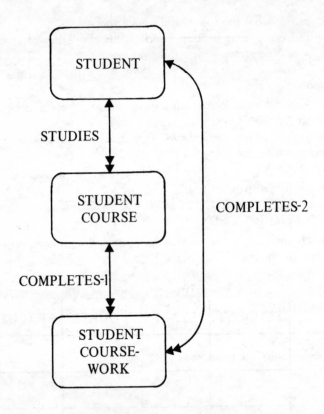

Clearly, one of the COMPLETES relationships is redundant. Given a STUDENT occurrence, the same STUDENT COURSEWORK occurrences can be arrived at by using the COMPLETES-2 relationship as by using the STUDIES and COMPLETES-1 relationships. Assuming STUDIES and COMPLETES-1 are operationally significant, the COMPLETES-2 relationship is redundant. Note, however, that to declare such a relationship to be redundant requires a full understanding of what the relationship means. For example:

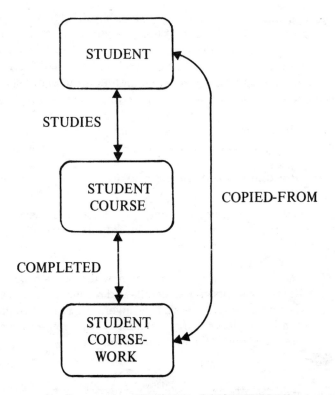

contains no redundancy; the STUDENT COURSEWORK occurrences obtained from a particular STUDENT occurrence being different when using the STUDIES and COMPLETED relationships than from when using the COPIED-FROM relationship.

8.2.4 Data needs for processes

The outline methodology requires the data needs for each process to be identified in terms of entities, attributes, and relationships, and for these (new) data needs to be used to refine the outline model. How this may be carried out in detail is now examined.

As was discussed in Chapter 6, processes may be regarded as being the means by which the given input is transformed into the required output. Chapter 7 described how processes may be analysed in terms of events and operations. Therefore the approach to be taken is to examine the input to each operation and, by using the required output, determine the data needs of the operation. The data needs for each operation then may be combined as an expression in terms of entities, attributes, and

201

relationships and used to refine the outline data model. Notice that what is being performed here is, at the functional area level, very similar to what is being performed at the global level: the problem is analysed into smaller sub-problems that can eventually be tackled in terms of a specific statement of data needs. There are parallels here with the step-wise refinement technique used in a top-down approach to program design.

Several examples are now given from the functional area of Course Registration at UniHyp.

Personal tutor and student choose courses

Prior to the start of each semester at UniHyp each student will choose, in consultation with their personal tutor, the courses they wish to study in the coming semester. In order for this to be carried out several operations need to be performed.

(i) Each personal tutor needs to know the Registration Number, Name, previous course details and results for their students so that informed advice can be given. This set of requirements can be depicted using a similar convention to a data model diagram, but at the attribute level, thus:

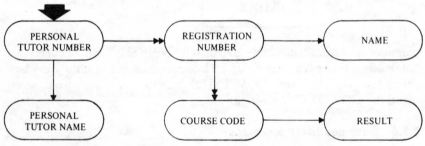

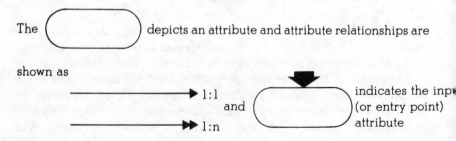

202

omitting any 'backward' arrow so that the flow from a given input attribute (or set of attributes) to the output attributes can be depicted. In the case above, a Personal Tutor Number is input and the required attributes are the Registration Numbers and Names of the students, along with the Course Codes and Results of the courses previously studied. The tutor's own Personal Tutor Name is also required so that he may check that he has quoted the correct Personal Tutor Number!

(ii) Each student needs to know the courses offered on their degree, including details of when the course is offered and of any pre-requisites.

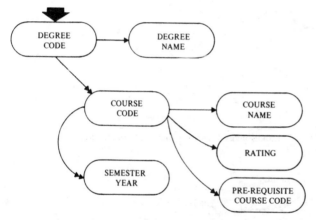

(iii) Students may enquire what courses successful study of a given course allows

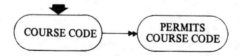

Student provisionally registers

(iv) Using this information the student will choose the courses to be studied in the following semester. They will then *provisionally register* for that set of courses. Course Administration will require, for a given course in a semester, a list of the students provisionally registered.

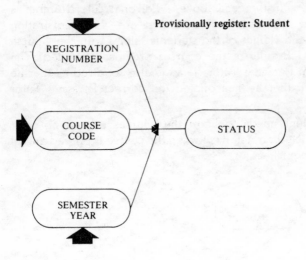

Provisionally register: Student

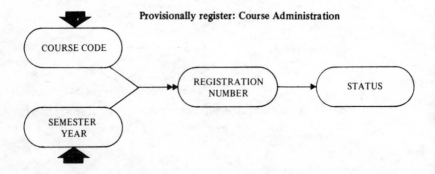

Provisionally register: Course Administration

Student finally registers

(v) After the first three weeks of a course a student is required to **finally register** for those courses that are to be counted by the student as academic credit. A personal tutor will need to know for each student tutored which courses are actually being studied and which courses have been withdrawn from.

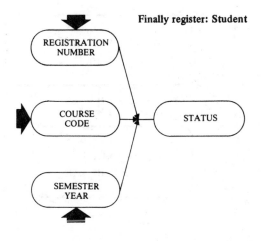

Finally register: Student

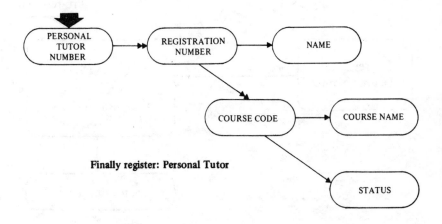

Finally register: Personal Tutor

Notice that the requirements of (iv) and (v) are not portrayed by creating 'report' or 'list' entities, but by representing the data needed by the operation for the production of the list or report. Notice also that for each operation information is recorded about the **functional dependencies** of the attributes involved.

The data needs of the operations can now be combined to give an expression in terms of entities, attributes, and relationships.

The picture given by (i) is:

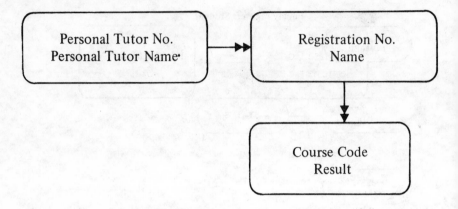

The picture given by (ii) is:

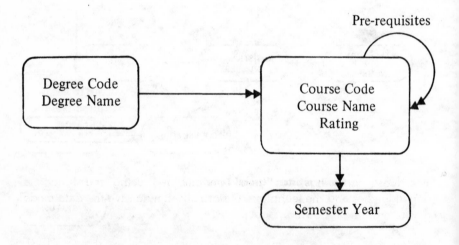

The picture given by (iii) is:

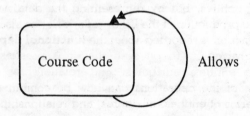

The picture given by (iv) is:

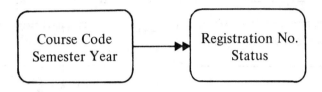

The picture given by (v) is:

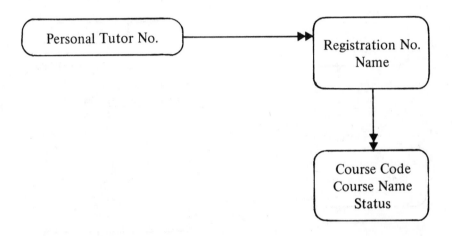

The loose groupings can then be combined using the functional dependencies and the technique of normalisation to give the data model diagram on the following page.

Notice the introduction into the combined model of the COURSE-OFFERING entity, with no non-key attributes. The addition of further views might reveal non-key attributes such as NUMBER-OF-STUDENTS, etc. Notice, also, the requisites relationship represented as m:n, made up from two views.

As a further check, it can be seen that it is possible to describe completely the entities, attributes, and relationships used by an operation by means of the combined model, i.e. the operational data needs verify the combined model.

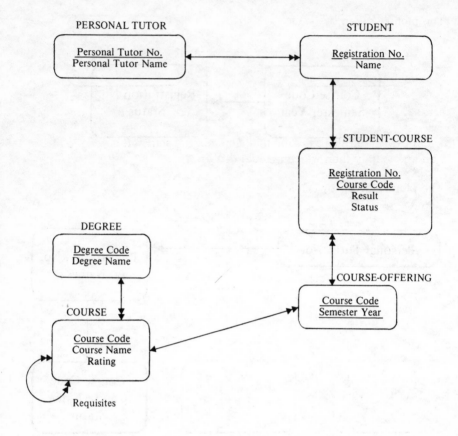

8.2.5 The unacceptable face of normalisation

The decision as to whether to represent data as an entity, attribute, or relationship relies heavily on the use of normalisation, as in the examples in the previous section. However, it is not the whole story: normalisation can produce unwelcome results which the data analyst should be aware of.

1. Resolution of m:n relationships

By its removal of repeating groups, normalisation will resolve an m:n relationship into two m:n relationships with an intersection entity *regardless* of whether there are any non-key attributes. For example, if the organisational structure at UniHyp is such that a member of staff belongs to just one faculty then we can model this as:

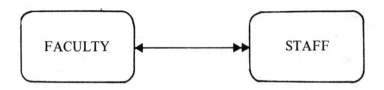

If, however, the rules are such that a member of staff can belong to more than one faculty then we can model this as:

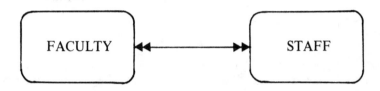

Normalisation will insist that we model it as:

even if there is no data that we wish to record about the relationship, i.e. there are no non-key attributes for FACULTY/STAFF. Since the conceptual data model should not make any assumptions about the structuring power of any logical data model that may be used for implementation, such an m:n relationship should remain in the conceptual data model.

2. Reliance on functional dependencies

Paradoxically, whilst normalisation can spuriously produce all-key entities in the handling of m:n relationships, it can fail to generate entities in certain circumstances. These circumstances exist when one component of a possible functional dependency is missing, namely the key or the non-key attributes. For example, Exercise 7.4 in S3NF is:

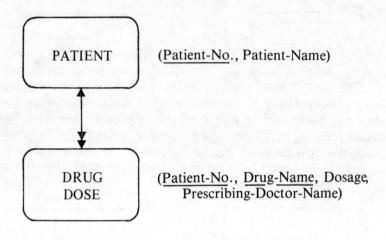

PATIENT   (Patient-No., Patient-Name)

DRUG
DOSE   (Patient-No., Drug-Name, Dosage,
Prescribing-Doctor-Name)

No recognition of a DOCTOR entity is produced. This could be the result of there being no attributes that are functionally dependent on Prescribing-Doctor-Name, if such names are unique. Consider the effect of introducing in this case, a Prescribing-Doctor-Telephone-No., attribute. A DOCTOR entity is produced by normalisation. Alternatively, the absence of a DOCTOR entity could be the result of the omission of a specific key that uniquely identifies Prescribing-Doctor-Names, if such names are not unique. Consider the effect of introducing, in this case, a Prescribing -Doctor-No. A DOCTOR entity is produced by normalisation. Similar considerations apply concerning a DRUG entity. Therefore, the data analyst should ask if the attribute is significant in itself — is it likely to have attributes dependent on it, or be determined by other (absent) attributes? If so, then it should be represented as an entity.

Normalisation, then, is a technique to be used in data analysis. It is not the only technique used and the data analyst needs to be aware of its limitations.

8.3 CONSOLIDATION

The task of analysing the data needs to produce a conceptual data model was broken down into the tasks of analysing the data needs of functional areas to produce conceptual data sub-models. These conceptual data sub-models need to be *consolidated* to produce the desired end result.

210

8.3.1 Two ways to consolidation

It is possible to use the local models to produce the global model in the manner depicted by Fig. 8.4. The initial local model produced is consolidated with succeeding local models, building towards the global model. Such an approach can be used, but suffers from the handicap that it lacks any framework in which to conduct the consolidation. Local models may be disjoint or may conflict in the views they take. Some outline is required to place the local models in context. Fig. 8.5 depicts an approach that provides such a framework. At the global level it repeats, in outline, what has been performed at the local level. A global outline model is initially defined which may then be refined by the consolidation of the local models.

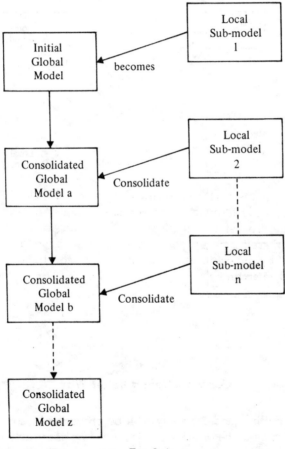

Fig 8.4
Consolidation: One Way

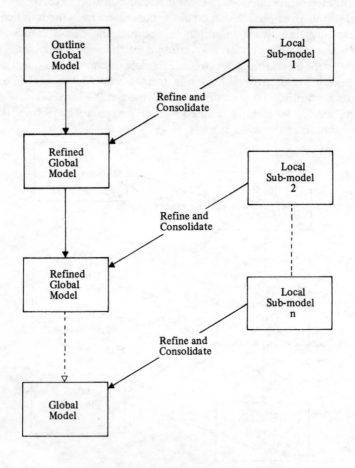

Fig 8.5
Consolidation: a Better Way

The global outline model, ideally, will be produced by someone with a wide experience of the organisation, and can be constructed in terms of the major entity types and relationship types using similar techniques as in the case of the local models. At the very least, it will broadly partition the data of an organisation into major areas and identify the relationships between these areas. For example, at UniHyp, such a broad brush stroke approach might yield something like Fig. 8.6. As well as providing a context for the process of consolidation and refinement, such an outline global model provides the organisation with a *planning tool* for data analysis. It may be used to define a strategy for the analysis of functional areas and to provide an indication of the degree of overlap between local models.

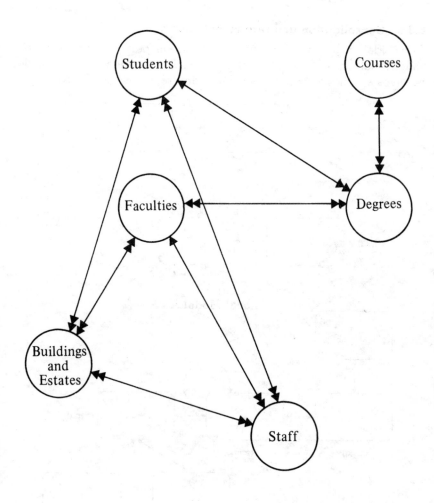

Fig 8.6
Major Data Areas and Relationships at UniHyp

However, both approaches emphasise two points about the global data model that is being produced.

(i)   The global data model is an evolving creation: it is added to and refined. It is not a static, final product.

(ii) The global data model is not just the sum of the local sub-models, i.e. a collection of application views. It has a *long term,* global element. It should, so to speak, *anticipate change.*

8.3.2 Consolidation and refinement simply.

Consolidation and refinement of local sub-models may be portrayed simplistically as in Figs. 8.7, 8.8, and 8.9. The consolidated data model receives a richer view of the attributes and relationships involved.

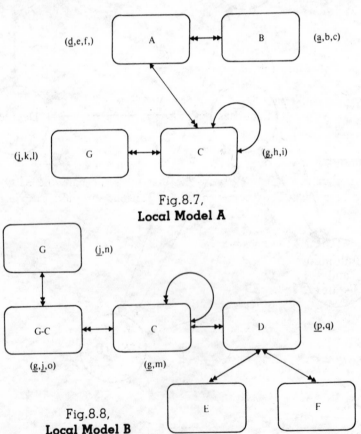

Fig.8.7,
Local Model A

Fig.8.8,
Local Model B

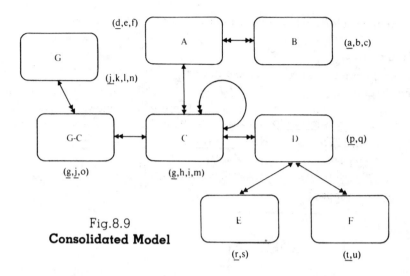

Fig.8.9
Consolidated Model

8.3.3 Consolidation in practice.

In practice, the principle of the above consolidation process holds, but it is unlikely that the neat overlapping of names will hold for entities, attributes, and relationships. Practically, the data analyst needs to unravel a conflicting tangle of terms.

Synonyms

A synonym is a word or phrase that has the same meaning as another word or phrase. They occur readily in consolidating local models. For example:

STUDENT (Registration No.,.........,   Date of Registration
,..........,..)

STUDENT (Registration No.,.........., Admittance Date ,..........,..)

Are Date of Registration and Admittance Date the same attributes with different names? The data analyst will need to resolve such questions, perhaps by reference back to the end-users.

PERSONAL TUTOR (Personal Tutor No.,..........,)

PERSONAL TUTOR (Staff No.,...........,)

Are Personal Tutor No. and Staff No. the same attributes with different names?

Similar problems can occur with entities and relationships.

Homonyms.

A homonym is a word or phrase that is used to refer to different things. For example:

ORDER (<u>Order No.</u>, ..., Price)

LINE-ITEM (<u>Order No.</u>, <u>Part No.</u>, Qty.,........., Price)

PART (<u>Part No.</u>, ..., Price)

in the data model

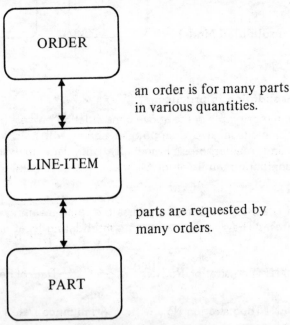

an order is for many parts in various quantities.

parts are requested by many orders.

Is Price the same attribute in each entity, or a different attribute? Here, clearly, it is a homonym. We might rename thus:

ORDER (<u>Order No.</u>,........., Price-for-Order)

LINE-ITEM (<u>Order No.</u>, <u>Part No.</u>, Qty.,.......... Line-Price)

PART (<u>Part No.</u>,..........., Unit-Price)

This introduces an interesting point. There is now a case of *derived redundancy*. The Line-Price value can be obtained by multiplying Unit-Price by Qty, and the Price-for-Order value can be obtained by summing the appropriate Line-Price values. Should such derived redundancy be present in a conceptual data model? There is no clear cut answer to this since an attribute such as Price-for-Order seems fundamental to the entity ORDER. The best answer would seem to be to record such derived redundancy in the model *and* to record the derivation as a form of consistency rule.

Homonyms are not restricted to attributes. Consider the following example:

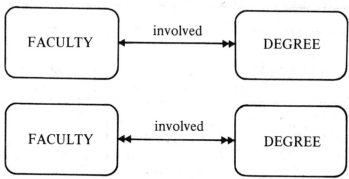

Is this the same *Involved* relationship, with a slightly richer view given in the lower depiction? Careful analysis at UniHyp will reveal that it is *not*, and that the more useful interpretation is:

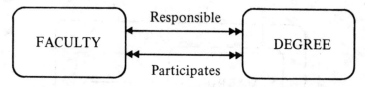

That is, many FACULTYs may *Participate* in setting-up many DEGREEs, but for a given DEGREE only one FACULTY will be *Responsible* for running a DEGREE.

Entity sub-types

An entity sub-type has as its occurrences some defined sub-set of the total occurrences of the entity type. For example:

Entity type: ORDER

Sub-types: (i)   Received - ORDER
                           (received, but not delivered)

	(ii)	Delivered - ORDER
		(received, delivered, but not paid)

	(iii)	Paid - ORDER
		(received, delivered and paid)

Pictorially:—

ORDER

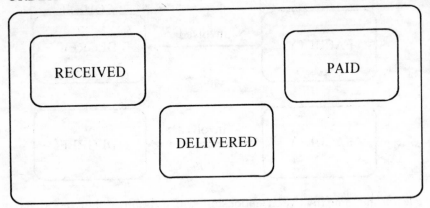

In this example the entity sub-types are *disjoint*, but this need not be the case. Consider:

PERSON

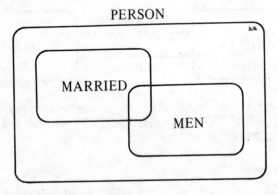

Entity sub types are important because:

*   they provide a means of recognising and reconciling differences in the local conceptual views.
*   they provide information important to storage model design, e.g. the ORDER entity could be implemented as several

distinct record types. Note that this consideration makes it desirable that the sub-types be disjoint.

The first of these considerations is now examined. Assume that we have two local views, thus:

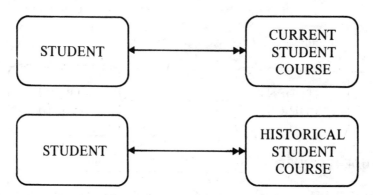

These can be consolidated thus:

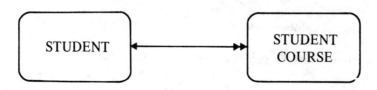

i.e. Entity type: STUDENT COURSE

    Entity sub-types: Historical STUDENT COURSE
                                   Current STUDENT COURSE

Using 1:1 relationships.

Normalisation whilst excluding m:n relationships says little on 1:1 relationships save that they sensibly would be combined. This may not always be desirable as the following example illustrates.

Local view (i)

STUDENT COURSE (Registration No., Course Code, Status)

Local view (ii)

STUDENT COURSE (Registration No., Course Code, Overall Coursework Mark, Exam Mark, Result)

Combining both these views into one entity disguises the fact that a STUDENT COURSE has a COURSE RESULT but

(a)   not until the course is completed

(b)   not for those STUDENT COUSES where the student has failed to finally register, as indicated by the value of Status.

A more useful consolidated view is therefore:

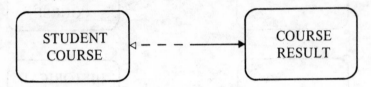

STUDENT COURSE (Registration No., Course Code, Status)

COURSE RESULT (Registration No., Course Code, Overall Coursework
Mark, Exam Mark, Result)

That is, the separation out of attributes that consistently move from null to meaningful values together.

Functional entities represented as relationships.

Consider the following local data models.

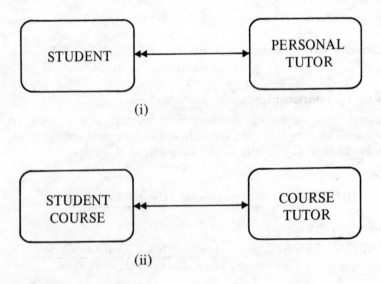

(i)

(ii)

Within the global data model they will be contained as:

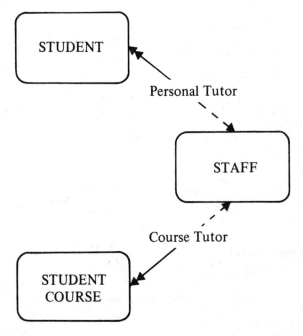

That is, the role of the entity is displayed as a relationship.

An example of consolidation.

To conclude, an example is given of consolidating two local sub-models.

Local conceptual model 1

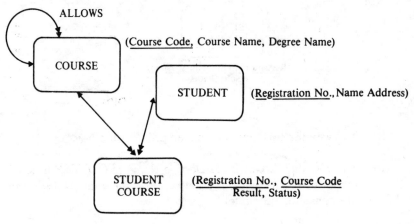

Local conceptual model 2

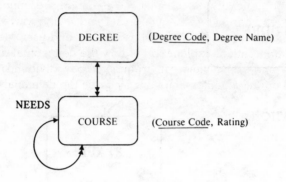

DEGREE   (<u>Degree Code</u>, Degree Name)

NEEDS

COURSE   (<u>Course Code</u>, Rating)

Consolidated model

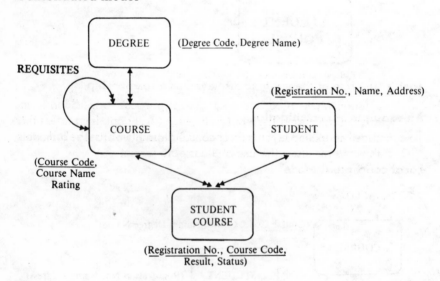

DEGREE   (<u>Degree Code</u>, Degree Name)

REQUISITES

(<u>Re</u>gistration No., Name, Address)

COURSE   STUDENT

(<u>Course Code</u>,
Course Name
Rating

STUDENT
COURSE

(<u>Registration No., Course Code,</u>
Result, Status)

Notice:

(i)   The way the two local models amplify each other.

(ii)   The way that the attribute Degree Name of COURSE in local
       model 1 finds its place as an attribute of the entity DEGREE in
       the consolidated model.

222

8.3.4   Validating with users

Many organisations *validate* the local models and the global model with end-users. This is not (hopefully) the simplistic situation of presenting a conceptual data model diagram before an end-user and saying 'Have we got it right?'. The conceptual data model is not an end-user view. However, a careful and patient explanation of how the conceptual data model contains the end-user's view can frequently pay dividends in trapping errors and unwarranted assumptions made by the data analyst.

8.4   DOCUMENTATION.

The outcome of data analysis will need to be documented. This documentation will take two forms:

(i) a data model diagram : a *summary* picture;

(ii) detailed documentation about the entities, attributes, and relationships recording the necessary information noted in Chapter 7. Such documentation is an example of *data about data,* and as such has a structure which can be analysed and can then be represented as some form of logical data model. The representation of such a logical data model with a database structure is explored in Chapter 12, but it is possible for a small exercise in data analysis to be supported by some form of clerical documentation system where each entity, attribute and relationship is recorded on a special purpose form. Such forms are not discussed here but Reference (8.1) contains papers that detail proposed layouts that are fixed format, whilst the following three forms show the use of a variable format.

Type	ENTITY	Name

DESCRIPTION: A brief description of the entity type.

SYNONYMS: Any other names by which the entity may be known within the organisation.

AUTHORISED TO
```
‖ CREATE
‖ MODIFY
‖ DELETE
‖ RETRIEVE
‖ COUNT
```
The names of the end users who are allowed to access the entity according to the options chosen.

CONTAINS: The names of the attributes which comprise the entity.

IDENTIFYING KEY: The name(s) of the attribute(s) which uniquely identify the entity, including any alternative candidate keys.

OCCURRENCES: The number of occurrences of the entity type.

COMMENT: Any additional information about the entity.

RAISED BY: DATE: SHEET   OF

224

| Type | ATTRIBUTE | Name | |

DESCRIPTION: A brief description of the attribute.

SYNONYMS: Any other names by which the attribute may be known within the organisation.

ENTITY DESCRIBED: The name(s) of the entity (or entities) the attribute describes.

AUTHORISED TO
‖ CREATE ‖
‖ MODIFY ‖
‖ DELETE ‖
‖ RETRIEVE ‖
‖ COUNT ‖

The name of the end users who are allowed to access the attribute according to the options chosen.

SOURCE: The source of the data within the organisation.

USE: The use made by the organisation of the attribute

FORMAT: The type and length of the attribute.

VALUES: The values that the attribute can take.

COMMENT: Any additional information about the attribute.

| RAISED BY: | DATE: | SHEET OF |

225

Type	Name

RELATIONSHIP

DESCRIPTION: A brief description of the relationship.

SYNONYMS: Any other names by which the relationship may be known within the organisation.

RELATIONSHIP BETWEEN: The names of the entities related, and the degree of the relationship — 1:1, 1:n, m:n.

RELATIONSHIP IS $\begin{Bmatrix} \text{MANDATORY} \\ \text{CONTINGENT} \\ \text{OPTIONAL} \end{Bmatrix}$ $\begin{Bmatrix} \text{FIXED} \\ \text{TRANSFERABLE} \\ \text{TRANSIENT} \end{Bmatrix}$ and the conditions governing the existence and permance of the relationship

RELATIONSHIP IS $\begin{Bmatrix} \text{EXCLUSIVE} \\ \text{INCLUSIVE} \end{Bmatrix}$: names of other relationships included or excluded by the relationship

OCCURRENCES: The numbers of each entity type involved in an occurrence of the relationship and the number of occurrences of the relationship

AUTHORISED TO $\begin{Vmatrix} \text{CREATE} \\ \text{MODIFY} \\ \text{DELETE} \\ \text{RETRIEVE} \\ \text{COUNT} \end{Vmatrix}$

The name of the end users who are allowed to access the relationship according to the options chosen.

COMMENT: Any additional information about the relationship.

RAISED BY:	DATE:	SHEET OF

226

SUMMARY

Data analysis begins by developing local conceptual data sub-models reflecting the data needs of functional areas within an organisation.

These local data sub-models can be developed by considering the data needed by the processes the functional area performs.

The local sub-models are consolidated to yield a global data model.

REFERENCES AND BIBLIOGRAPHY

(8.1)   **Data Analysis for Information Systems Design,** proceedings of BCS conference, Loughborough, June, 1978. All the papers are worth attention, but in particular those of H.C. Ellis, and R.M. Tagg are relevant to the topic of data analysis

(8.2)   BCS DDSWP **Report**, see Ref. (7.6). Again, there is material here relevant to data analysis.

(8.3)   King, P.J.H. **Information Analysis for Database Design,** Online Database Conference, London, 1977. Proceedings published by Online Conferences Limited, Uxbridge, England. An interesting outline of some of the problems associated with the determination of entities and their relation to 'real world' objects.

(8.4)   Tsichritzis, D. and Lochovsky, F. **Views on Data,** in **The ANSI/SPARC DBMS Model,** ed. D.A. Jardine, North Holland, 1977.

(8.5)   Robinson, H.M. **Data Modelling and Database Design: Practicalities and Problems,** paper presented at IUCC Colloquium 1979, University of Warwick.

EXERCISES

8.1   "Customers place purchase orders with an automobile spare-parts company for a variety of parts. Each purchase order must clearly identify the parts required and the appropriate quantities. The company meets the orders for the various parts by obtaining them from a range of suppliers. Each potential supplier for a part is requested to submit a quotation. The

227

quotations are used to determine, for a given part, who the suppliers will be and how many units of a given part they will supply."

Draw a data model diagram for the entities and relationships implied in the above extract.

8.2   For each of the entities in the data model diagram for Exercise 8.1 list likely attributes. Include key and non-key attributes.

8.3   "A distribution company maintains a series of depots throughout the country from which it distributes goods for a range of companies. Goods are distributed according to the orders received at each depot from the salesmen of the various companies whose goods are being distributed. Each salesman operates in area that coincides with the depot's distribution area. A company may have more than one salesman in an area. The depot distributes goods via vehicles attached to the depot. When a vehicle requires maintenance, this is carried out by one of the larger depots that has the necessary facilities."

Draw a data model diagram for the entities, relationships, and attributes implied in the above extract.

8.4   UniHyp maintains a convential file concerning its lecturing staff. Which of the following statements are about the conceptual view of the data on the files?

(a) There are separate records for each lecturer, held in alphabetical name sequence.
(b) Each lecturer has a marital status.
(c) The marital status can be married, widowed, divorced, single, or separated.
(d) The coded values for marital status are A — E.
(e) A faculty can have a number of members of staff.
(f) The number of members of staff held on file for a faculty is not allowed to exceed 200.
(g) A program lists lecturers who are entitled to sabbatical leave.

8.5　A personal tutor needs to know the following information in connection with his tutees:

(i) the Registration No., Name, Degree Code, and Degree Name for his tutees.

(ii) The Course Codes, Course Names and Ratings for a given degree,

(iii) the Course Codes and Results for each of the courses currently being taken by his tutees.

For each of these operations draw an attribute data needs diagram and consolidate these to yield a conceptual data model.

DESIGN

The aim of this Part of the book is to define the design needed to translate a conceptual data model into a set of computer-based data structures. The design needed is not radically different in kind to that which traditionally *should* be practised by systems designers. It differs by being a more rigorous and coherent treatment than that meted out in conventional file design.

9.2.3. Architectural limitations

The overall approach to database analysis and design depicted in Fig. 6.8 is based upon, and assumes, the generalised architecture discussed in Chapter 2. That is, it assumes something like Fig. 9.2.

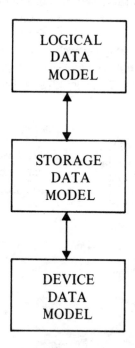

Fig. 9.2
Architectural Assumptions

Decisions concerning the logical structure and characteristics of the data are expressed in the logical data model, decisions concerning the access and storage patterns of the data are expressed in the storage data model, and decisions concerning the allocation of data to machine devices are expressed in the device data model. Importantly, the assumption of the top down approach is that these decisions can be kept separate and can be made in that order.

It has already been noted, in Chapter 6, that the architectural limitations of conventional file systems — that they have no distinct storage data model — forces conventional file design to make decisions at the logical level that are really storage level decisions. The point was made that the richer architecture of a database system avoided this dilemma. An astute reader will have noted in the first Part of this book that there is no widely used commercial system available at the moment that explicity incorporates a storage data model. The only database approach that has a systematic and distinct storage data model — CODASYL '78 — has yet to make such an architectural feature *formally* part of its specifications, and no implementor has yet produced a CODASYL database system that incorporates a storage schema. As a consequence the *actual* architecture of available commercial database systems is as portrayed in Fig. 9.3. The storage data model does not appear as a distinct architecture component, and is conflated with the logical data model (usually) and/or the device data model.

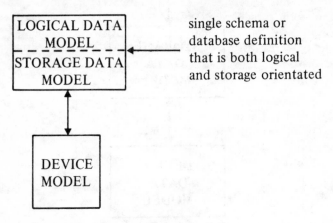

single schema or
database definition
that is both logical
and storage orientated

Fig. 9.3
Actual Architecture

The consequence for logical database design is exactly as for conventional file systems: decisions about the *access* and *storage* of data need to be made at the *logical* level. Importantly, logical database design becomes directly concerned with *efficiency*, where this is a prime objective.

9.2.4 Software limitations.

Just as the architectural limitations of current database systems force logical database design to consider efficiency, so do *software limitations*. These limitations are now examined in three areas.

1. Access Control

To a varying degree database systems provide a measure of access control: that is, they provide features for implementing privacy decisions. For example, CODASYL provides the facility of an ACCESS CONTROL LOCK. Similar features are available in other database system approaches. For example, suppose we have two relations:

PERSONAL-TUTOR (PERSONAL-TUTOR-NO., PERSONAL-TUTOR-NAME)

STUDENT (REGISTRATION-NO., NAME, ADDRESS, PERSONAL-TUTOR-NO.)

and the privacy decision made by UniHyp is that PERSONAL-TUTORs may only see the NAMEs, etc. of the STUDENTs they tutor. The access control for such a decision may be expressed as the condition

PERSONAL-TUTOR-NO. IN PERSONAL-TUTOR = PERSONAL-TUTOR-NO. IN STUDENT.

Ideally, the granularity of such locks and conditions should be as fine as possible: down to the data-item type and data-item occurrence level in CODASYL, for example. Many database systems do indeed provide this level of control. However, the cost, in terms of efficiency can be unacceptably high. If every time, say, a record is accessed a whole range of locks or conditions need to be evaluated then clearly this will slow down processing.

As a result of this, logical database design will frequently take steps to minimise this inefficiency by reducing the number of locks or conditions needed to implement privacy decisions. The usual technique employed is to try to arrange matters so that all data items in a record require the same level of privacy protection and can therefore be encompassed by one lock or condition. Similarly, if the database is partitioned in any way, as are CODASYL databases by AREAs, all record types with the same level of privacy requirement may be grouped into one partition and can therefore be controlled by one lock or condition.

2. Logical model: logical sub-model mapping.

As we discussed in Chapter 2 this mapping generally needs to be complex: sub-model objects being constructed from model objects. However, a complex construction or derivation incurs penalties: it takes processing time. As a consequence many database systems reduce this mapping to a simple sub-set. Even within this simple sub-set, processing penalties are frequently incurred if the sub-setting goes below the record level, i.e. if only certain data items are selected from a model record to form a sub-model record. Therefore logical database design will frequently take steps to minimise the processing required to derive a sub-model. Typically, the logical data model may be designed so that only a simple sub-set mapping is required even where a more complex mapping is available. If only a simple sub-set mapping is available then steps may be taken to ensure that this sub-setting does not go below the record level. Logical data model objects may therefore be designed with these objectives in mind.

3. Physical placement control.

Whilst currently available database systems conflate the logical data model and the storage data model they also frequently give little adequate control over the mapping to the device data model. For example, suppose we have the schema depicted in Fig. 9.4. in a CODASYL database.

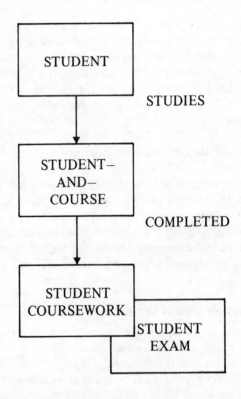

Fig. 9.4.

Notice, in passing, that the records are now both logical schema records *and* storage schema records. The processing pattern may well be that all four record types need frequently to be accessed together. If this is the case then, ideally, we would like to ensure that the appropriate occurrences of these four record types are stored *together* — on the same page or block or on nearby pages or blocks. Whilst many database systems allow some recognition of this place-near logic (or more correctly, 'physic') they do not allow fine enough control. As a consequence, logical data model design is frequently forced to ensure the situation by, for example, collapsing a set, as in Fig. 9.5.

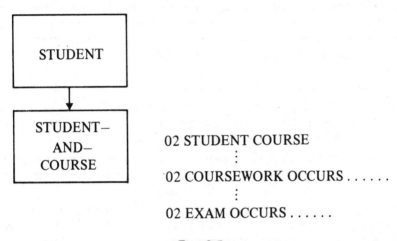

02 STUDENT COURSE
:
02 COURSEWORK OCCURS . . . . . .
:
02 EXAM OCCURS . . . . . .

Fig. 9.5.

Thus the course, coursework, and exam details of a student will be physically stored together.

9.2.5 Consequences.

We may conclude from the above that logical database design

(i)   needs to consider a range of objectives that may possibly conflict,

(ii)   needs to consider the data structuring capability of the database system approach used,

(iii)   needs to consider requirements of storage and access — implementation features that should more correctly be part of physical database design,

(iv)   needs to consider requirements of efficiency, where this is an important objective.

241

9.2.6 A partial solution.

The main brunt of the characterisation given above of logical database design results from the architectural and software limitations of *current* database systems. Things, hopefully, will change. However, it would be convenient if an approach to logical database design could be given that

(a)   works for current systems and their limitations

and

(b)   will work, with some modification, for future systems that do not incorporate such limitations.

Such an approach will not only have attractions for the author of an undergraduate text, but will also have direct benefit for database design practitioners since it will insulate the effort of their design to an extent from evolutionary changes in database systems.

The approach to logical database design can be summarised thus:—

1. Perform a *naive translation* of the conceptual data model into the logical data model constructs of the database system approach used. This is termed a *first-cut* logical data model.

2. If the architecture and software constraints mentioned above are no longer present then this *first-cut* logical data model becomes, essentially, the final logical data model.

3. If the architecture and software constraints mentioned above are present then the *first-cut* logical data model is subjected to a *collapse and fragmentation* to yield what becomes the final logical data model.

4. If the architecture and software constraints mentioned above are not present then the *first-cut* logical data model is subjected to a *collapse and fragmentation* to yield what becomes, eventually, the *storage data model*.

9.3 NAIVE TRANSLATION.

In this section a set of rules is given for each major database system approach that allows, within data structuring limitations, a direct translation of a conceptual data model into the appropriate logical data model.

9.3.1 CODASYL '73 Structures.

(i)   Entities.

An entity is translated to a record, e.g.

(ii) Attributes.

An attribute is translated into a data item.

e.g.

STUDENT (Registration No., Name, Address, Personal Tutor
No.,..........)

becomes

RECORD NAME IS STUDENT

02 REG-NO;	PIC 9(4)
02 STUDENT-NAME;	PIC X(12)
02 ADDRESS;	PIC X(20)
02 PERS-TUT-NO;	PIC 9(4)

The inclusion of a PIC clause emphasises only that decisions
need to be taken about the format (size and type) of data items
at this level. The actual storage of data items is discussed in
Chapter 10.

(iii) Relationships.

1:1 and 1:n relationships that are not involuted become sets.

e.g.

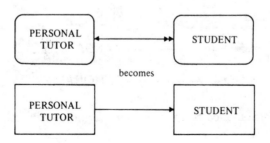

The existence rules for *members* in a 1:n relationship can be expressed in a limited fashion since we have the following correspondence.

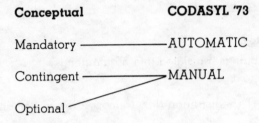

Conceptual   **CODASYL '73**

Mandary —————————AUTOMATIC

Contingent —————————MANUAL

Optional

The existence rules for *owners* in a 1:n relationship cannot be expressed, i.e.

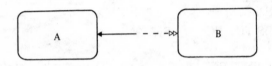

cannot be expressed.

The permanence rules for *members* of a 1:n relationship can be expressed thus:

Conceptual   **CODASYL '73**

Fixed ————————————— FIXED

Transferable ————————— MANDATORY

Transient ————————————— OPTIONAL

Permanence rules for owners cannot be directly expressed.

m:n relationships cannot be directly handled. They are converted thus:

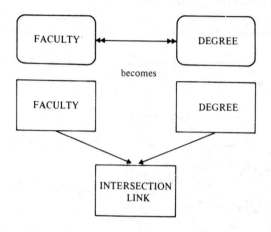

in a manner we are already familiar with.

Involuted relationships cannot be handled directly.

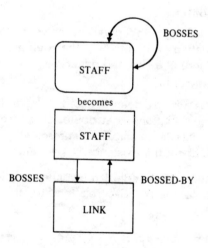

where the BOSSED-BY set is 1:1. That is, to find out who someone bosses the LINK members in the BOSSES set are found, each of which will own just one STAFF record in the BOSSED-BY set. To find out who someone is bossed by the single LINK owner in the BOSSED-BY set is found and the owner in the BOSSES set for that LINK is located.

Involuted m:n relationships are handled in a similar fashion, i.e.

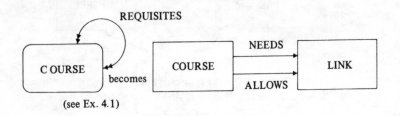

(see Ex. 4.1)

9.3.2   Relational structures.

(i)   Entities.

An entity type is translated into a relation; entity occurrences becoming the tuples.

(ii)   Attributes.

An attribute (conceptual) becomes an attribute (relation): this translation will involve the definition for the attribute (relation) of a size and data type.

(iii)   Relationships.

As has already been detailed, relationships are represented between relations by attributes drawn from common domains. Since this is an implicit representation no mention can be made about the existence or permanence of a relationship.

Relations can handle 1:n involuted relationships directly. For example, the BOSSES relationship, above, can be dealt with thus:

STAFF (STAFF-NO., NAME, POSITION, BOSS-STAFF-
NO.,..........)

providing the attributes STAFF-NO. and BOSS-STAFF-NO. are declared as being from the same domain.

Relations cannot handle m:n relationships directly. A link relation is required. For example, the m:n relationship between FACULTY and DEGREE has to be represented as

FACULTY (<u>FAC-CODE</u>, FACULTY-NAME,..........)

LINK (<u>FAC-CODE,</u> <u>DEGREE-CODE</u>)

DEGREE (<u>DEGREE-CODE</u>, DEGREE-NAME,.........)

Involuted m:n relationships cannot be handled directly and need a link relation, as was discussed in Chapter 3.

9.3.3 Other approaches

Within IMS entities become *segments,* attributes become *fields,* and relationships become represented by *hierarchies.* The structuring limitations of such an approach have already been discussed and the use of incestuous pointers to overcome them outlined (Chapter 5).

Within ADABAS entity types become *files,* entity occurrences become *records,* attributes become *fields,* and relationships are represented by *coupling indexes.* Note that m:n relationships can be treated directly.

Within TOTAL entity types become *files,* entity occurrences become *records,* attributes become *fields*, and relationships are represented by *linkage paths.* The data structuring limitations of TOTAL are similar to those of CODASYL '73 and similar solutions are adopted. One limitation peculiar to TOTAL is that it cannot represent multiple level hierarchies directly: LINK master files need to be introduced.

e.g.

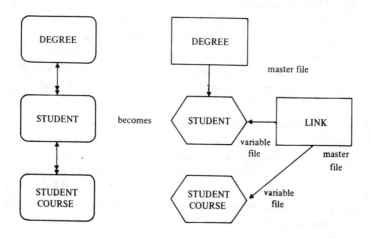

9.3.4 A means of evaluating database system approaches.

This naive translation provides two things that are not directly connected with the task of logical database design, but are concerned with *evaluation,* and can be usefully remarked upon at this point.

1. The naive translation provides a basis for understanding and comparing the various database system approaches at the logical data model. We would expect a good logical data model approach to provide a naive translation that involved as little distortion from the conceptual data model as possible. On these grounds, clearly our two best candidates are the relational approach and CODASYL (we note in passing that CODASYL '78 can handle involuted 1:n relationships). The computing profession has debated long and hard on the merits of these two approaches and the issue has become one of almost theological import. It is not the intention of this book to become embroiled in this debate, but it is worth nothing that

    (i) the data structuring power of the two approaches is equivalent,

and

    (ii) the differences between the two approaches are largely the result of the difference in the level of procedurality in the languages that manipulate the database in the two approaches.

2. The naive translation provides a basis for a particular organisation to choose a particular database system. The ability of each database system being considered to model directly the organisation's conceptual data model can be assessed. Thus, for a particular organisation, this may reveal that, say, a TOTAL or IMS database approach is well suited.

    It should be stressed that this is not the only basis on which such evaluations should be made. Other criteria are important, such as the degree of data independence provided, the complexity of model to model mappings, data dictionary facilities, etc.

9.3.5 The benefits of normalisation.

Normalisation was deliberately postponed until Chapter 7 and was introduced as a technique for ordering a conceptual data model — for ensuring that one fact was represented in one place. The relevance of normalisation to logical models of data can now be seen. If we refer to the normalisation process carried out in section 7.4.1. onwards we can see that if the unnormalised entity STUDENT were naively translated into a record or relation, then from a processing point of view it would possess the following undesirable characteristics.

* there is duplication of data — COURSE NAME is repeated. Therefore if a COURSE NAME is changed a program will need to change *all* these occurrences — otherwise the data will be inconsistent.

* similar remarks hold for PERSONAL TUTOR NAME and DEGREE NAME.

* we cannot record data about a COURSE until at least one STUDENT studies that COURSE.

* similar remarks apply to TUTORs and DEGREEs.

In other words, an unnormalised record or relation presents processing and storage anomalies. Notice that these anomalies are removed by the normalisation process.

Normalisation, therefore, applies equally well for conceptual data models and logical data models. The appropriate definitions for S3NF and the precursor forms can easily be given for relations or records (see the Exercises at the end of the Chapter). However, the place to do normalisation is obviously at the start of things — at the conceptual data model.

9.4 COLLAPSE AND FRAGMENTATION.

As a result of a naive translation a first-cut logical data model has been obtained. If none of the architecture and software limitations described in Sections 9.2.3. and 9.2.4 are present then this first-cut logical data model will become the final logical data model. The naive translation described above has been performed mainly by the use of diagrams. Therefore, the final logical data model will need to be described in the appropriate logical data model definition language. Where this language cannot express, or cannot fully express, the existence and permanence rules for relationships consideration may be given to producing generalised programs that can be run against the database to check for any violation of these rules. The ability of the logical data model definition language to define the degree of access control required, and the validation and consistency rules for the data will also be exploited fully.

There are circumstances where, even if none of the architecture and software limitations are present, this logical data model will require some modification.

If compatability is a prime objective then some form of collapse and fragmentation may be needed to meet the demands of other (less well designed) systems.

If implementability is a prime objective then some form of collapse and fragmentation may be desirable where the conceptual data model is particularly complex. A similar consideration applies to maintainability.

Conversley, even where architecture and software limitations are present, it may be desirable not to collapse or fragment the first-cut logical data model if *flexibility* is a prime objective. The first-cut logical data model will represent an implementation, within the chosen database system's constraints, of the inherent structure of an organisation's data, and to accommodate change in the organisation easily this structure should be modified as little as possible. If efficiency *and* flexibility are both prime objectives then a problem arises as we shall see later.

9.4.1 The aims of collapse and fragmentation.

The aims of collapse and fragmentation can be demonstrated by an example. Consider the conceptual data model diagram of Fig. 9.6. Fig. 9.7 shows a naive translation of such a conceptual data model to a CODASYL '73 structure. Assume that one of the processes that this structure must support is the ability to retrieve for a given PERSONAL TUTOR the COURSE NAMEs and RATINGs of the COURSEs currently being studied by the tutor's STUDENTS. This process may operate as follows:

(i) Locate the appropriate PERSONAL TUTOR record.

(ii) Locate the STUDENT members in the TUTORS set owned by this record.

(iii) For *each* STUDENT record locate the STUDENT COURSE members in the STUDIES set.

(iv) Examine each of these STUDENT COURSEs members to determine which are currently being studied, (i.e. examine SEMESTER YEAR and STATUS).

(v) For *each* current STUDENT COURSE locate the owner in the TAKEN-BY set.

(vi) For *each* COURSE OFFERING locate the owner in the OFFERED set.

of *pointers.* Therefore, our process will involve a possibly high number of physical I/Os and disc head movements. In fact the number may be prohibitively high: desired response times will not be achieved.

For any reasonably complex conceptual data model a naive translation will produce a database that certainly works *but* will certainly work too *slowly.* The aims of collapse and fragmentation are therefore

(i)   to take steps to minimise access times

without

(ii)   destroying the inherent structure and flexibility of the first-cut logical data model.

It is therefore a process of compromise and trade-off.

For example, the number of accesses could be reduced by a fragmentation, as in Fig. 9.22, where the current STUDENT COURSEs are made a distinct record type. The number of accesses could be reduced by a collapse, as in Fig. 9.18, where the COURSE-OFFERINGs are made a repeating group of COURSE.

Exactly what is done can only be decided on the basis of *how* many accesses need to be made to the first-cut schema, *how* often the process is run, and *how* important it is that the process be efficient. That is, we again have to look at data usage, and we have to attempt to quantify that usage.

9.4.2 Documenting data usage.

The use of the first-cut logical data model by each process it must support needs to be documented. Before this can be described two important questions need to be asked.

(i)   What do we mean by process?

(ii)   What do we assume concerning the implementation features of the first-cut logical data model?

Ideally, at this stage, usage in terms of *programs* is required. Usage in terms of operations may give a false picture of access costs, since several operations may be subsequently grouped into one program on the basis of their access to common data. Thus the access cost of the program they make up will be less than the sum of their individual access costs. Conversely, usage in terms of some unanalysed, ill-defined process may also give a false picture of access cost, since the programs that eventually represent the process may have a higher net access cost than the ill-defined process. *Access cost* is defined as being the total number of logical data model records accessed by a program. It may not be the case that program definitions are available — program definition is clearly dependent to an extent on the definition of the logical data model. What is needed, therefore, is a description of usage in terms that are as close to the final program definitions as can practically be achieved.

Concerning the implementation features of the first-cut logical data model: clearly we want to make as few assumptions as possible so that as many implementation details as possible are left to physical database design. In other words, despite the (possible) conflation of logical and physical aspects in one architectural component there will still remain distinct activities of logical design and storage design. The exact assumptions made as to the implementation features of the first-cut logical data model will depend upon

(i)   the database system approach used

       and

(ii)   the particular implemention of that approach used.

Generally, however, what is needed is a set of assumptions that create, albeit in a 'virtual' fashion, a true *logical* data model for the database system approach used. To illustrate this idea in practice let us assume that UniHyp has an implementation of the CODASYL '73 proposals. For such a situation the following assumptions about implementation are made to give a working definition of a logical data model that can be used to document usage.

1. A program may enter the logical data model on any uniquely identified record occurrence.

    e.g. the access cost to locate a STUDENT record
    with REG-NO equal to '1234' is 1.

    Notice that no mention is made of how this access is achieved, i.e. LOCATION MODEs are excluded.

2. A program may enter the logical data model on a record type and search for the record occurrence required for that type against some selection criteria. The average access cost to locate such a record occurrence will be: $(n + 1)/2$ if the occurrence exists, where n is the number of occurrences of that record type.

254

The access cost when the occurrence does not exist will be n. From this it is clear that no *ordering* is assumed for record occurrences.

3. The issue of set implementation is more complex since what is assumed must be consistent with what is available at the storage design stage. Implicit in the CODASYL notion of a set, such as that given in Fig. 9.8, is an occurrence picture given in Fig. 9.9.

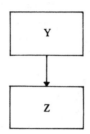

Fig. 9.8.

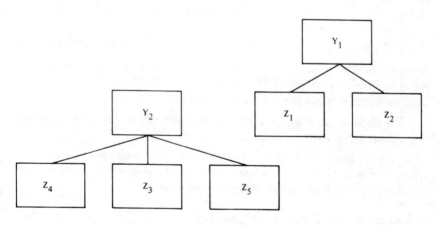

Fig. 9.9.

That is, a set is treated merely as a logical association between members and owner. As a result we have the following.

(a) To find a particular Z_a for a particular Y_m requires

— $(n + 1)/2$ accesses on average if the Z_a is present.

— n accesses if the Z_a is not present.

255

Where n is the number of Zs in the set occurrence.

(b) To find a particular Y_m for a particular Z_a requires 1 access.

(c) To create a record occurrence, say Z_6, once the Y_m, say Y_2, is located costs 1 access.

(d) To modify the contents of a record occurrence costs nothing other than the access cost to locate it.

(e) To delete a record occurrence costs nothing other than the access cost to locate it plus the access cost to locate the owner records in any set occurrences in which it participates.

(f) To modify set membership requires the owner to be located, the member to be located, and (where necessary) the new owner to be located.

The exact details of *these* assumptions given are not important as such. What is important is that a set of coherent assumptions are made that reflects the concept of a logical data model for the particular database system used. For example, it may be the case that a set is assumed to be a circular linked list — a different assumption to that made above.

It is now possible to document data usage. For each program that the database must support the following information will be required (again using a CODASYL example — the *principles* are precisely the same for the other approaches):

1. The records and sets the program uses in its navigation of the logical data model.

2. The use the program makes of these records and sets.

3. The logical access cost for each record.

4. The data items used, and the nature of the use, for each record type accessed.

This information can conveniently be recorded on forms such as those given in Fig. 9.10, 9.11: these are *example* forms which in practice may need modification to record more detailed usage.

The form shown in Fig. 9.10 allows the records and sets used by a program to be recorded along with information about the logical access cost for each record. The logical access cost is split into two parts: the number of occurrences ACCESSED and the number of occurrences USED, i.e. the number that must be examined in order to obtain the number that are required. Generally, ACCESSED will be greater than USED and the amount of discrepancy will be a measure of the (potential) inefficiency of the first-cut logical model for the process. Fig. 9.12 shows such a form completed for the process outlined in Section 9.4.1. Notice that to complete the form information is required about the occurrences of records and sets. In the example used this information is

— a PERSONAL TUTOR has, on average, 10 STUDENTs

— each STUDENT has, on average, 10 STUDENT COURSEs

— of these 10 STUDENT COURSEs, 2, on average, will be currently studied.

ACCESS FOR PROGRAM ....

RECORD	SET	ACCESSED	USED
TOTAL ACCESS COST		

Fig. 9.10

DATA ITEM USAGE FOR PROGRAM ....

RECORD	DATA ITEM	ACTION

Fig. 9.11

RECORD	SET	ACCESSED	USED
PERSONAL TUTOR	Direct entry	1	1
STUDENT	TUTORS	10	10
STUDENT COURSE	STUDIES	100	20
COURSE OFFERING	TAKEN-BY	20	20
COURSE	OFFERED	20	20
TOTAL ACCESS COST		151	71

Fig. 9.12
ACCESS FOR PROGRAM Student details for Tutor

RECORD	DATA ITEM	ACTION
PERSONAL TUTOR	PERSONAL TUTOR NO. PERSONAL TUTOR NAME	Key, Retrieval Retrieval
STUDENT	REG. NO. NAME	Retrieval Retrieval
STUDENT COURSE	SEMESTER YEAR STATUS COURSE CODE	} Selection criteria Access only
COURSE OFFERING	COURSE CODE SEMESTER YEAR	} Access only
COURSE	COURSE CODE COURSE NAME RATING	Retrieval Retrieval Retrieval

Fig. 9.13
DATA ITEM USAGE FOR PROGRAM Student details for Tutor

This information, recalling Chapter 7, was collected for the conceptual data model in terms of entity occurrences and relationship occurrences and will therefore be fairly directly available from the naive translation.

The form shown in Fig. 9.11 allows the detailed data item usage of a program to be recorded. For each record accessed the data items used are listed along with the actions taken by the program on the data item. This action can vary from a mere access in order to navigate further within the database, to retrieval or modification or deletion. Fig. 9.13 shows such a form completed for the process outlined in Section 9.4.1.

The recording of program usage in this manner flows naturally from data analysis and functional analysis where the use of data by processes was used as an analytical tool.

9.4.3 Inversion of data usage.

The documentation of data usage by program gives a *detailed record* of the (potential) inefficiency of the first-cut logical data model which will be used in the detailed design of the final logical data model. However, to obtain the *broad* indications needed for collapse and fragmentation the usage needs to be *inverted*. A variety of inversions can be used: three significant types are now described.

Record/program matrix.

A table or matrix is constructed as in Fig. 9.14. The entry made in each box of the table is the ACCESSED value for the appropriate record by the appropriate program taken from the form of Fig. 9.10. These values are summed by column to give the TOTAL COST for the program (this information can be cross-checked with the same value on the form of Fig. 9.10). They are also summed by row to give the Total accesses for the record.

This basic idea can be elaborated on in a variety of ways. For example, the efficiency of the logical model for some programs may be more important than for others — say, certain critical, frequently run, real-time programs. In this case the entries in the table may be weighted to reflect this relative priority. Or, if more detailed information is available — such as the number of creation accesses or deletion accesses — this can be used to form appropriate record/program tables that concentrate on the critical actions of record creation and deletion.

	Program 1	Program 2	....	Program n	Total
Record 1					
Record 2					
Record 3					
⋮					
Record n					
TOTAL COST					

Fig. 9.14
RECORD/PROGRAM TABLE

Set/program matrix.

A table is constructed as in Fig. 9.15. A '1' is entered in each box of the table if the appropriate set is used by the appropriate program. No entry is made if no use is made by the program of the set. The '1' may be weighted to reflect the relative importance of programs. The values in the rows are summed to give a Total for each set.

	Program 1	Program 2	....	Program n	Total
Set 1					
Set 2					
Set 3					
⋮					
Set n					

Fig. 9.15
SET/PROGRAM TABLE

Data item/program matrix.

A table is constructed as in Fig. 9.16. A '1' is entered in each box of the table if the appropriate data item is used by the appropriate program. No entry is made if no use is made of the data item by the program. The '1' may be weighted to reflect the relative importance of programs. Alternatively, the actual number of accesses made (this can be obtained from a combination of the two usage forms) can be entered, weighted if necessary. The values in the rows are summed to give a Total for each data item.

This inversion now gives a picture for each construct in the logical data model of its overall usage. The usage of records and sets may be pictorially displayed by means of a *database traffic diagram,* as in Fig. 9.17. Here the relative size of the objects in the diagram reflects the relative use made of them.

	Program 1	Program 2	....	Program n	Total
Data item 1					
Data item 2					
Data item 3					
⋮					
Data item n					

Fig. 9.16
DATA ITEM/PROGRAM TABLE

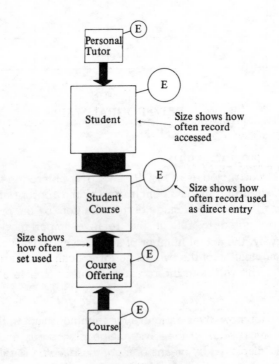

Fig. 9.17
Database Traffic Diagram

9.4   Define a specific set of assumptions that create a 'virtual' logical
       data model for a database system with which you are familiar (see
       section 9.4.2.)

9.5   Even if architectural and software limitations are present, are
       there circumstances where a naive translation would be
       acceptable?

9.6   Produce definitions of S3NF for *relations* and *records*.

9.7   Outline the conceptual data structure of this text in terms of
       entities BOOK, CHAPTER, and REFERENCE. What design
       decisions have been taken to implement this conceptual
       structure as a logical/storage structure, i.e. the present volume?

Chapter 10

PHYSICAL DATABASE DESIGN

"No - Gatsby turned out all right in the end...."

F.Scott Fitzgerald, The Great Gatsby

In this Chapter the final tasks involved with the design of a database are considered - the issues of storage data model design and device data model design. The principles outlined in this Chapter apply to all database systems, but the very nature of storage and device models dictates that the details be expressed in terms of some particular database system approach or even in terms of some particular implementation. The approach centered upon (but not exclusively), as in Chapter 9, is that of CODASYL '73 since this seems to provide some common ground between the various approaches. However the discussion is kept as general as possible, and it should be noted that one feature of the mapping to a storage model assumed in Chapter 9 — the ability to combine logical model records into storage model records — does not form a part of the recent CODASYL draft proposals on a storage schema. It is worth remarking that at the storage and device level all the database system approaches begin to look very similar. This is a reflection of the limited alternatives offered by current hardware and software facilities.

10.1 THE TASK OF PHYSICAL DATABASE DESIGN

The design activity described in Chapter 9 will have resulted in a logical data model that will take two forms depending on the impact of architecture and software constraints.

1. A true logical data model, resulting from a naive translation. In this case the fragmentation and collapse exercise will have resulted in the *storage model records* for this logical data model.

2. A 'virtual' logical data model, resulting from a naive translation and a fragmentation and collapse. In this case the record objects are both

logical model records *and* storage model records as a result of the conflation in the architecture. However, this 'virtual' data model has not considered all aspects of storage model design.

In both cases what now needs to be done is to consider the following issues:

i) How direct entry to records is supported in terms of access mechanisms.

ii) How associations between records (sets) are implemented in storage.

iii) How data items are implemented in storage.

These issues can then be said to conclude storage model design for both the forms above.

There then remains the issue of how these storage model records are grouped together and allocated to device configurations. This is the issue of device model design.

10.2 STORAGE MODEL DESIGN

10.2.1 Access mechanisms

Neither of the two forms of logical data model resulting from logical database design properly considered the issue of how direct entry to a record is implemented, this being a storage model design problem. The relevant options available, using CODASYL terminology, are DIRECT and CALC.

DIRECT requires that whenever a program wishes to access a record the database key — a *logical* address of the record — must be supplied. However, the majority of implementations have treated the database key as being a unique *storage* address — the identification of a *page* of device storage plus some information as to the position of the record within the page. Thus DIRECT provides a fast (*the* fastest, in fact) direct entry mechanism since the appropriate unit of physical transfer is immediately located. The penalty paid for such high performance is a severe loss in data independence. Should the database be reorganised — that is, the storage model and device model are changed to reflect some new or better understood pattern of usage — it becomes necessary to change programs since in all likelihood storage addresses, and hence database keys, have changed. It follows that DIRECT should be used with extreme caution. Typically, it will only be used in situations where the record type

i) has few occurences

ii) is extremely stable and not subject to change in its use or structure

iii) has a very high usage for which a fast response is essential.

Control records that are used by every program within the system — say, to validate passwords against, or to update summary totals — are examples of cases where the use of DIRECT may be considered. With the database key concept implemented as a storage address DIRECT will result in retrieval in one physical I/O* at the most (the record may actually be already in the DBMS buffer).

CALC requires that when a program wishes to access a record a named logical application data item — a record key — will be given to a named procedure as input and a database key will be produced as output. Inevitably, implementations of CALC have treated the output database key as being a storage address. CALC procedures generally take two forms : hashing (or randomising) algorithms and indexes. Both achieve the same result, but their manner of so doing has led many implementations to distinguish between hashing algorithms and indexes by providing a syntactical distinction, e.g.

LOCATION MODE IS CALC (hashing)

LOCATION MODE IS INDEX SEQUENTIAL (index)

are options available in the DMS 1100 implementation of CODASYL '73.

a) Hashing algorithms operate by performing some transformation on the input key to produce, ultimately, an output key that can be used to locate the record. Distinct input keys will not necessarily produce distinct output keys, that is, *collisions* may occur and a technique is needed to deal with this overflow. Hashing algorithms do not have the same data dependence characteristics of DIRECT, and they do allow a record to be located with an average number of physical I/Os that is close to one. The exact performance of a hashing algorithm will depend on a variety of factors, such as:—

i) the time taken to evaluate the hashing transformation: an unduly complex transformation can require considerable processing,

ii) the range of keys input to the algorithm: rarely are the keys evenly spread through a (theoretical) range and hit groups create problems with collisions,

---

*physical I/O is an access to the unit of physical transfer — a page — to **in**put data or to **out**put data.

iii) the range of output values: the number of collisions should be minimised and overflow techniques should not result in lengthy searching.

Investment in producing a suitable hashing technique for the range of keys involved will frequently pay dividends in terms of performance. The one undesirable feature of hashing algorithms is that they do not provide a direct facility to process records in key sequence and this *may* be an important requirement that a storage model must support. However, it should be remarked that the need to process in key sequence may be unfounded in many systems. It is frequently an unquestioned assumption carried over from tape-based conventional file systems that dictated sequential processing for efficiency reasons.

b) Indexing techniques — in particular index sequential techniques — have traditionally been associated with data processing systems. Index techniques have the advantage that they are capable of directly supporting the processing of records in key sequence. The penalty that is paid is that the index *itself* needs to be *accessed* in order to obtain eventually a location where the record may be *accessed*. Where the number of record occurrences is large, as it typically may be in a database, the number of entries in the index will be correspondingly large. Therefore physical I/Os are spent in merely accessing the index. Index sequential techniques reduce the number of index entries that are needed by requiring an entry only for the highest key for each partition of storage. They can therefore be an attractive proposition : they allow a degree of direct access to a record, they support sequential processing, and they reduce the amount of index required. This reduction in the amount of space needed for the index, however, may not be enough. Typically index sequential techniques require *indexes* to indexes in an attempt to reduce the amount of index searching needed. Even with a two-level index the number of physical I/Os needed to locate a record will be in the order of three : one to access the index-to-the-index, one to access the index proper, and one to access the record. Compared to hashing techniques (where the average is close to one) this may be an unacceptable performance for processes that require some form of real-time response. Furthermore, a large number of record insertions can cause problems once they need to be placed in an overflow area. The index is not usually dynamically maintained and begins to give 'false' information about the location of records. That is, the indicated partition of storage is searched only to find that an overflow partition must be accessed and searched.

The available implementations of CODASYL '73 frequently supply ready-made CALC procedures - both hashing algorithm and index based. These obviously need to be evaluated carefully before embarking upon the production of CALC procedures by the organisation using the database system.

SEARCHING. In some cases the analysis of data usage in logical database design may be ambiguous as far as direct entry is concerned. For a given record type direct entry may be required by some (low priority, possibly) processes, but may not be required by other (higher priority, possibly) processes. The use of DIRECT, CALC, or their analogues may be an unwarranted complication to the database. An access mechanism that may be used in this case is a simple serial search : record occurrences are examined one after another until the desired occurrence is located. Such a mechanism can result in many occurrences being examined and large areas of storage being accessed. This may be ameliorated by the database system supporting a sequential search and some form of direct placement of storage records. A sequential search reduces the time taken to ascertain that a record occurrence is *not* present: once a record with a higher key value has been accessed then the desired occurrence is not present. Directed placement attempts to minimise the amount of storage accessed by storing records contiguously. This is the storage model analogue of the VIA SET location mode. Consider the set depicted in Fig.10.1.

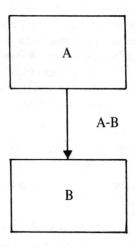

Fig. 10.1

Assume that direct entry is definitely required for record A, but that direct entry for record B is less-well established: a significant number of processes access Bs after having accessed an A. In this case, the location mode of B may well be declared as VIA A-B SET. In storage model terms this will be implemented by directing placement of B occurrences so that all Bs for a given A are *clustered* together and, if necessary, also around the A occurrence that owns them. This technique is sometimes referred to, somewhat inappropriately, as 'place near logic'. Notice that this clustering of storage model occurrences assumes a corresponding clustering of occurrences at the device model level - that is, in the example, all Bs for an A would be located on the same page or on adjacent pages.

Given these techniques for supporting direct entry on a record, storage model design needs to decide for a given storage model record which technique is to be actually used. The data usage documentation performed as part of logical database design will have identified those records requiring direct entry and an inversion of this data usage can reveal, along the lines of Fig. 9.17, the relative importance of a record entry point. Generally, therefore, the aim will be to implement direct entry for the most important direct entry points as efficiently as possible — usually by means of some CALC (hashing) procedure. Consideration can be given to not implementing certain direct entry points as such : that is, where they are infrequently used by low-priority processes. Here, searching may be an acceptable mechanism. The aim, as throughout storage data model design, is to maximise the support of high-priority, high-frequency processes without producing a structure that is unacceptably inefficient for the remaining processes. As will be seen with storage structures to support logical associations (sets), the impact of alternative structures in terms of their efficiency may be quantified by documenting data usage at the storage data model level and comparing *storage* access costs for different structures.

Whilst efficiency is generally the prime consideration, regard needs to be made to other factors such as

* the volumes of records that need to be stored and accessed,

* patterns of insertions and deletions,

* possible exploitation of hit group situations,

* the ease with which physical placement reorganisation may be performed.

It is clearly not satisfactory to have a structure that works efficiently for a given population of records and then proceeds to degrade dramatically in performance as a result of a trivial number of insertions or deletions. Even with a high level of physical data independence and the ability to tune the database to meet changing requirements, the designer does not want to be faced with exploiting such an architecture for every change in usage and storage patterns.

10.2.2 Set implementation

Neither of the two forms of logical data model resulting from logical database design contained any detailed consideration of how the associations between records were implemented. Indeed, as we have seen, such a consideration should not form part of the logical data model. A set of *navigational* *assumptions* about this logical association between records was made, but nothing more. The particular assumptions made concerned the logical association between records known as a set. Several implementation possibilities for the set construct are now described. Two points need to be borne in mind when examining them:

   i)   although centered around set implementation, these techniques may also be regarded as general techniques available for implementing associations between records at the storage model level;

   ii)   it is unlikely that all the techniques described below would be available in one database system.

The three chief techniques are:
   *   linked lists
   *   indexes
   *   aggregates

LINKED LISTS. We have already encountered linked lists in the examination of TOTAL in Chapter 5, but notice that there the mechanisms for implementing associations between records intruded into the logical data model.

The exact form taken by a linked list can vary and reflects the processing that needs to be supported. The basic form is as in Fig. 10.2: a simple linked list.

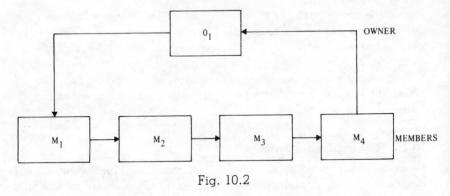

Fig. 10.2

In a particular set occurrence, each record contains a pointer - often known as a NEXT pointer - to the succeeding record in the set. Notice how closely such a storage structure mirrors processing of the GET NEXT record variety. Indeed, early versions of CODASYL allowed such storage considerations to intrude into the (logical) schema with a MODE IS CHAIN clause for the set entry. Such a storage structure efficiently supports processing where an owner record and all its members need to be examined. It also efficiently supports insertions into associations between records where the new member occurrence is to be inserted immediately *after* the record just accessed (i.e. ORDER IS NEXT in CODASYL terms). However, such a structure becomes inefficient if a new member occurrence is to be inserted immediately *before* a particular record occurrence. For example, if record M3 has just been accessed and a new record occurrence, M7, is to be inserted into the set occurrence immediately before M3, it becomes necesary to traverse the whole set in order to change the pointer in M2. In circumstances such as these (i.e. ORDER IS PRIOR in CODASYL terms) additional pointers may be introduced as in Fig. 10.3. Such extra pointers are often referred to as PRIOR pointers. In traditional computing terms what we then have is a *doubly linked list.*

Variations on the theme of NEXT and PRIOR pointers are possible when the record relative to which new occurrences are to be inserted is the owner (i.e. ORDER IS FIRST or LAST in CODASYL terms). In these instances, single FIRST or LAST pointers within the owner may be used.

Both NEXT and PRIOR pointers properly speaking refer to a 'logical' sequence. This sequence may be a sorted sequence. The sequence is maintained by NEXT and PRIOR pointers irrespective of any physical ordering, as shown in Fig. 10.4.

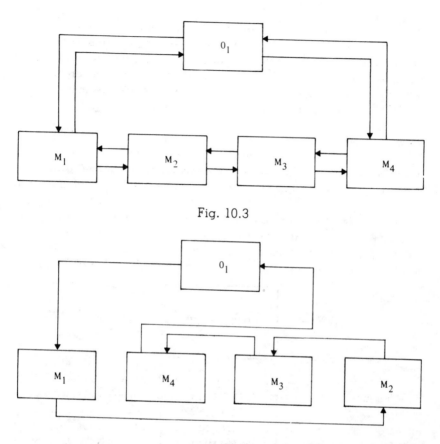

Fig. 10.3

Fig. 10.4

Clearly such an approach can reduce processing time by avoiding the need to examine all the members of a set merely to ascertain that a particular occurrence is not present in the set. This is the conventional advantage of a sequential or lexical ordering over a simple serial or physical ordering. However, given the electro-mechanical nature of current backing store devices, such as moving head discs, the use of such a sorted order can create problems in a linked list structure. For example, to insert a new record occurrence, M7, into the sorted set occurrence of Fig. 10.4 requires the sort chain to be followed until the logical insert point is found. With a large sorted set this may involve unacceptable physical I/O overheads. The member records that need to be accessed may, typically, be contained in several pages, thus involving several physical I/Os. Furthermore, the order of access to these pages may, typically, not be in their physical serial order. This will

279

result in uneven time-consuming head movements that are graphically referred to as 'thrashing'. Such sorted set implementations should therefore be used with caution. Frequently the desired ordering can be maintained by use of FIRST or LAST insertion. For example an insertion of LAST in the TAKES set of Fig. 10.5 will effectively maintain the STUDENT-AND-COURSE records in year of study sequence.

As was noted above, the linked list concept provides a measure of support for processing from owner to member; that is, from the "1" to the "n" in a 1:n relationship. Where the processing pattern also involves access from member to owner - from the "n" to the "1" - such a storage structure can be inefficient. Returning to Fig. 10.2, consider the case where M1 has been accessed via its membership in the occurrence of another set type and it is necessary to access O1. Accessing O1 then involves following the linked list all the way around to the owner. This processing situation is common for structures such as that of Fig. 10.5.

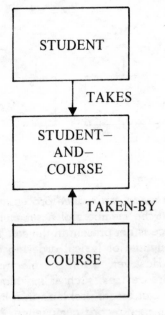

Fig. 10.5

In order to find the COURSE NAMEs of the COURSEs taken by a STUDENT, the members in a particular TAKES occurrence (that owned by the STUDENT) are first accessed, and then, for each of these, the *owner* in the TAKEN-BY set needs to be accessed. We have already

280

examined one way of supporting such processing in Chapter 9 when the inclusion of COURSE NAME in the STUDENT-AND-COURSE storage record was suggested (i.e. a partial collapse of TAKEN-BY). Such a duplication of data items* is frequently unacceptable. An alternative is to link members to owners, as illustrated in Fig. 10.6, by the provision of OWNER pointers (this is the meaning of the LINKED TO OWNER clause in '73 CODASYL).

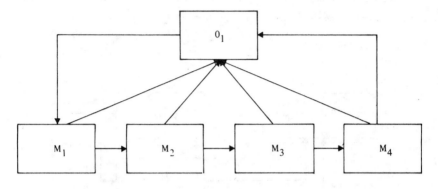

Fig. 10.6

Thus, linked lists, adapted in a variety of ways, provide a storage structure for implementing the set construct. Their chief weakness lies, somewhat paradoxically, in the fact that they mirror too closely the set construct in the logical data model and therefore may not always offer the necessary scope for optimising storage and access in the storage data model.

INDEXES. Early versions of CODASYL contained a set entry clause MODE IS POINTER-ARRAY, and this is the essential idea behind the use of an index as a means of implementing a logical association between records. If we consider the TAKES set of Fig. 10.5 this could be implemented using an index as in Fig. 10.7.

The owner record, O_1 contains a pointer to the INDEX which consists of a series of entries that are pointers to the member records in the set. Each member record contains a pointer back to the owner record. The entries

---

   *   To echo a point in Kent's paper (Ref. (7.7)): notice that we have discussed **three** ways of implementing a relationship - by some pointer system, by duplicating data items, and by structuring of the storage record (complete collapse of owner into member).

in the index may consist of only the pointers to the members, or they may also include (application) key values along with pointer values. Such a storage structure may not provide quite as an efficient implementation as a linked list structure in its support of member-to-member processing, but it does have two advantages:

i) Processing that needs to establish the membership of a record in several set types can now be efficiently supported. For example, consider the set structure of Fig. 10.8

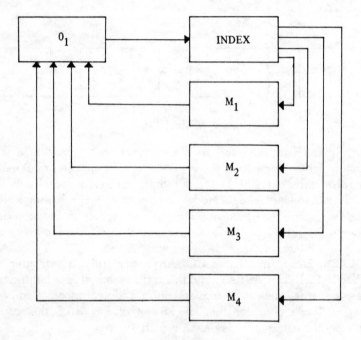

Fig. 10.7

Each COMPANY storage record occurrence contains a pointer to an INDEX-A that contains pointers to the related STUDENT storage records. Similarly, each STUDENT storage record occurrence contains a pointer to an INDEX-B that performs the same function. This is strongly reminiscent of the coupling indexes of ADABAS discussed in Chapter 5. It has the merit of extending the separation of data and relationships in the storage structure with the consequent benefits when a physical placement reorganisation takes place.

The last storage structure for representing logical associations by means of indexes that will be examined is an indirect technique. Certain sets may be so little used that consideration may be given to *not* explicitly representing them in the storage structure at all. When such a set is required by a run unit, the stored database may be scanned by the DBMS to construct the required set, based on data item values in storage records. Potentially, even for little used sets, this will be a lengthy process. The process may therefore be enhanced if indexes on these data item values are maintained. We then have, basically, an inverted file approach as a storage structure for supporting logical associations.

AGGREGATES. Consider the logical association depicted in Fig 10.15

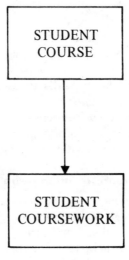

Fig. 10.15

An alternative storage structure to linked lists or indexes for representing this association is an embedded aggregate or repeating group, which we may depict as in Fig. 10.16

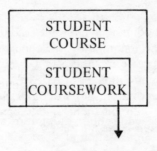

Fig. 10.16

The ↓ depicts the repeating group. This has similarities to the collapse technique discussed in Chapter 9 as a means of designing storage records, and serves to emphasise two points:

i)   it is a perfectly correct *implementation* of the *logical* association that is the set construct; we have a separation of the logical level from the storage level,

ii) it is a way of representing an association by storage record design (as opposed to pointers and indexes). It is assumed here that the decision to collapse STUDENT COURSE and STUDENT COURSEWORK was not made as part of logical database design.

However, such a storage representation clearly presents problems if STUDENT COURSEWORK is itself an owner record in other sets.

Other techniques besides the three discussed above have been used in the implementation of sets. Prime's DBMS product, for example, makes use of B-tress as described in References (10.2) and (10.12). B-trees themselves can be used as an access mechanism for direct entry to records; this is well described in Reference (10.13).

10.2.3 Choosing a set representation technique

Given the range of techniques discussed in the previous section it becomes important to have a set of criteria for deciding which particular technique should be used when considering how to implement a given logical association. It needs to be remarked that, in practice, not all these alternatives will be available. For example, the database system used may only provide linked lists as a means of representing logical associations at the storage level. However, even within a limited context, we can identify three major (somewhat interconnected) criteria that will affect the choice of storage technique:-

288

- efficiency : the storage structure chosen should enable processing of the logical association to be performed with the minimum number of storage record accesses.

- lack of complexity : the storage structure chosen should enable the insertion and deletion of records to be performed with the minimum of pointer/index adjustments.

- ease of reorganisation : the storage structure chosen should enable reorganisation of storage records to be performed with the minimum of pointer/index adjustments.

These criteria can be in conflict : an efficient storage structure may well be unacceptably complex and may be difficult to reorganise. Present hardware/software configurations tend to make efficiency the prime objective. If this is the case different structures may be evaluated by means of usage matrices, in a fashion similar to that described in Chapter 9. The difference is that, here, the *storage* access cost is being determined and compared, and not the *logical* access cost. In addition, the set of navigational assumptions is replaced by the actual storage structure under consideration.

However, it is likely that lack of complexity and ease of reorganisation will figure as increasingly important objectives in the future. It is by no means clear how the attainment of such objectives by alternative structures may be compared and quantified.

10.2.4 Data item implementation

The final issue that needs to be examined in storage model design is that of data item implementation. It is helpful here to review what has happened at this level in the analysis and design process. At the conceptual data model stage attributes were defined without any consideration as to how they may be represented in a computer model. That is, an attribute such as an ADDRESS was defined as being, say, from 20 to 200 (and exceptionally beyond) alphanumeric characters in length and as consisting of 2 to 7 (and exceptionally beyond) lines. Alternatively, an attribute such as MARITAL STATUS was defined as having permissible values of 'MARRIED', 'SINGLE', etc. As part of logical database design attributes are translated into data items. This involves some considerations about the way in which they will be represented in a computer model. For example, ADDRESS may be defined as being a data item consisting of up to 70 alphanumeric characters and of being up to 5 lines in structure. Alternatively, MARITAL STATUS may be defined as being a single character alphabetic field having coded values, 'M', 'S', etc. denoting 'married', 'single', etc. Such decisions are made on the basis of the work of analysis: the assumption in the case of ADDRESS being that all ADDRESSes may be amended without loss of information content to fit the more restrictive logical definition. Such decisions are necessary since current logical models do not provide satisfactory facilities for coping with such natural variations. However, given that the format and size range has been considered in logical database design it is *not* part of logical database design to consider *how* such data items may be represented in storage. That is, aspects of logical data models, such as that of CODASYL, that provide PIC and TYPE clauses for data items that have connotations as to storage, are not really true logical data model constructs. *How* a data item is represented in storage is a decision for storage model design.

To begin, a decision needs to made as to whether the data item needs to be stored at all. The VIRTUAL/ACTUAL feature of the SOURCE/RESULT option in CODASYL '73 (see Chapter 4) is really a storage consideration, and it is of note that it has been removed in later versions of CODASYL. Therefore, where a data item in a storage record may be derived from other data items consideration should be given as to whether the data item is explicitly stored or merely derived on run-unit request. Derivation can make for inefficiency, but it minimises storage requirements and provides a measure of control over duplication of data item values.

Conversely, data item duplication may be considered for reasons of efficiency in the storage model. Notice that this is the correct place to consider such duplication - although we may be forced to consider it in logical model design for the reasons discussed in Chapter 9. Duplication of data items carries with it all the potential inconsistencies that have been discussed earlier. However, data item duplication at the storage data model level places the onus for maintaining consistency on the DBMS rather than on individual application programs. This should, in theory, be a much more reliable solution.

Given that the contents of each storage model record in terms of data items has been determined, it becomes necessary to consider how they may be represented in storage. That is, whether a data item is representd as a binary field, a packed decimal field, a character field, etc. and whether alignment on addressable units of physical storage (words) is required, and so on. The decision will be made in the light of the *use* that the data item in question must support. For example, a data item such as

290

DATE-OF-BIRTH may be implemented as a character field *if* it is used predominantly for retrieval only and is not subject to arithmetic computation and comparison. On the other hand, *if* it is used frequently for arithmetic computation and comparison it may be implemented as a binary field. Frequently the usage pattern will be by no means as clear cut as that outlined above. The representation chosen then will be a compromise balancing ease of storage and retrieval against ease of computation.

10.2.5 The connection with device model design : pages and areas

The mapping to device model requires objects that are intermediate between the storage model and the device model. The objects are *pages* and *areas*. An area is simply the storage aspects of the CODASYL AREA concept : that is, a division of the (storage) data model that will correspond to its placement on some portion of a device — such as a fast access disc pack, or particular cylinders of a disc pack, etc. It therefore follows that if we have the situation described in Fig. 2.5 of Chapter 2 — where STUDENT occurrences may be partitioned according to their frequency of use (an extreme case being where a hit group is present) — we would wish to place these partitioned occurrences in *different* storage areas on the assumption that this will result in them being ultimately stored on devices with appropriate characteristics to meet the frequency of use. Notice that this may be done, as in Fig. 2.5, by partitioning logical *occurrences* into separate storage *types*, or it may be done by partitioning the actual storage occurrences.

Mention was made in previous sections to storage records being placed 'near' one another. We may define 'near' a little more formally by means of the notion of *page*. Areas will be divided into a number of pages, each page containing a number of storage records. Each page will be allocated a unique page number. To say that records are stored 'near' one another now means that they are either on the same page or are on consecutive (in terms of page number) pages. Clearly the expectation is that a page becomes the unit of physical transfer between the DBMS and the operating system and that 'near' storage records are contiguously laid out on whatever device the area is mapped to. The determination of page size and the number of pages in an area is discussed in the next section.

10.3 DEVICE MODEL DESIGN

Although throughout this book we have been discussing programs, processors, and data that are all effectively resident at one site, it is possible to consider systems where data is stored at a series of distinct geographical locations. Much current research and experimental work is being devoted to this idea of a **distributed database system.** It is not the place in an undergraduate text to examine such ideas at this stage in their development. However, there are two remarks that may be usefully made at this point about distributed database systems that are in keeping with general themes in this book.

Firstly, the level at which distribution takes place in a distributed database should not be confused with the distribution of data to devices that forms the subject matter of this section. The former is a *geographical* distribution of *logical* data model occurrences performed for a variety of reasons, none of which are directly concerned with efficiency of *placement*. The latter is a machine *device* distribution of *storage* data model occurrences performed for a variety of reasons, most of which are directly concerned with efficiency of device placement.

Secondly, a distributed database system should exhibit a form of data independence known as *geographical* data independence. This may be illustrated by considering the subschema view developed in Chapter 4 : it is given again here as Fig. 10.17

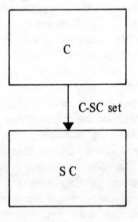

Fig. 10.17

Such a subschema was developed and presented with the (now stated) assumption that all the data relating to that subschema was resident on one site. The point about geographical data independence is that *even if* the data relating to that subschema was distributed over several sites, the subschema would still remain the same. That is, an application program does *not need* to know where the data is geographically distributed. Importantly, therefore, it does not need to be changed when that distribution changes. However, the DBMS *does* need to know where the data is distributed, but the architecture and systems involved in this are beyond the scope of this text.

10.3.1 Allocation to operating system files

In the previous section the notion of a storage area was introduced as a means of specifying the mapping to the device model. The device model will not be directly described in terms of discs and tapes but, recalling Chapter 2, will be defined in terms of objects manipulated by the operating system : that is, operating system files. These will then be allocated, via the operating system facilities, to particular machine devices. Certain factors need to be decided about this allocation.

1. What is the size of the file - i.e. what is the size of the area?
2. What is the block size of the file - i.e. what is the area page size?

This assumes, as one reasonably can, that the mapping between areas and files, and pages and blocks will be 1:1.

Area Size

Clearly, the size of an area must be at least sufficient to contain all actual storage model occurrences. However, it is also obvious that in the majority of cases the area size needs to be larger than that required to contain actual occurrences. This is because new occurrences will typically be added. Even if a similar rate of deletions occur and deleted record space is made available, store 'near' and overflow conditions will still dictate the need for more storage space unless physical placement reorganisation is frequently performed. Typically, therefore, space is left for expansion. This space allocation may be dynamic in the sense that many storage models (or rather those portions of 'logical' data models that really relate to storage models) permit clauses such as

AREA SIZE IS 8000 PAGES EXPANDABLE TO 10000 PAGES

However, allocation of free space for expansion at the end of an area may not always be the best policy, since store 'near' considerations require space to be distributed within an area, rather than at its end. Again, many current storage models permit such an approach and it is, as we shall see below, an important factor in load program design.

Page Size

The determination of page size is a compromise between two requirements.

i)   The need where storage records are stored 'near' - clustered representations of sets, for example - to obtain all the 'near' records in as few page accesses as possible. This favours a large page size.

ii) The need to minimise the amount of unwanted data transferred. This favours a small page size.

The actual compromise chosen will obviously depend upon device characteristics such as the amount of core storage available to the DBMS buffer, transfer rates of peripheral storage devices, page control data required, and so on.

The actual choice of device to which the operating system file is allocated will obviously reflect the decisions taken in storage model design. Storage records requiring fast access will be allocated to appropriate high speed devices, and so on.

10.3.2   Fine placement

So far we have considered only a form of *coarse* placement to ensure that storage records are physically near each other when necessary. *Fine* placement is achieved by

i)   the definition for the mapping from the logical data model to storage data model,

and/or

ii) a *load* program.

The mapping definition

The mapping definition for the transformation of logical data model objects into storage model objects may take two general forms depending on the actual architecture of the database system.

a)   Where the architecture has a distinct logical data model and a distinct storage data storage model, the storage data model will usually contain a mapping definition that specifies how logical data model objects are represented as storage data model objects. As part of this mapping definition there will be some form of fine placement control. For example, considering Fig. 10.1, the storage data model definition for B might read

STORAGE RECORD B

.
.
.

PLACEMENT CLUSTERED VIA SET A-B

.
.
.
.

or for Fig. 10.11

INDEX ......
PLACEMENT NEAR OWNER

More complicated possibilities involving conditional placement exist and are well catered for in the proposed CODASYL Data Storage Definition Language. The reader is referred to Reference (10.8) for a particularly cogent worked example.

b) Where the architecture has a conflated logical data model and storage data model — i.e. current CODASYL implementations — the mapping definition is implicit by the inclusion of clauses relating to AREA size and page size, as in the example given in section 4.6 of Chapter 4. The fine placement control that is present is usually restricted to the implication that a LOCATION MODE of VIA SET will involve clustering at the storage level.

Therefore, in practice, fine placement control as administered by the DBMS is frequently inadequate. This is usually overcome by the use of a *load* program. A load program reads the data in the form of a conventional file (or a set of conventional files) and stores it within the database to give the necessary fine placement. A load program is also required to create the database in the first instance. This special creation will be necessary for two reasons

i) Not all data will necessarily be capable of being inserted by application programs. For example, some parts or all of the database may be for retrieval purposes only.

ii) Even if application programs existed, that could create the database given the necessary input data, it is unlikely that such an approach would be adopted in practice since the degree of fine placement control present in the data definitions is inadequate. The consequence would be that the application programs used in creation would become progressively less efficient as placement in physical storage began to reflect less and less the efficient access paths that had been assumed. Time would be spent attempting to place members near owners when no 'near' space existed, overflow conditions would occur, hashing collisions would become more frequent, and so on.

The load program attempts to alleviate these problems by precisely placing records in storage so as to reflect the efficient storage structures that have been designed. Clearly, such a program (or set of programs, as is frequently the case) needs careful design to ensure its efficiency. Good load programs for large databases can take many hours to run; bad load programs for large databases can take many days to run. Two sets of techniques that are frequently used to ensure the efficiency of load programs are *load data models* and *load strategies*.

Load data models*

If we refer to the logical data model definition under which application programs will run as the *production logical data model* we can refer to a *load logical data model* as being a logical data model describing the same logical data structure as the production model, but omitting certain clauses for the sake of efficiency. For example, considering CODASYL '73 implementations a *load schema* may differ from the *production schema* in the following ways.

— SET SELECTION clauses in the load schema may always be CURRENT OF SET — placing the burden for selection on the load program (which can do it efficiently) rather than on the DBMS (which is generalised and therefore less efficient in practice).

— Where the set ORDER clause is SORTED in the production schema it may be declared to be NEXT in the load schema. The data files consumed by the load program will be sorted to present records in the correct sorted order. Thus the need to traverse *all* the members of a sorted set *for each* new member inserted is avoided.

---

* Here we refer to a load data model as being a load *logical* data model on the assumption that the architecture in use conflates logical and storage models. Where such conflation is not present we should more correctly refer to a load *storage* data model.

- DUPLICATES NOT ALLOWED clauses in the production schema may be omitted in the load schema. The load program (or prior programs that create the load files) will ensure that no duplicates are present, thus avoiding the need for DBMS checking of set members every time a new insertion is made.
- LOCATION MODEs of VIA SET in the production schema may be replaced by LOCATION MODES of DIRECT in the load schema, the load program ensuring that clustering occurs.
- Recovery statements (see Chapter 11) may be omitted in the load schema, thus avoiding the need to write to any journal file.
- Access control locks may be omitted in the load schema thus avoiding the need to provide and evaluate keys.
- Procedures and clauses concerned with data validity may be omitted from the load schema. The load program (or programs prior to it) perform all necessary validation, thus removing the need for DBMS validation.
- SOURCE and RESULT clauses may be omitted from the load schema and the actual data item values supplied in the load files. Again this avoids the need to invoke DBMS procedures.

It is interesting to note that whilst many of the above techniques are designed to minimise physical I/Os, a significant number are designed to avoid the use of DBMS procedures. This reflects the fact that general purpose software, such as a DBMS, frequently involves a heavy CPU overhead.

Load strategies

These complement the use of a load schema and may include the following.

- The load program allocating distributed free space rather than relying on the DBMS to do this.
- Passing records whose LOCATION MODE is CALC through the CALC procedure first to obtain the database keys. The records may then be sorted by

database key, ensuring smooth head movements on the disc devices when the records are loaded.

— CALC records may be loaded first, followed by a second pass that loads any VIA records.

— The records may be sorted into sets prior to the load, so that serially reading the load file produces a sequence such as

$$O_1M_1M_2M_3M_4O_2M_7M_8M_9O_3M_{10}M_{11}\ldots\ldots$$

Load programs and load schemas obviously do not exhibit much data independence, but this is the price that is paid in order to have efficiency and the necessary fine physical placement.

SUMMARY

* A variety of storage structures are available for implementing a logical data model. The choices of storage structure made will reflect the usage pattern of the data.

* The allocation of storage structures to devices will reflect the usage patterns used in designing the storage structure.

* Fine placement can be aided by a powerful mapping definition for the transformation of logical data model objects into storage data model objects, but present day systems need a load program for fine placement.

* The efficiency of the load program is important. The use of a load schema and a load strategy can ensure that efficiency.

REFERENCES AND BIBLIOGRAPHY

(10.1) Knuth, D.E. **The Art of Computer Programming,** Vol.1, **Fundamental Algorithms,** Addison-Wesley, 1972

(10.2) Knuth, D.E. **The Art of Computer Programming,** Vol.3, **Sorting and Searching,** Addison-Wesley, 1973

(10.3) Lefkovitz, D. **File Structures for On-line Systems,** Spartan Books, 1969

(10.4) **DMS 1100 Schema Definition Manual,** Sperry Univac

(10.5) CODASYL **Data Base Task Group Report,** April, 1971

(10.6) **BCS/CODASYL DDLC Data Base Administration Working Group Report,** British Computer Society, 1975

(10.7) CODASYL DDLC **Journal of Development,** 1978, particularly the **Appendix**

(10.8) Stacey, G.M. **The Data Storage Description Language,** paper given at **Database Developments-CODASYL 1978** conference, Polytechnic of the South Bank, 1978. A similar exposition is contained in Reference (4.14).

(10.9) Davenport, R.A. **Distributed or centralised data base,** Computer Journal, **21,** 1

(10.10) Champine, G.A. **Six Approaches to distributed data bases,** Datamation, **23,** May, 1977.

(10.11) Severance, D.G., Carlis, J.V. **A Practical Approach to Selecting Record Access Paths,** ACM Computing Surveys, **9,** 4, December, 1977

(10.12) **User's Guide for the Database Administrator,** IDR 3043, Prime Computer Incorporated, 1977.

(10.13) Comer, D. **The Ubiquitous B-Tree,** ACM Computing Surveys, **11,** 2, June, 1979.

EXERCISES

10.1 Draw a storage structure similar to Fig.10.2 to show the use of FIRST and LAST pointers.

10.2 What storage data model would you recommend for the schema and processing discussed in section 9.4.1, Fig.9.7 of Chapter 9?

10.3 What storage data model would you recommend for the *requisites* example of Fig.3.4 of Chapter 3?

10.4 Which storage structures for supporting sets would you consider allocating to a magnetic tape device?

Chapter 11

DATABASE ADMINISTRATION

'And covenants, without the sword, are but words, and of no strength to secure a man at all.'

Thomas Hobbes, Leviathan

11.1 THE ROLE OF DATABASE ADMINISTRATION

Chapter 1 introduced two key components needed if data is to be treated as an organisational resource :

* the database administrator,
* the database management system.

So far, little explicit mention has been made of the database administrator, whilst much has been made of the database management system. However, as the astute reader will have realised, both the Analysis and Design Parts of this text have been discursive treatments of what being a database administrator can involve. Given the magnitude of the tasks described and the range of expertise required — from analysis to storage model design — it is unrealistic to imagine one person performing all these tasks within an organisation. Typically, several people will be involved, and we shall now refer to database administration rather than a database administrator. The organisational structure within database administration, and its relation to other components within a company's organisational structure are discussed later, in section 11.4. Here we begin by identifying the responsibilities of database administration.

1. Defining the data needs of the organisation

That is, conducting the data analysis necessary for the definition of the global conceptual data model.

2. Defining the logical data model

That is, conducting logical database design and expressing the results in the logical data model of the appropriate database system(s) in use.

3. Defining the storage data model

That is, mapping the logical data model to a storage data model by deciding on access mechanisms, storage representation of logical associations, and data item representation in storage. The results of the exercise are expressed in the storage data model of the appropriate database system(s) in use.

4. Mapping to the device data model

A mapping of the storage data model onto the device data model must be defined, both at a high level — placement as defined within the database definition — and at a low level — placement as defined by a load program.

5. Defining access constraints

Privacy *rights* need to be *ascertained* and appropriate *access constraints* defined to *implement* these privacy rights.

6. Application support

Application systems analysts and programmers using the database will need advice in areas such as

- logical data sub-model definition

- data validation checks that can be performed by the database

- navigation of the database where the data manipulation language operates at a record-at-a-time level.

7. Defining a strategy for back-up and recovery

Since data is being treated as an organisational resource and is being modelled as such by a database system, it is necessary to define a strategy to deal with situations where the database system model fails or is corrupted.

8. Responding to change

Very few organisations are static. Typically, organisations change. This change must be reflected in the database system that is modelling the organisation's data needs. Such change will impact on the database system at a variety of levels :

302

— at the logical data model level, requiring a change, or **restructure,** of the logical data model.

— at the storage data model level, requiring a **reorganisation** in terms of a change to access mechanisms, pointers or indexes, storage records, etc.

— at the mapping to the device data model level, requiring a **physical placement reorganisation.**

Several important issues are bound up in the above list of responsibilities.

(a) It should be appreciated that they are tasks which database administration is *responsible for:* exactly who performs the tasks is examined in section 11.4 of this Chapter.

(b) Essentially the responsibilities of database administration mirror the stages and tasks involved in the analysis and design of a database system. So far we have examined in some detail the first four responsibilities listed above. The remaining responsibilities connected with analysis and design are examined in this Chapter under the headings of **Security** (section 11.2) where access constraints and back-up and recovery are discussed, and **Organisational structure and impact** (section 11.4) where application support is discussed.

(c) The major exception to the generalisation that the responsibilities of database administration mirror the tasks of analysis and design is in the last area listed — that of response to change. Techniques for carrying out the necessary changes are discussed under the heading of **Reorganisation and restructuring** (section 11.3) in this Chapter. How the need to change is ascertained, the means by which the necessary change is determined, and the impact of the database change predicted are discussed in Chapter 12.

(d) It is significant that the fourth responsibility in the list is entitled "the *mapping* to the device data model", rather than "defining the device data model". The device data model is not defined in terms of DBMS objects; rather, it is defined in terms of operating system objects. However, the mapping to the device data model does involve DBMS objects in the sense that partitions of the storage data model — storage areas and pages — are involved. This architectural distinction is reflected in an administrative distinction: the definition of the device data model is the responsibility of operations management. Operations management, however, will need some input for the definition of the device data model. This input is in terms of DBMS objects — the mapping to the device data model — and is the responsibility of database administration. Similarly, database administration are responsible for defining a *strategy* for back-up and recovery. The *implementation* of that strategy is the responsibility, again, of operations management.

11.2 SECURITY

This section examines the issue of data security by beginning with data privacy: that is, the rights of individuals and organisations to decide who may obtain information about them, the manner by which they obtain that information, and what they may then do with that information. A fundamental distinction, then, needs to be made. The determination of *what* these privacy rights are is something to which a computer scientist has no professional expertise whatsoever to offer. It is an issue of social dimensions involving ethical, legal, and judicial questions. Reference (11.2) gives the report of one body that attempts to answer these questions. However, *how* privacy decisions are implemented is a matter on which a computer scientist has considerable professional expertise to offer. This is the proper subject matter of this section.

Given that a privacy decision has been made concerning a unit of information, any computer system that models that unit of information with some unit(s) of data must:

(i)   ensure that the unit of data is accessed only by those persons who are authorised to do so;

(ii) ensure that once the unit of data is stored in the computer system measures are taken to ensure that it is not corrupted, lost, or destroyed within the terms of the privacy decision.*

---

*A privacy decision may involve the specification that data must not be held in a computer system beyond a certain duration, or that data must not be retained after the reasons for which it was collected have been satisfied.

The above two themes, in the context of a database system, are now examined in detail below.

11.2.1 Access constraints

It is useful to make some preliminary distinctions. *Access control* refers to the ability to restrict the use of database resources to authorised persons or software. It consists of two components: access constraints and access control mechanisms. An *access constraint* is a statement specifying the restriction of a given data unit to given persons or software. An *access control mechanism* is the implementation of an access constraint.

It is the responsibility, initially, of database administration to *ascertain* the access control required in a database system. Database administration does not *determine* access control: that is the responsibility of groups and individuals within the organisation. Recalling Chapter 7, it will be remembered that this process of ascertaining access control requirements began at the conceptual data model level with data analysis. For each entity, attribute, and relationship the privacy rights of individuals and groups within the organisation are ascertained and documented. This will not be a trivial task, since it is rare to find privacy rights *formally* defined. Users of existing manual systems rarely formulate privacy decisions explicitly since they are usually implemented in an informal (but nevertheless, effective) fashion. That is, access to a file of manual records is controlled by the staff in the office knowing the people who are allowed to look at the file. A stranger walking in to examine the file would (hopefully!) be immediately questioned as to what he/she wanted in the office. This mutually understood set of unwritten rules based on the recognition of individuals is by no means easily translated into a set of formal rules specifying privacy rights. In fact, the data analyst may be the first person who asks users to consider formally the access control that they operate. Users of existing computer files pose a similarly difficult, but different, problem. Since access control to a conventional file is on the all-or-nothing basis discussed in Chapter 1, it is unlikely that they have given much thought to the level of access control that they might require in a more flexible system. Furthermore, both the manual and conventional file cases are application orientated, and therefore the issues of access control in a shared data environment have not been issues requiring consideration. Access to an application orientated manual file centres around those people involved in the application, and those people are usually concentrated in some physical location(s). Access to an application orientated file centres around the application programs, and those programs are concentrated into application suites under operating system control. Therefore, the formal specification of access control requirements in the conceptual data model will require considerable skill and persistence on the part of the data analyst.

Given a statement of access control requirements in the global conceptual data model, these need to be translated into access constraints within the logical data model. Before discussing the techniques available for specifying access constraints it is of use to consider the range of access control requirements that access constraints must be able to handle. Following Reference (11.1) we can summarise that, in terms of a CODASYL database, we potentially have access control requirements for the following objects:

* schema
* area
* record — both type and occurrence
* data item — both type and occurrence
* set — both type and occurrence

The type/occurrence distinction is significant here. It may well be that a given user — say, the Chief Architect at UniHyp — is denied access to *all* ADDRESS data items in STUDENT records; that is, an access control requirement at the type level only. However, student John Doe may deny access to the ADDRESS data item in *his* STUDENT record to everyone except certain individuals; that is, an access control requirement at the occurrence level.

Notice also that access control is required on the associations (sets) between records. Access to the set FUNDS in Fig. 11.1 yields information that may be just as private as that obtained by access to the records RESEARCH PROJECT and BODY.

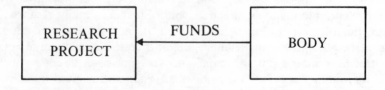

Fig. 11.1

It is also clear that access control to these logical data model objects must also be expressed in terms of *levels* of action. An ADDRESS data item may only be retrieved by a set of users, but it may also only be modified by a set of users. The two sets of users are unlikely to be the same and access constraints must be capable of distinguishing the level of action allowed in access.*

We can also distinguish between *data independent* access control and *data dependent* access control. An example of access control that is data independent is the decision to restrict a user from ever seeing a data item named ADDRESS. An example of access control that is data dependent is the decision to restrict a user to seeing only ADDRESS data item values that are within a fifty mile radius of UniHyp. Another example is the decision to restrict a user to updating ADDRESS data item values only from a terminal in Student Administration, and then only between the hours of 9 a.m. and 5.30 p.m. on working days.

Notice that the dependent/independent distinction does not map directly onto the occurrence/type distinction. For example, the last illustration above, concerning ADDRESS, is at the type level, but is also data dependent.

Given these considerations, if we examine the techniques available for expressing access constraints in database systems we find some confusion. Typically, there is a conflation of the access constraint with the access control mechanism. For example, if we consider a CODASYL database system, we have the system of access control locks described in Chapter 4. We had for instance:

> 02 RESULT; ......
> .
> .
> .
>
> ACCESS-CONTROL LOCK IS RESULT-BOX.

The lock and key technique confuses *what* access control is required (the access constraint) with *how* access control is implemented (the access control mechanism). In the CODASYL example above, nowhere is it

---

*CODASYL provides excellent features in this respect: see the DDLC JOD 1978, for example.

stated who is being allowed to access RESULT and who is not being allowed to access RESULT: this may only be ascertained by presenting the key to the lock and seeing if it "opens". This is particularly evident with data dependent access control decisions. Returning to the example of the updating of ADDRESS only from certain terminals and only inside certain hours, we can see that this would need to be expressed as something like

02 ADDRESS:
.
.
.

ACCESS-CONTROL LOCK IS PROCEDURE
I-WILL-DECIDE

The access constraint and access control mechanism are here bound up together in the program code of the procedure I-WILL-DECIDE. A similar set of considerations apply to the expression of access constraints involving access control of occurrences: the *logic* of the situation is never displayed.

This situation is not restricted to CODASYL databases: it can be seen as a feature of those database systems whose architecture conflates the logical model with the storage model.* Therefore, database systems whose initial development paid little attention to a storage considerations at all — relational systems in particular — do exhibit the ability to declare access constraints separate from access control mechanisms. For example, consider the conceptual data model of Fig. 11.2, where one of the access control requirements is that DATE-OF-BIRTH of a STUDENT may only be accessed by a PERSONAL TUTOR if the PERSONAL TUTOR actually TUTORS the STUDENT.

---

*It should be remarked here that no consideration is being given to the use of logical sub-models as a means for expressing access constraints. They **may** in practice be used for such purposes, but properly speaking their purpose is to provide an application orientated view and a measure of data independence. That this also involves some practical degree of access control is neither here nor there.

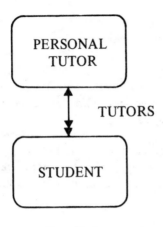

Fig. 11.2

In a relational schema this may be expressed as an access constraint thus:

RELATION PERSONAL-
TUTOR

(PERSONAL-TUTOR-NO.,
PERSONAL-TUTOR-NAME,....)

RELATION STUDENT

(REG-NO., NAME, ADDRESS,
PERSONAL-TUTOR-NO., ...)

.
.
.
.

ACCESS CONSTRAINT FOR GET (REG-NO., ADDRESS)

PERSONAL-TUTOR-NO. IN PERSONAL-TUTOR = PERSONAL-TUTOR
NO. IN STUDENT.

However, as will be seen in Chapter 12, even this can be considered unsatisfactory since it still does not clearly define the mapping, over access constraints, between users and data objects. Even if the above relational schema were extended it would still not be clear what data objects a particular user had access to, and, for a given data object, what users had access to it. There is a case, as Chapter 12 will illustrate, for removing the specification of access constraints from the logical data model definition altogether.

Be that as it may, the issue of access control mechanisms needs to be examined. It could be argued that the correct place for their specification was within the storage data model. However, a more appealing solution is not to re-invent the wheel again, but to pass the issue of mechanisms for access control to a piece of software that has traditionally been involved with the allocation and restriction of processing **and** data resources, viz. the operating system. In practice such an alternative is used anyway, since any specification of access control in the logical data model is frequently part of an overlapping "onion-layer" system of access control that involves the use of passwords and other techniques for identification and authentication.

Whatever system of access control is employed, thought needs to be given to the action taken when access to some data object is denied to a user by the operation of an access constraint. This could range from the logging of attempted breaches to some form of positive action such as the denial completely of database resources. This is a complex and somewhat under-developed area within database systems: many database systems operate without any mechanism for informing database administration that a wrong "key" has been applied to a "lock".

11.2.2. Back-up and recovery

A user stores data within the database and, as discussed in the preceding section, a system of access control operates to ensure that only authorised users can access and manipulate that data. We must now examine the less prosaic problem of ensuring that once that data is stored (and possibly changed at a later time) in the database, it stays stored (and changed) as the user intended. That is, we must examine ways of preventing the loss, destruction, and corruption of data stored in the database.

Before embarking on an examination of back-up and recovery, it would be as well to recall that we have already examined one problem and one solution in this area. Chapter 4 examined the corruption problems that can be encountered with concurrent usage of a database, and detailed a locking scheme for resolving those problems. This is of importance to this section, since the recovery techniques that will be described.

a) assume the locking scheme described in Chapter 4,

b) can be used in the resolution of the deadly embrace or deadlock situation described in Chapter 4.

310

Some form of back-up and recovery will be needed due to a variety of reasons.

i)   A deadlock situation has been identified and the resolution of the situation requires that one of the embracing run-units effectively has its processing on the database reversed: that is, it is 'backed-out' of the system. Usually this is done on the basis of choosing the run-unit with the lowest priority as being the run-unit to be backed-out. The other run-unit may then perform its processing to completion, with the backed-out run-unit being reinitiated. There is, therefore, a requirement to recover the database *from* the effects of *one* run-unit.

ii) A run-unit fails. This may be due to a variety of reasons. It may detect a situation in the database that it cannot resolve by futher processing, or it may be something less esoteric such as the failure of an on-line terminal or communications line. Again, there is a requirement to recover the database *from* the effects of *one* run-unit.

iii) A software failure, such as a failure within the DBMS. Here, effectively, there is a failure of all active run-units. There is, therefore, a requirement to recover the database *from* the effects of *all* active run-units.

iv) A hardware failure, such as a head crash on a disc or the discovery that areas on a disc are flawed and unreadable. There is a requirement to 'back-up' the database so that all the stored data on the affected device is restored to its state immediately prior to the disaster. Hence there is a need to recover the database *for* the actions of *many* run-units that are no longer active.

v)   A corruption of the database by faulty logic in an application program or invalid input to an application program. Typically this situation is only discovered some time after the error occurred. It therefore becomes necessary to recover the database *from* the action of a no longer active run-unit.

Notice that reasons (i)—(iii) concern action to be taken about active run-units, whilst (iv) and (v) refer to action about run-units that are no longer active.

A variety of recovery procedures are possible to deal with these situations — Reference (11.8) gives an excellent summary of such techniques. However, in this section, we shall concentrate on one particular technique that uses the concept of *images* of database objects recorded on a *journal file.* This technique is used successfully by several large-scale commercial DBMSs and more complex variations (see Reference (11.9)) have been proposed for some prototype relational systems. As mentioned above, it assumes a locking scheme for handling the problems of concurrent usage similar to that described in Chapter 4. The scheme described in Chapter 4 was defined in terms of a CODASYL database, but clearly the technique could (and does) apply equally well to other database systems. For example, within a relational database system the unit of locking could be at the tuple level or at the level of a storage unit such as a page. In what follows a record orientated database is used to define the technique and the granularity of locking is assumed to be at the record level.*

IMAGES

An *image* is a copy of a record taken in order to provide a means for recovery. It is written to a sequential *journal* file. Two versions of an image may be taken:-

i) **before- image** : a copy of the record immediately *prior* to alteration by a run-unit,

ii) **after-image** : a copy of the record immediately *after* alteration by a run-unit.

A particular image is uniquely identified by, say, a time-date stamp and run-unit identification.

RECOVERY

Using these images on the journal file the recovery situations listed above can be catered for as follows.

---

*For practical reasons the granularity of locking and recovery may be at the *page* level. This is the situation in Sperry Univac's DMS 1100 DBMS, for example. The recovery techniques successfully employed in DMS 1100 are similar *in principle* to those outlined in this section.

1. Roll-back

This procedure reverses the effects of a run-unit on the database.

— the journal file is scanned to identify the before-images for the run unit;

— these before-images are applied to the database;

— internal DBMS tables (such as currency tables) are restored.

Thus the effects of a run-unit are backed-out from the database. Several points can be made about this procedure.

* Notice that it depends on the records for that run-unit being protected from any update by other run-units by means of the concurrency locking scheme.

* If the journal file is written to a serial medium such as tape, then the scanning of the file can be a lengthy business. For this reason several database systems employ *transient before-images* that are written to a fast-access device, such as a disc. These transient images exist, effectively, until successful completion by the run-unit. Normal before-images are also written to the journal file.

* The locking scheme can operate down to the level of a success-unit. Therefore roll-back can operate down to the level of a success unit, i.e. the application program may define the unit of recovery. In the case of roll-back of a success-unit, transient before-images would only exist for the duration of the success-unit. The application program would need to record the state at which it can continue processing after the roll-back of the success-unit.

* In practice, for a given record altered by a run-unit, only the *first* before-image would be applied to the database. The scanning of the journal file could achieve this by means of the time-date stamp on the image. Clearly, this theoretical possibility is made more practical by the use of transient before-images written to disc, as this enables direct access to the necessary before-images. Otherwise, if the journal file is on tape considerable re-winding is necessary.

* Roll-back does not require other active run-units to cease processing since the locking scheme has isolated the backing-out to the effects of only the run-unit in question.

313

2.Quick-recovery

This procedure reverses the effects of *all* active run-units on the database. Essentially, it is roll-back applied to all active run-units.

— the journal file is scanned to identify the (earliest) before-images for all active run-units;

— these before-images are applied to the database;

— internal DBMS tables (such as the list of active run-units) are restored.

Again, such a process can be optimised by a transient before-image file along with the journal file, since this isolates a "hit-group" of before-images that need to be scanned.

3. Roll-forward

Both roll-back and quick-recovery adequately deal with deadlock resolution, run-unit failure, and software failure. For hardware failure and database corruption a similar, but somewhat different, set of techniques may be employed. This set of techniques may be termed roll-forward. Roll-forward requires

(i) physical copies, or dumps, of the database to be taken periodically;

(ii) the journal file with some combination of **checkpoints,** before-images, and after-images written to it.

In its simplest form the checkpoint is a simple marker written to the journal file, i.e. an indication of a point in time to which the system can return and be secure. The exact nature of a checkpoint determines the nature of the recovery strategy. Two possibilities will be considered.

* A checkpoint may only be written when no run-units are active. This may be done taking advantage of a natural quiet point, or it may be achieved by allowing active run-units to complete and denying any new run-units temporarily the right to start. Alternatively, quick-recovery may be performed and a checkpoint written. Either way, the fact that no run-units are active allows the requirement that only after-images need to be written to the journal file. In this case, the use of transient before-images has an additional attraction.

314

* A checkpoint may be written when run-units are active. The checkpoint may be a simple marker or it may be a checkpoint record that contains a list of all active run-units at the time the checkpoint was written. In either case both before-images and after-images may be written to the journal file.

Roll-forward with checkpoints and after-images

Where the checkpoint may only be written with no active run-units present, the following sequence occurs:

— the required checkpoint is determined, i.e. the latest checkpoint prior to the corruption occurring;

— the appropriate database dump is loaded, i.e. the latest dump prior to the checkpoint,

— the journal file is scanned and all after-images are applied up to the specified checkpoint, i.e. the database is rolled-forward to a point where no run-units were active.

This process is illustrated in Fig. 11.3.

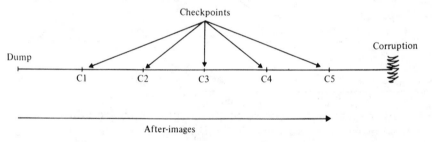

Fig. 11.3

Where the checkpoint may be written when active run-units are present, the journal file is scanned, and after-images for these run-units are *not* applied to the database. If the checkpoint does not contain a list of active run-units a pre-scan of the journal file is necessary to construct this list.

Sensibly, a new journal is begun after each dump.

Roll-forward with checkpoints, after-images, and before-images

This technique will be used where run-units are active when checkpoints are written. Notice, however, that the previous approach also applies to this situation. There after-images for active run-units were *not* applied to

315

the database, in order to bring it to a stable position where no run-units were active. In this approach the same effect is achieved, but use is made of before-images to roll-back the database after having rolled-forwards.

The first two steps in the process are as before. Then the following sequence occurs.

— all after-images up to the checkpoint are applied to the database. This yields an accurate restoration of the database at the time when the checkpoint was written, but the checkpoint was written when run-units were active;

— before-images for the active run-units are applied to the database, backing-out their effects, i.e. the database is rolled-back after being rolled-forward.

This process is illustrated in Fig. 11.4.

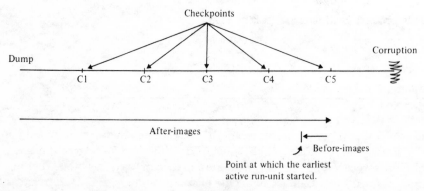

Fig. 11.4

If the checkpoint does not include a list of active run-units then the sequence is as above, except an extra scan of the journal file is required to construct this list of active run-units. Clearly, this can be potentially time-consuming if the journal file is kept on tape. As before, a new journal file will be commenced after each dump.

Both these versions of roll-forward do not recover the database from the corruption, but they do allow the database to be restored to a point in time close to that at which corruption occurred. *This* could have been achieved by loading a dump and re-running all the necessary run-units. However, to do this would involve:

316

- complete re-processing, which may be a lengthy business, and involve the retention of input data;
- keeping a record of the run-units;
- keeping a record of the *sequence* of run-units since this is frequently an important factor in determining the eventual state of the database.

The use of roll-forward and the journal file provides us with the last two facilities effectively, and a means of achieving the first by only applying the *effects* of processing.

Given a recovery system in principle similar to that outlined above, database administration needs to define the strategy to be employed. This involves such decisions as:

* how often dumps are taken;
* deciding on which type of checkpoint will be employed (no run-units active versus run-units active) if both facilities are available in the DBMS used;
* deciding on the use of before-images if active checkpoints can be written.

The frequency of dumps will be determined by a variety of factors. Dumping of the whole database can be lengthy and it may involve the database being unavailable to run-units, and therefore to users. Hence there is a tendency to dump only infrequently. However, infrequent dumps involve roll-forward taking a longer time - there are more images to apply. Conversely, therefore, there is a tendency to dump frequently. The exact pattern chosen will be a compromise and make take advantage of natural processing breaks. For example, many organisations divide their processing into an on-line 'day' and an off-line 'night'. Dumps may be taken at the beginning and end of the on-line day. Alternatively, the whole database need not be dumped en masse: different areas may be dumped at different times and with different frequencies. This is particularly useful where the database may be partitioned into logical 'chunks' that have differing processing and recovery patterns. Such an approach, taken to its logical conclusion, leads to dumps of individual pages being taken, giving what is termed a 'fuzzy' dump, since it is a snapshot of the database over a period of time, rather than at one particular time. The reader is referred to Reference (11.9) for details of such a scheme. An approach similar to a 'fuzzy' dump is available in some commercial systems. For example, Sperry Univac's DMS 1100 has a dynamic dump facility allowing a dump to be taken whilst run-units are active.

The choice of checkpoint facility again depends on how important it is that database processing is not interrupted by checkpointing. However, the price that is paid for uninterrupted processing is the need to back-out the effects of active run-units, either by not applying their after-images, or by applying the before-images for such run-units.

In making these decisions it is vital that database administration involve both application teams and operations staff. Recovery is being performed for the former, and will be carried out by the latter. Finally, any particular data processing system is unlikely to depend soley on database structures, as outlined in Chapter 9. Data that has a low frequency of use may be stored on conventional files; this is particularly the case with data of an archival nature. Input data for application programs may also be stored on conventional files, for example, on a key-to-disc file. Therefore, any recovery strategy has to take account of the need possibly to recover the database *and* conventional files *together*. Typically, conventional file recovery is under the control of the operating system, whilst database recovery is under the control of the DBMS. Hence, there is a need for an *integrated* recovery system that allows operations management to use one recovery system for failure in the one data processing system. This integrated recovery system co-ordinates the use of the DBMS and operating system recovery systems, and attempts to provide a unified view and a unified service to operations management. Such facilities are available in commercial DBMSs - for example, Sperry Univac's DMS 1100.

11.3 REORGANISATION AND RESTRUCTURING

Very few organisations are static. Most organisations change and evolve. This change may range from:

* entering entirely new areas of business;

to

* changing the way business in current areas is conducted.

to

* merely changing the volume of business conducted.

Any data processing system, and in particular any database system, that models and supports the organisation's business must be capable of responding to such changes. In terms of a database system we may translate such changes into a need to *restructure* and *reorganise* the database.

Restructuring the database refers to changes made initially to the logical data structure - to the logical data model. In its simplest form it involves

318

precisely the same sorts of decisions that were discussed in logical database design, and alternative solutions will be evaluated in the same way.

Once the restructuring of the logical data model has been identified, it needs to be performed. Trivial changes to the logical data model, such as the addition and/or deletion of, for example, records, sets, and data items can usually be carried out by simply changing the logical data model definition and re-translating it into the internal DBMS form. New logical data model types introduced may then be populated with occurrences by the appropriate application programs. Populations of deleted logical data model types may be removed at the next reorganisation. More complex changes cannot be performed so easily. In practice what needs to be done is to restructure the database by *unloading* and then *loading*. An *unload* program (potentially a suite of programs) *logically* writes the database to a set of conventional files somewhat in the reverse manner to a load program. Notice that such an unload program is different to a physical dump. An unload program will write records out in some logical sequence - such as each owner record followed by its member records - whilst a dump program will write records out in their physical serial ordering - such as adjacent page after adjacent page. The logical data model definition is then amended and retranslated, and the database loaded by means of an *amended* load program. Notice that the load program needs to be amended to take account of the new logical data model structure. The files unloaded will need to be amended in a similar fashion to take account of necessary changes. This is obviously a lengthy and expensive business and is one of the least satisfactory aspects of currently available DBMS software. Some DBMS packages provide a restructure utility, but this is usually capable of handling only simple changes, database administration needing to specify the old and new logical data model definitions.

Not only is the form of restructuring described above expensive, but it is also an off-line process that makes the database unavailable to users whilst restructuring takes place. Work has been done on investigating means by which restructuring may be performed dynamically employing some form of incremental change. However, such work is not complete and commercial implementations offering such a form of dynamic restructuring are unlikely to be available for several years.

Once restructuring has been performed one task remains outstanding for database administration. That task is to identify the *impact* of the logical

321

data model change. The degree of data independence offered by the DBMS may require the rebinding of logical sub-model to logical model mappings and the possible re-compilation or even amendment of application programs. These changes need to be accurately and completely identified and then performed in a quick and coordinated manner. *What* is required is a record of the relationships between logical data models, logical data sub-models, and application programs. *How* this may be provided forms part of Chapter 12.

The complications involved in a serious restructure of the database serve to emphasise that it *ought* to happen as a result of a genuine change in conceptual data structure. That is, it should not occur as a corrective measure to poor logical database design. It counts as further evidence for a systematic, structured approach to database design. As a corollary, a well designed database should be capable of accommodating change without major restructuring surgery. There is an analogy here with structured program design that has as one of its objectives the production of maintainable programs.

11.3.2 Strategy reorganisation

Strategy reorganisation will be necessary for several reasons:-

   i)   it may be consequent to a restructuring;

  ii)   it may be necessary because patterns of usage and storage are better understood;

 iii)   it may be necessary because patterns of usage and storage have changed.

Database administration will be aware of the need to reorganise in case (i), but cases (ii) and (iii) ideally require some form of *monitoring* of database performance. That is, some measure of *actual* patterns of usage and storage, as opposed to the calculated patterns involved in the design process. Clearly, such monitoring can be performed by software, and this is discussed as part of Chapter 12.

The task of deciding exactly what changes are required to the storage data model - what *tuning* is required - is the same task as storage model design. As with restructuring, a sensible aid to carrying out this tuning is a record of previous storage model design decisions - a record of how logical model structures are mapped onto storage model structures. Again we postpone discussion of such a tool to Chapter 12.

The techniques available for performing reorganisation are also similar to those available for restructuring. This is to be expected, since commercial database systems nearly all conflate the logical model and the storage model. Therefore, apart from trivial changes, it is usually a question of an unload/load operation which, again, may be performed by a general purpose reorganisation utility made available by the DBMS supplier.

Reorganisation, in theory, should be more frequent than restructuring. After all, the point of having a storage data model within the overall architecture is largely the result of isolating a level of modelling where access and storage considerations, and changes to them, can be explicitly expressed. Changes in patterns *of* business, rather than changes *in* business, will naturally occur and will need to be reflected in the tuning of the storage data model. Therefore, the penalty of an off-line load/unload reorganisation becomes more onerous. As with the case of restructuring, work has been carried out in the area of *dynamic* reorganisation. Notably, the BCS/CODASYL Data Base Administration Working Group has extended the Draft Data Storage Description Language to incorporate facilities that allow dynamic reorganisation. This extended DSDL is defined in Reference (11.10). Such a DSDL has yet to be implemented, but it is worth examining briefly the ideas involved in dynamic reorganisation.

Essentially, dynamic reorganisation recognises from the start that a storage data model is an evolving description. A storage data model object — such as storage data model record — will have several *versions*. Each version relates to a change, for that storage data model object, in the mapping between the logical data model and storage data model. For example, consider the logical data model record shown in Fig. 11.7

STUDENT–
LOGICAL–
RECORD

Fig. 11.7

If STUDENT-LOGICAL-RECORD were initially mapped to a single STUDENT-STORAGE-RECORD, then the declaration of this mapping along with the declaration of the storage model record would constitute the initial version. If reorganisation dictated that the mapping became more complex, for example that the single storage record be replaced by two storage records, STUDENT-ESSENTIAL-STORAGE-RECORD and

STUDENT-DETAIL-STORAGE-RECORD, then the declaration of this mapping and of the appropriate storage records would constitute the next version.

Dynamic reorganisation may then be carried out using these versions in two possible modes: background mode and incremental mode. In background mode the reorganisation process progresses through the data base making the necessary changes to storage model objects in accordance with the latest versions. The reorganisation process may operate concurrently with application run-units. Until the reorganisation process has completed its progression through the database the response time for these application run-units may be degraded as a result of competition with the reorganisation process for database resources. In incremental mode the reorganisation is performed when storage model data *occurrences* are accessed as a result of application program processing. Therefore, the most frequently accessed occurrences (those in most need of reorganisation) are reorganised first. Notice that background mode reorganisation is complete once the reorganisation process has completed its progression through the database. Incremental mode reorganisation is complete only when the last storage model data occurrence requiring reorganisation has been accessed by an application program. Which mode is used will depend upon

(a) the processing overhead incurred in incremental mode when an application program accesses an occurrence requiring reorganisation;

(b) the degradation of run-unit response time produced in background mode.

In both modes the reorganisation is performed by the DBMS.

Complications can clearly occur when changes are made to storage model records that involve representations of set structures : the representation of the set structure itself may require reorganisation. This, in turn, may involve reorganisation of further representations of set structures leading to what has been termed a **cascade reorganisation**. Notice that stress was laid in storage data model design on set representations that provided ease of reorganisation at the (possible) cost of extra accesses.

As with restructuring, once reorganisation has been performed it is necessary to accurately and completely identify any changes needed in application systems. This will be necessary if the degree of physical data independence in the database system is not high. Again, how this need can practically be met will be discussed in Chapter 12.

324

11.3.3 Physical placement reorganisation

The task of consolidating space, tidying of indexes, etc. is considerably less complex than either restructuring or strategy reorganisation. Practically, it should be performed by a standard utility made available by the DBMS supplier. This is not always the case, and some DBMS's require the change to be made in the fashion of "old"/"new" data model definitions. This can be very unsatisfactory when the data model in question is a conflation of logical model and storage model (and even device model). However, whichever way the reorganisation can be performed, it is still necessary to have some form of monitoring, as in strategy reorganisation, to indicate when a physical placement reorganisation is necessary.

11.4 ORGANISATIONAL STRUCTURE AND IMPACT

Before beginning an examination of the organisational structure within database administration and its relation to other components within a company's organisational structure, it would be as well to clarify two points.

1. Database administration is the topic examined. A distinction is sometimes made between data administration and database administration. The grounds for this distinction are seen to be that data administration is a corporate level function concerned with a company's overall data policy, whilst database administration is a department level function (specifically the data processing department) concerned with the specific task of producing computer-based data models. The data administrator is seen as fulfilling a *strategy* role on a par with, say, the chief accountant. The database administrator is seen as fulfilling a *tactical* role on a par with, say, the chief programmer. The notion of data administration is appealing since, in one sense, it represents an embodiment of the "data as an organisational resource" dictum. However, it is the author's opinion that the practical realisation of such a role is (a) not sufficiently advanced enough for any general conclusions to be drawn, and (b) would not properly form part of this text anyway. Several organisations, notably in the U.S.A., have data administrators in this sense, and that the reader is referred to Reference (11.5) for details.

2. The list of database administration responsibilities given in section 11.1 is a potential list. The actual responsibilities of database

administration will vary according to the level reached in the analysis and design iteration, and organisational structure may reflect these considerations. Indeed, in some organisations where databases and file systems have been implemented in an ad hoc and intuitive fashion without any serious attempt at analysis and design, database administration may be pre-occupied exclusively with data analysis as a means to comprehend and reconcile a series of muddled application-orientated views.

11.4.1 The organisation of database administration

Fig. 11.8 illustrates an obvious approach to the organisation of database administration.

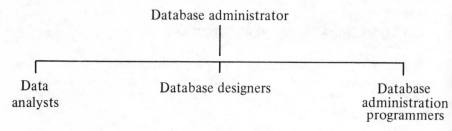

Database administrator

Data analysts

Database designers

Database administration programmers

Fig. 11.8

A **database administrator** fulfills a management role in coordinating and planning the activities of three sets of people:-

i) **Data analysts** whose responsibilities centre around the determination of the global conceptual data model.

ii) **Database designers** whose responsibilities centre around the task of translating the conceptual data model into some form of computer data model. In practice, no distinction is made between logical database designers and storage database designers since commercially available database systems conflate the two levels in their architecture, as has previously been described.

iii) **Database administration programmers** whose responsibilities centre around several tasks:

— provision of load/unload programs in connection with fine placement, and restructuring and reorganisation,

— provision of database administrator defined procedures where these are required by the database system used,

326

— provision of database administrator defined procedures where these are necessary to meet deficiencies in the database system software provided, e.g. monitoring routines, physical placement reorganisation, etc.

— provision of advice and support to applications programmers concerning the use of the database. This may be a significant task where the data manipulation language in use operates at the record-at-a-time level (such as the CODASYL COBOL DML) and advice on *navigating* the database is required.

Such an organisational structure has an appealing simplicity since it mirrors the main themes of analysis and design. However, in practice this simplicity may need modification.

Firstly, the database administrator will fulfill more than a mere management role. He/she will be required to be involved at a technical level in a number of decisions, such as

— the methodology and standards used in analysis and design,

— the strategy required for back-up and recovery,

— the possible evaluation and selection of a DBMS,

— the possible evaluation and selection of a data dictionary system.

Secondly, the distinctive split between data analysts and database designers has attractions since it reflects a logical split between *what* is required and *how* it is achieved. However the amount of work and the stage that it has reached may make such a distinct job split impractical. At least in the early years of using database systems, many organisations concentrate their efforts on the successful creation of *one* database system covering some well-defined area of the organisation's activities. In such a situation it is usual to find database analysts/designers fulfilling both the roles of analysis and design during the different stages of the development. At the beginning of a project, everyone works on data analysis, through to logical database design, and onto storage database design. Such an organisational structure may revert to the structure of Fig. 11.8 as the use of database systems achieves a certain maturity, i.e. there is a series of database systems in various stages of development.

Thirdly, the simplified structure of Fig. 11.8 implicitly assumes that data analysis and database design are not only the *responsibility* of database administration, but that they will also be *exclusively performed* by database administration. Any review of Chapters 8 and 9 will show that this sensibly will not be the case.

Data analysis requires a fine and detailed understanding of the functional areas under investigation in order to produce the needed local conceptual models. This *could* be done exclusively by a data analyst from database administration, but this ignores an existing body of people who are well versed in such investigations, albeit lacking formal tools, viz. systems analysts. This was the central thesis of Chapter 6. If systems analysts are trained in the techniques of data analysis and functional analysis they can develop the necessary local conceptual models *and* gain a much clearer understanding of *what* their application system must achieve. This does *not* mean that this dispersion of data analysis techniques results in a 'withering away of the state' for data analysis in database administration. The local views need still to be consolidated into a global conceptual view, and this crucial task can only be performed by database administration. All it *does* mean is that techniques and expertise are spread to those people who need them. Consequent upon this, there is a need for the database administrator to fulfill a missionary role by ensuring adequate training in, and comprehension of, the techniques of data analysis and functional analysis, and their crucial role in the overall development of computer-based systems. It should be noted that practically, as discussed in section 11.4.2, such a distribution of techniques is needed if the introduction of database techniques is to be politically successful within a data processing department.

Database design, similarly, requires a fine and detailed understanding of the objectives of the computer-based system under development, in particular of the data usage and storage patterns that the computer database system must support. The source for such a detailed understanding already exists in the shape of systems analysts, designers, and programmers working in the various application teams. Clearly, the ultimate design of the database will be a task for database administration, but the detailed consideration of the provision of logical sub-models, for example, will be a task requiring the joint efforts of database designers and applications staff. Similarly, the question of the degree to which data validation and data consistency rules can be a function of the DBMS rather than being distributed and replicated through application systems, is a matter for joint discussion and decision. Unless this coordination is carried out, one at least of the objectives of the database approach — consistency of standards for data — will not be achieved.

Fourthly, database administration programming will not be the sole perogative of database administration. Applications teams will be involved at a detailed level in the design of load programs, since they will be ultimately responsible for providing the files of application data that the load program(s) will consume. The specification of database administration defined database procedures — such as CALC procedures, validation procedures, etc — again requires the involvement of those with the detailed knowledge of the applications that such database procedures must support, viz. application analysts, designers, and programmers. Similarly, the provision of database administration defined procedures to meet deficiencies in the database system software *should* involve a group of people with expertise in such areas, viz. systems software programmers.

To summarise, therefore, the organisational structure shown in Fig. 11.8 will in practice

a) exist, because it reflects a set of distinctions inherent in the analysis and design of database systems,

but

b) will be considerably more complex than the structure shows, since the analysis and design of database systems is not an activity that can occur in isolation from the other activities of a data processing department.

11.4.2 The impact of database administration within the data processing department

The previous section has covertly discussed the danger inherent in the introduction of database administration into a data processing department : the introduction of an *elite*. The organisational structure of many data processing departments approaches the basic structure of Fig. 11.9

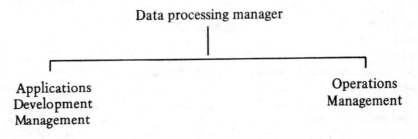

Fig. 11.9

329

Applications development management is responsible for the analysis, design and implementation of computer-based systems to support the organisation's business activities. Its formal organisation may take a variety of structures. The most usual approach is that of **applications teams** responsible for the development of computer-based systems within certain functional areas. These application teams consist of systems analysts and programmers. More complex structures can be overlaid on this basic structure : chief systems analysts and chief programmers may exist having as their responsibility the conduct of analysis and programming over the individual application teams.

Operations management is responsible for the operational running (and possibly maintenance) of applications systems. As such it has control over hardware and systems software, and consists of a variety of personnel ranging from data control clerks to systems software programmers.

It is possible to integrate database administration within this existing structure by making the interactions discussed in the previous section part of the formal structure, as in Fig. 11.10

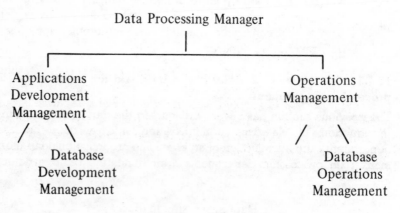

Fig. 11.10

Database analysis and design falls under the control of applications development management, and the operational running and maintenance of the database falls under the control of operations management. This certainly achieves the necessary integration of analysis and design techniques into application teams, and software considerations into systems software programming. The cost of such an integration is the loss of any recognition of the database approach as being something over and above a set of file organisation techniques. The net result will tend to be a series of application-orientated databases with the attendant problems of uncontrolled redundancy and inconsistency. An alternative structure is that outlined in Fig. 11.11

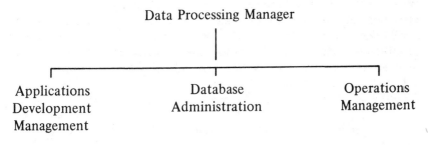

Fig. 11.11

Database administration is a distinct organisational grouping on a par with applications development management and operations management. This provides the basis for the exploitation of database as a technique that transcends and co-ordinates the application views : the recognition of data as an organisational resource. The danger inherent in such a structure is that an elite is created. Database systems are a radical departure from conventional file systems, and this in itself can cause resentment among data processing staff, since there is a traditional conservative reaction in any organisation to the introduction of new technology. If this is coupled with the creation of a separate group of people initiated in the rites and practices (data analysis and database design) of this new technology, then this resentment is increased possibly to the point where the successful use of database systems is jeopardised. This situation currently can be exacerbated because the traditional roles of systems analyst and programmer are changing. The introduction of structured programming and related techniques relieves (not entirely willingly) the analyst of the concern to design program by making program design the proper business of programmers. At the same time, the introduction of database and database analysis and design techniques relieves the analyst of the concern to design data structures. Despite the introduction of the notion of a *business systems analyst*, systems analysts can frequently be left with a sense of confusion as to exactly what their job now involves. Such considerations can percolate into a distrust of database administration by the conventional groupings within a data processing department.

It is the burden of this text that a distinct database administration section at the level of Fig. 11.11 is needed. It is the burden of the previous section that database administration cannot, however, exist in isolation. Missionary as well as messianic zeal is required. The techniques of database analysis and design should not be represented as radical departures from the past that are the exclusive practice of the elect of database administration. They should be represented as evolutionary techniques* for tackling commonly recognised problems in analysis and design that need to be practised by all concerned with the development of computer-based systems to meet operational needs. In many ways, the prime task of database administration is to achieve this working relationship with the other groups within data processing.

11.4.3 The impact of database administration within a company

The recognition and treatment by the data processing department of data as an organisational resource will have an impact on other departments within a company. This impact will not be so much that they no longer have their 'own' application orientated data : they still do (this is the point of logical sub-models). Rather it will be that they are now being asked to think of data as being the resource it should be, without the constraints of application orientated conventional files. Potentially, this should mean less time spent on application system maintenance, and more time on application system development. In the final analysis, the impact of a database system on a company should be computer-based systems that meet, and are responsive to, users needs. *That* is the ultimate aim of the exercise.

REFERENCES AND BIBLIOGRAPHY

(11.1) Conway R.W., Maxwell W.L., Morgan H.L., **On the Implementation of Security Measures in Information Systems**, Comm. ACM, **15**, 4, April 1972.

(11.2) **Report of the Committee on Data Protection**, Chairman: Sir Norman Lindop, HMSO, December, 1978.

(11.3) Curtice R.M., **Integrity in Data Base Systems**, Datamation, May, 1977.

---

* For example, although this text has not addressed the problem specifically, data analysis is as much a pre-requisite for conventional file design as it is for database design.

(11.4) Gray J.N., **Notes on Data Base Operating Systems**, in **Lecture Notes in Computer Science: Operating Systems (an Advanced Course)**, ed. Goos and Hartmanis, Springer-Verlag, 1978.

(11.5) Yasaki E.K., **The Many Faces of the DBA**, Datamation, May, 1977.

(11.6) **BCS/CODASYL DDLC Data Base Administration Working Group Report**, British Computer Society, 1975.

(11.7) **DMS 1100 System Support Functions Manual**, Sperry Univac.

(11.8) Verhofstad J.S.M., **Recovery Techniques for Database Systems**, ACM Computing Surveys, **10**, 2, June, 1978.

(11.9) Lindsay B.G., **Recovery Facilities**, Proceedings Advanced CREST/SRC Distributed Data Bases Course, Sheffield City Polytechnic, July, 1979.

(11.10) CODASYL **DDLC Journal of Development**, 1981.

(11.11) Bennetto B.W., **Experience at the Open University**, Online Database Conference, London, 1977. Proceedings published by Online Conferences Limited, Uxbridge, England.

(11.12) Manhood (ed.) D.W., **Storage level control of a CODASYL database:** Part II, Computer Bulletin, December, 1980.

EXERCISES

There are no formal exercises associated with this Chapter, but the reader is encouraged to consider how database administration might carry out its responsibilities in a data processing department with which they are familiar.

Chapter 12
DATA DICTIONARIES

"Once you know what the word stands for, you understand it, you know its whole use."

— **Ludwig Wittgenstein,** Philosophical Investigations

It is customary to write some form of a concluding chapter to a book. This is the purpose of this Chapter. It attempts to summarise the ideas presented so far by showing how they may be applied to themselves: that they are, in a sense, recursive. The topic examined is that of data dictionary systems. A data dictionary system (or DDS) formed an important feature of the generalised architecture examined in Chapter 2, but its structure was not examined in detail. References to the role and use of a DDS in the analysis, design, and operational running of a database system have been made throughout the text. This Chapter attempts to establish the *principles* of a DDS, its *role* in the architecture of a database system, and its *use* in analysis, design, and operational running. It does not attempt to examine DDSs in detail, nor to survey and evaluate commercially available DDSs. *That* needs a separate book in its own right.

12.1 META-DATA

A central thesis of this book has been that data as an organisational resource has an inherent structure that may be modelled in the process of database analysis and design. Data analysis is seen as an essential feature in this process, since it attempts to define this inherent structure prior to its modelling in a computer system. The central thesis of this Chapter will be that the very data generated by this process of analysis and design must itself be subjected to the process of analysis and design since it, too, is an organisational resource. That is, data about data has an inherent structure that may be explicitly modelled. In this section we shall establish the nature of such data-about-data structures or **meta-data models.**

Imagine that we have the conceptual data model for an area of UniHyp depicted in Fig. 12.1. This shows that a member of STAFF may fulfil two tutoring roles: one as a PERSONAL TUTOR giving general educational advice to a STUDENT, the other as a COURSE TUTOR giving specific academic advice to STUDENTs on a particular COURSE. An attribute of both STAFF and STUDENT is ADDRESS, which is a variable length alphanumeric string that does not contain, at the moment, a post code.

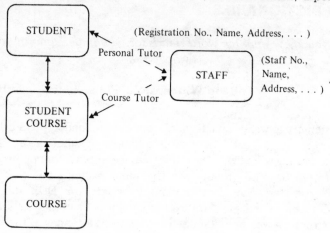

Fig. 12.1

This conceptual data model has been mapped by the database design process to the CODASYL schema shown by the schema diagram of Fig. 12.2.

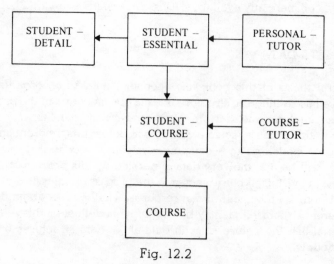

Fig. 12.2

Notice that the STAFF entity has been implemented as two record types, as indicated in Fig. 12.3.

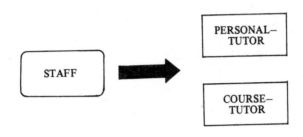

Fig. 12.3

The reasons for this fragementation need not concern us here. What is of interest is the record declarations for these two record types:

RECORD NAME IS PERSONAL TUTOR;

```
    .
    .
    .
02 STAFF-NO;                        PIC 9(4).
02 PERSONAL-TUTOR-NAME;             PIC X(12).
02 PERSONAL-TUTOR-ADDRESS;          PIC X(58)
    .
    .
    .
```

RECORD NAME IS COURSE-TUTOR;

```
    .
    .
    .
02 STAFF-NO;                        PIC 9(4).
02 CRSE-TUT-NAME;                   PIC X(12).
02 CRSETUTADDR;                     PIC X(58).
    .
    .
    .
```

Note that the attribute ADDRESS has been implemented as the same fixed number of alphanumeric characters in each case, but that it is named quite differently.

Similarly the STUDENT entity has been implemented as two record types, with declarations:

RECORD NAME IS STUDENT-ESSENTIAL;

    ⋮

02 REG-NO;	PIC 9(4).
02 NAME;	PIC X(12).
02 STUDENT-ADDRESS;	PIC X(58).

    ⋮

RECORD NAME IS STUDENT-DETAIL;

    ⋮

02 REG-NO;	PIC 9(4).
02 NAME;	PIC X(12).
02 STUDADDR;	PIC X(58).
02 MARITAL-STATUS;	PIC X.
02 SEX;	PIC X.

    ⋮

Imagine now that UniHyp decides that ADDRESS must include post code. Database administration needs certain information to be able to effect this restructure; specifically:

*   which records in the schema need changing;

*   which subschemas need changing;

*   which programs need changing;

*   which subschemas/programs need recompiling.

How can database administration obtain this information? It could be obtained by a manual search of the schema DDL looking for data item declarations that could be implementations of ADDRESS. This would be tedious, impractical, and error-prone. In the simple example we have generated above we have four implementations of ADDRESS: PERSONAL-TUTOR-ADDRESS, CRSETUTADDR, STUDENT-ADDRESS, and STUDADDR. It is by no means obvious that all four of these data items are implementations of the same attribute!

338

Given such a meta-database, database administration can now, in our example problem, determine the records and data items that are, at the logical level, involved in the implementation of ADDRESS. That is, they can identify STUDADDR in STUDENT-DETAIL, PERSONAL-TUTOR-ADDRESS in PERSONAL-TUTOR, and so on. In addition, if the logical data model portion of the meta-database is suitably structured, they can determine the subschemas that require change and/or recompilation.

It is now easy to see that this idea may be extended to provide the information needed completely. The meta-database may be extended to model data about programs, perhaps as in Fig. 12.11, where the data about the programs and the modules that comprise them may be recorded.

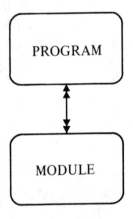

Fig. 12.11

The relationship of programs to logical data model objects may now be recorded. That is, the *use* programs make of records, sets, and data items. Our meta-database now looks like Fig. 12.12

We can now complete our task by using such a meta-database to determine, for the changed logical data model objects, the programs that need to be changed and/or recompiled.

It is this idea of a meta-database as a structure for

* documenting the various components of a data processing system;

* recording the relationships *within* the components and *between* the components of a data processing system;

in such a manner that information about the data processing system can be stored and extracted that forms the core of the notion of a DDS.

So far we have discussed three components in such a DDS. A little reflection will show that six major components can be identified, as in Fig. 12.13*

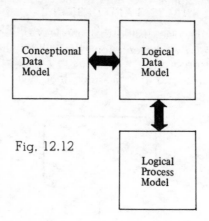

Fig. 12.12

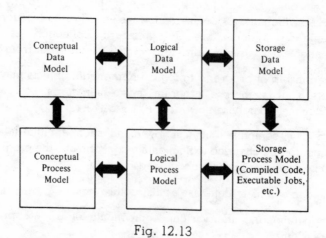

Fig. 12.13

---

* Notice how this structure begins to lay bare the structure of a database system - a representation of the architecture.

Such a DDS is a powerful tool in structuring the documentation produced about any data processing system - a way of structuring the data produced by the data processing department itself. As such, it has been termed a **systems encyclopaedia**. It can play a vital role in both analysis and design and operational running in a database system. These aspects are examined in the next two sections.

12.2 AN AID TO ANALYSIS AND DESIGN

The previous section established that one way of regarding meta-data was simply as being documentation: data about the data processing system. Recalling Fig. 8.1 of Chapter 8, any conceptual data model may be implemented as:

* a manual file system;

* a conventional file system;

* a database system.

Conceptual meta-data models may also be implemented in these three ways. Indeed, a manual file system has been the traditional way (if at all) of recording documentation about data and processes in a data processing system. However, the previous section illustrated the use of meta-data by assuming an implementation as a meta-database. The advantages of such an approach will be only too obvious to any one who has worked with manual documentation systems. Typically, such manual documentation systems are a haphazard collection of reports, specifications, listings and definitions. Such systems suffer from a variety of problems:

* they are frequently incomplete;

* they are frequently out-of-date;

* they are notoriously difficult to amend when the system changes;

* they are notoriously poor at providing any form of cross-referencing between different components in a system.

As a consequence such documentation systems are rarely *used* by any one. They are rarely capable of producing any *information* - such as that outlined in the previous section. Data processing departments have traditionally attempted to counter these problems with a well defined set of documentation *standards*, but such standards are more usually acknowledged by non-compliance than by adherence.

The use of a DDS incorporating a meta-database does *not* guarantee a documentation system that is well-used and useful. What it does do is to remove many of the problems that stand in the way of a well-used and useful documentation system*. As a meta-database it provides the ability to:

* check for completeness of documentation by means of software validation procedures;

* update documentation easily by means of, say, on-line terminal facilities;

* retrieve information easily by means of, say, on-line terminal facilities or listings;

* cross-reference documentation, because of a database system's ability to represent relationships.

We shall now examine some of the way in which a DDS can be used as a true documentation aid.

1. The conceptual data model

Fig. 12.9 displayed the meta-data model for the conceptual data model as involving m:n relationships between ENTITY, ATTRIBUTE, and RELATIONSHIP. If we re-draw this meta-data model so as to replace the m:n relationships with link entities, then we have the model of Fig. 12.14

ATTRIBUTE ROLE and ENTITY ROLE are the link entities and there is meaningful intersection data for such entities. In the case of ATTRIBUTE ROLE non-key attributes might be:

* the role the attribute plays in the entity - say as part of the identifying key;

---

* It is interesting to consider, in this context, the work of Reference (12.8) which suggests many of the facilities of a DDS, but which was written at a time when database systems were in their infancy.

12.3 AN AID TO OPERATION AND MAINTENANCE

The previous section emphasised the use of a DDS as a tool in analysis and design. In this section the use of a DDS in the running and maintenance of a database system is discussed, emphasising the aspect of the DDS as an interactive component with the DBMS.

One of the major responsibilities of database administration discussed in Chapter 11 was that of responding to *change*. As part of that discussion several key questions were identified:

*   determining *when* change was needed;
*   determining *what* change was needed;
*   carrying out the change;
*   determining the *impact* of the change on other components in the data processing system.

The use of a DDS as a vehicle for recording information that may answer several of these questions has already been covered in the preceeding two sections.

The determination of the change required to either the logical data model or the storage data model is aided by having within the DDS a record of

— the conceptual data model and its structure;

— the mapping, or design, of the conceptual data model to the logical data model;

— the logical data model and its structure;

— the mapping, or design, of the logical data model to the storage data model;

— the storage data model and its structure.

On the basis of this information database administratior. can make a coherent and systematic change to the logical data model and/or the storage data model, *and* record that change.

The impact of change on other components in the data processing system can be provided by using the mappings between the various components in a DDS to predict the subschemas, programs, etc. that require change and/or recompilation. This feature is sometimes termed *impact analysis.* Automatic generation of subschemas can aid the change and/or recompilation needed.

However, what has not been examined are the facilities required for determining *when* change is required. In the case of a restructuring change this, as discussed in Chapter 11, falls outside the province of a DDS in the sense that the need for such change is articulated initially by a change in the organisation's data requirements. In the case of a reorganisation change the DDS provides the ideal vehicle for the monitoring and statistics collection that is required for determining when change is necessary.

The DDS, as the DBMS's *own database*, can be used to record:

*   how often an access mechanism is used;
*   how often a linked list or index structure is used as a storage representation of a logical association between records;
*   the pattern of use — owner to member, member to member, member to owner — of a logical association between records;
*   the use of a data item for computational purposes or for printing or display purposes;
*   the run time for programs using the database.

Such information sensibly may be recorded in the DDS as data about storage records, set representations, programs, etc.

DBMS utilities may then access this data to produce statistics representing the patterns of storage and access for use by database administration as guidelines for deciding when strategy reorganisation or physical placement reorganisation are needed. The DBMS may *monitor* such data against pre-defined parameters and automatically produce statistics when performance falls outside these pre-set limits. This interaction between the DDS and DBMS, forming a unified software mechanism for supervising and controlling the database, will undoubtedly be extended in the future as the mechanism for automatic reorganisation and optimisation.

Such interaction between the DBMS and DDS will also result in consideration being given to the DDS as being the proper place in which to record *access control* for the database. For example the relationship between users and data constituted by access control requirements can be modelled in outline by the meta-data model of Fig. 12.19.

The intersection entity, ACCESS CONTROL REQUIREMENT, records the access a particulr USER has to a particular CONCEPTUAL DATA

MODEL OBJECT. The latter is a generic term, since, in detail, this may be an entity, attribute, or relationship, either at the type or occurrence level. As indicated, each of these three entity types in Fig. 12.19 will be mapped to appropriate computer model objects, as shown in outline in Fig. 12.20.

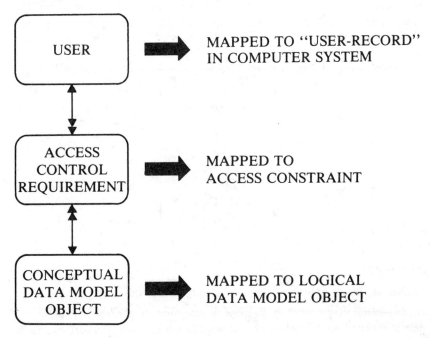

Fig. 12.19

Implemented in a DDS, such a structure as Fig. 12.20 could be accessed by whatever software component is responsible for providing an access control mechanism to determine whether access to a logical data model object should be allowed/not allowed for a particular user of the computer system.

In conclusion, it should be emphasised that the structure and use of a DDS outlined in this Chapter reflects the intent stated at the beginning of the Chapter - as a summary for the essential ideas that have gone before. Data dictionary systems currently available for commercial use do not incorporate, yet, several of the advanced features discussed above. Conversely, they do incorporate many features not covered in the main thrust of this Chapter.

Fig. 12.20

SUMMARY

Database structures themselves have a structure which may be modelled by the same techniques of analysis and design initially used to produce such database structures.

Such models about data models are known as meta-data models and may be implemented as meta-databases.

The use of such a meta-database as a means for recording and retrieving information about the analysis, design and operational use of a database system forms the essential idea of a data dictionary system

REFERENCES AND BIBLIOGRAPHY

(12.1) **British Computer Society Data Dictionary Systems Working Party Report**, March, 1977. In ACM SIGMOD **Record**, **9,** 4, December, 1977, and ACM SIGBDP **Database**, **9,** 2, Fall, 1977.

(12.2) **Proceedings of the Conference on Data Dictionary Systems,** London, November, 1978. In **Computer Bulletin,** December, 1978.

(12.3) Bourne T.J., **Implementing a Comprehensive Data Dictionary System,** Online Database Conference, London, 1977. Proceedings published by Online Conferences Limited, Uxbridge, England.

(12.4) Lefkovits D., **Data Dictionary Systems,** Q.E.D., 1978.

(12.5) **The ICL 2900 Data Dictionary System, Technical Overview,** International Computers Ltd., 1977.

(12.6) **Fundamentals of the ICL Data Dictionary System,** International Computers Ltd., 1979.

(12.7) Bibby M.E., **The Role of a Data Dictionary,** Online Database Conference, London, 1977 (see 12.3).

(12.8) Fisher D.L., **Data, Documentation, and Decision Tables,** Comm. ACM, **9,** 1, January, 1966.

EXERCISES

12.1 Suggest attributes for the RECORD and SET entity types of Fig. 12.16.

12.2 Suggest attributes for the DOMAIN entity type of Fig. 12.17.

OUTLINE SOLUTIONS TO SELECTED EXERCISES

1.2
As Chapter 10 illustrates, inverted file structures can be used in database systems as a means for expressing relationships between records. However, they are *storage structures*, and their direct use by an application program would cause problems of data independence.

1.4

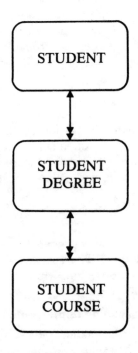

The new relationship that has been introduced is that between a STUDENT and the STUDENT DEGREEs he may be registered for - here a STUDENT may be registered for more than one degree at any one time. Hence a STUDENT COURSE that is being studied is related to study under a particular STUDENT DEGREE.

2.1

For COBOL the logical data model and the storage data model are conflated into one data model. That is, the data described in a COBOL program incorporates elements of *how* the data is stored and accessed as well as *what* the data structure is. In addition the logical data sub-model of COBOL is very limited, being confined to REDEFINES and the use of FILLER as a means for providing a sub-set of a central file definition in the COBOL LIBRARY.

2.2

Introduction of controlled redundancy

Redundancy may be controlled because, properly, it is a feature of either the logical data sub-models or the storage data model. As such the central role played by the logical data model places the burden for controlling such redundancy (or replication) onto the DBMS, rather than onto a set of application programs. Redundancy within the logical data model may be present as a result of *normalisation* considerations (see Chapters 7 and 9), but this is again *controlled* since it is the direct result of the application of a set of rules, and is limited to concerns of unique identification.

Sharing of data

The centralised data resource, in the form of the logical data model, can support the expansion or introduction of logical data sub-models with the minimum of effort since *how* the data is stored and accessed does not form part of such a definition, and will be transparent to the application program.

Standards for data

The logical data model focusses consideration on conflicting data definitions, whilst the logical data sub-models provide the means for expressing the application orientated views of data.

Access control decisions can be implemented

The logical data model and the logical data sub-models provide vehicles for defining the access constraints (see Chapter 11) that are the means for representing access control decisions. The centralised control of the DBMS can be used to implement these access constraints with some form of access control mechanism. Alternatively, as Chapter 12 argues, the data dictionary system provides a vehicle for defining the association between users and data over access control.

Security

Again, consider the central role of the DBMS which can co-ordinate the *prevention* of corruption, loss, or destruction of data, or may co-ordinate the *recovery* from corruption, loss or destruction.

3.1

DOMAIN   COURSE CODE ALPHANUMERIC 7

DOMAIN   COURSE NAME ALPHABETIC 30

.
.
.

RELATION REQUISITES (MAJCOURSE CODE   DOMAIN COURSE CODE,

MINICOURSE CODE   DOMAIN COURSE CODE)

RELATION COURSE   (COURSE CODE   DOMAIN COURSE CODE,

COURSE NAME   DOMAIN COURSE NAME,

..........................)

3.2
The relation REQUISITES is simply added to the relational schema. The algorithms do not need to be changed.

3.3

PROJECT(JOIN(JOIN(SELECT COURSES WHERE FACULTY = 'MATHEMATICS')
AND STUDENTS-AND-COURSES OVER COURSE CODE)

AND STUDENTS OVER REG NO.)

OVER NAME GIVING ANSWER.

3.4
Four occurrences are:

'9491,B.ROBERTS,9 INKERMAN ST.,8.6.58,1.10.77,PHI 121,THE EARLY WITTGENSTEIN,1,PASS'

'9491,B.ROBERTS,9 INKERMAN ST.,8.6.58,1.10.77,PHI 102,KANTIAN METAPHYSICS, 2,PASS'

'9491,B.ROBERTS,9 INKERMAN ST.,8.6.58,1.10.77,LIT 312,THE EXPATRIATES,2,PASS'

'9491,B.ROBERTS,9 INKERMAN ST.,8.6.58,1.10.77,ENG 111,BASIC SURVEYING,1,FAIL'

3.5
MAPPING

JOIN(JOIN(PROJECT COURSES OVER COURSE CODE,COURSE NAME,RATING)

AND STUDENTS-AND-COURSES OVER COURSE CODE)

AND STUDENTS OVER REG. NO. GIVING STUD-ADMIN-VIEW.

4.1
Say:

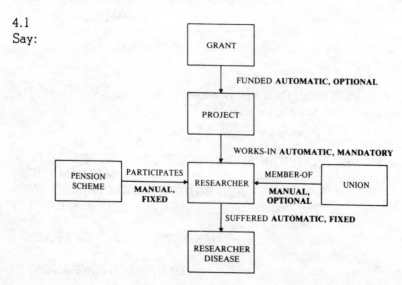

The example centres around a biological research station. The FUNDED set is AUTOMATIC since every PROJECT when set up will always have a GRANT. It is OPTIONAL since it may continue after the expiration of the GRANT where the PROJECT becomes self funding. WORKS-IN is AUTOMATIC and MANDATORY since a RESEARCHER must be associated with a PROJECT, but may move from PROJECT to PROJECT. SUFFERED is AUTOMATIC, FIXED since the disease has to be suffered by someone, and that suffering is certainly not transferable. PARTICIPATES is MANUAL, FIXED since a RESEARCHER does no have to join a PENSION SCHEME, but once joined a RESEARCHER must remain in that particular PENSION SCHEME. MEMBER-OF is MANUAL OPTIONAL since a RESEARCHER does not have to join a UNION, and once joined may leave the UNION and need not join another UNION.

4.2

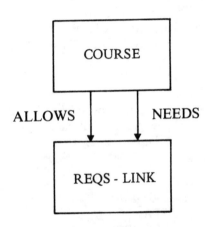

4.3
SCHEMA NAME IS COURSES-SCHEMA;
ACCESS-CONTROL LOCK IS 'LINDOP'.

AREA NAME IS COURSES-AREA;
ACCESS-CONTROL LOCK IS 'LINDOP'.

RECORD NAME IS COURSE;
      LOCATION MODE IS CALC RAND-COURSE USING
            COURSE-CODE IN COURSE;
      WITHIN COURSES-AREA.
      02 COURSE-CODE;   PIC X(7).
      02 COURSE-NAME;   PIC A(30).
           ⋮

```
RECORD NAME IS REQS-LINK;
    LOCATION MODE IS VIA NEEDS SET;
    WITHIN COURSES-AREA.
    02 MAJ-CRS-CD;           PIC X(7).
    02 MIN-CRS-CD;           PIC X(7).


SET NAME IS NEEDS;
  OWNER IS COURSE;
  ORDER IS PERMANENT IMMATERIAL
  MEMBER IS REQS-LINK FIXED AUTOMATIC;
  SET SELECTION IS THRU NEEDS OWNER IDENTIFIED BY CURRENT
  OF SET.


SET NAME IS ALLOWS;
  OWNER IS COURSE;
  ORDER IS PERMANENT IMMATERIAL
  MEMBER IS REQS-LINK FIXED AUTOMATIC;
  SET SELECTION IS THRU ALLOWS OWNER IDENTIFIED BY
  CURRENT OF SET.
```

4.4

Clearly the domain concept could be useful, but there are problems inherent in the CODASYL approach that make it less useful than would appear at first sight. See Chapter 12, section 12.2.

4.5

Possible candidates for removal would be:

> AREAs
> SET ORDER
> PIC clauses
> ACCESS-CONTROL LOCKS (they are
> really access control mechanisms)

4.6

The mapping *could* be defined in some high-level mapping language that was similar to a form of predicate calculus. However, given the navigational emphasis of CODASYL DML, it is possible that complex mappings (that requiring, say, all members for a given owner as a single subschema record) would be defined by a data-base-procedure that contained the necessary DML commands (to navigate the schema set, and thus construct the single subschema record).

The mapping would obviously form part of the MAPPING DIVISION in the subschema definition.

4.7
Less of the database would be locked out to other run-units at a given time.

5.1
Say:

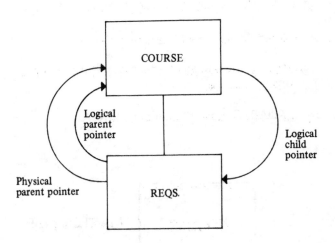

5.2
Say:
(i) **loop:**   Get next STUDENT;
              If STUDENT not found then **exit;**
              Get STUDENT AND COURSE for this STUDENT where
              FACULTY = 'MATHEMATICS';
              If none found then **loop;**
              Display NAME for selected STUDENT;
              loop;

     exit;

(ii) **big loop:** Get STUDENT where DATE-OF-BIRTH '31.12.59';
                If none found then **exit;**

     little loop: Get next STUDENT AND COURSE for STUDENT;
                   If none found then **big loop;**
                   Display COURSE NAME;
                   little loop;

     exit

5.3

The two algorithms are not symmetric, even though they attempt to answer symmetric queries.

5.4

The database key of CODASYL is used as:
— a data item in the schema;

— an application program provided value;

— part of the mechanism in currency indicators;

— implicitly as the values of pointers in linked list structures, etc. for representing sets.

Is the ISN in ADABAS used in analogous ways?

5.5

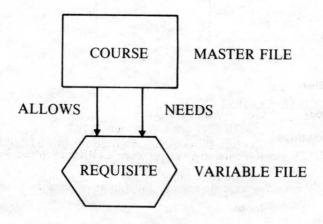

That is, exactly as in CODASYL.

6.1

One possible file structure is:

```
01   COURSE-RECORD
     02   COURSE-DETAIL
          03   COURSE-CODE
```

```
        03  COURSE-NAME
                  .
                  .
                  .

    02  COURSES-NEEDED
        03  COURSE-CODE OCCURS n TIMES
    02  COURSES-ALLOWED
        03  COURSE-CODE OCCURS m TIMES
```

That is, the full course data is held once, and the relationships are shown as repeating groups of **keys** only.

6.2

(i) A DEFINITION OF THE DATA ITEMS TO BE PROCESSED.

Names of elementary data items

COURSE CODE, COURSE NAME ......

Groupings

Natural grouping: COURSE
Data items: COURSE CODE, COURSE NAME ......

Identifiers

For COURSE: COURSE CODE.

Relationships

A COURSE may be related to many other COURSEs in two ways:

(a) it may **need** satisfactory study of other COURSEs in order to be studied;

(b) successful study of it may **allow** (further) study of other COURSEs.

Formats

COURSE CODE: 7 alphanumeric (up to 4 alpha, followed by 3 numeric)
COURSE NAME: Up to 30 alphabetic.

Measurement units

Not applicable.

Ranges and states

Not applicable.

(ii)   A DEFINITION OF THE MAINTAINED DATA

Contents of conceptual records

COURSE: COURSE CODE, COURSE NAME ......

Size of conceptual file

COURSE file contains (say) 150 COURSE records.

Processes acting on the file

(say) Retrieve *needed* COURSEs; Retrieve *allowed* COURSEs.
Both processes hit 20% of the COURSEs 80% of the time.

Volatility of file

Very few insertions/deletions - (say) 2 per year.

7.1
DEGREE:STUDENT

Existence: Contingent, a STUDENT will always be related to a
            DEGREE, but a DEGREE need not have any STUDENTs.

Permanence: Transient for DEGREE, transferable for STUDENT.

PERSONAL TUTOR:STUDENT

Existence: Contingent, a STUDENT will always have a PERSONAL
            TUTOR, but a PERSONAL TUTOR need not have any
            STUDENTs.

Permanence: Transient for PERSONAL TUTOR, transferable for
            STUDENT.

STUDENT:STUDENT COURSE

Existence: Contingent, a STUDENT COURSE will always be related to
            a STUDENT, but a STUDENT need not have any STUDENT
            COURSEs.

Permanence: Fixed for both STUDENT and STUDENT COURSE once
            course registration has occurred.

PERSONAL TUTOR (<u>Personal Tutor No.,</u> ......)
STUDENT (<u>Registration No.,</u> Name, ...)
DEGREE (<u>Degree Code,</u> Degree Name, ...)
STUDENT COURSE (<u>Course Code, Registration No.,</u> Result, ...)
COURSE (<u>Course Code,</u> Course Name, Rating, ...)

Notice that PERSONAL TUTOR has, as yet, no non-key attributes. Note also that the nature of the DEGREE:COURSE relationship is unresolved: it may be 1:n or m:n but nothing is given to indicate which.

9.1 and 9.2

Collapse

PERSONAL TUTOR could be collapsed into STUDENT, but this would result in duplication of data about PERSONAL TUTORs. Such data - say ADDRESS - is relatively large and is subject to change. In addition such a collapse would result in a loss in flexibility, since any relationships involving PERSONAL TUTOR would then be difficult to implement. Therefore this is not a suitable collapse.

Similar considerations argue against other collapses, with the possible exception of COURSE OFFERING into COURSE, and STUDENT COURSE into STUDENT. The latter collapse would involve a large repeating group, whilst the former would not significantly decreases the access cost.

Fragmentation

The chief candidate for fragmentation is STUDENT COURSE into CURRENT STUDENT COURSE and HISTORICAL STUDENT COURSE. This reduces the access cost by ensuring that only the STUDENT COURSEs that are required - CURRENT STUDENT COURSEs - need to be accessed. Little flexibility is lost by this move since a COURSE OFFERING will either have CURRENT STUDENT COURSEs or HISTORICAL STUDENT COURSEs. The major drawback is that a yearly maintenance run would be required to transfer CURRENT STUDENT COURSEs into HISTORICAL STUDENT COURSEs.

It now becomes possible to consider a suitable collapse: CURRENT STUDENT COURSE into STUDENT, as this now involves a smaller number of repetitions. In addition, COURSE OFFERING could be fragmented into CURRENT COURSE OFFERING and HISTORICAL COURSE OFFERING. CURRENT COURSE OFFERING (one occurrence in fact) could then be collapsed into COURSE. This would not significantly decrease access cost in this case, but might well be significant for processes looking at CURRENT STUDENT COURSEs from the COURSE aspect.

Exactly *what* collapse and fragmentation is carried out in practice depends on the numbers of records involved and the importance of the various processes.

9.3

See Chapter 11, section 11.2.1 concerning access control decisions. Attribute value constraints - such as the constraint that RATING can only have values of 1 to 4 - can be expressed as part of the DOMAIN declaration in a relational system. See for example section 3.1.5 of Chapter 3. Such declarations can also be made at the attribute level where attributes drawn from the *same* domain can have different sets of values. Within the CODASYL'73 logical data model the chief mechanism is the specification of allowable values at the data item level. See the schema example in Chapter 4, for example. More powerful facilities are available in CODASYL '80.

9.5

A naive translation might be acceptable where, for example, flexibility was a prime consideration. It might also be acceptable where the number of record occurrences in the database was very low. In short, the *objectives* of the design need always to be considered.

9.6

REFERNCE has been collapsed into CHAPTER, resulting in some data duplication.

10.2

As it stands, PERSONAL TUTOR could be accessed by an index or a hashing algorithm, preferably the latter. All the sets could be implemented as linked lists, with NEXT pointers. TAKEN-BY and OFFERED could have OWNER pointers, whilst STUDIES could have a SET ORDER of FIRST that would ensure that the most recent STUDENT

COURSEs (i.e. the current ones) were accessed first in processing the set. Such a structure would undoubtedly need to be re-evaluated when other processing demands were considered.

10.3
Firstly, some knowledge about the patterns of storage and access would be required in order to make a recommendation. However, a reasonable assumption would be that the processing involved leads to the COURSE:REQUISITES logical association being represented as a linked list with OWNER pointers, or as an index.

10.4
None, except perhaps aggregates!

11.1
For RECORD - LOCATION MODE, names of database procedures to be invoked on storing, modifying, etc. the record,

For SET - SET ORDER, SET OCCURRENCE SELECTION clauses, names of data base procedures to be invoked on insertions, deletions, etc. in the set.

11.2
Format, measurement units, allowable sets of values.

INDEX